Oh My Goddess!

ああっ女神さまっ **13**

STORY AND ART BY
Kosuke Fujishima

ORIGINAL TRANSLATION BY
Dana Lewis AND Toren Smith

LETTERING AND TOUCH-UP BY
Susie Lee AND Betty Dong
WITH Tom2K

DARK HORSE MANGA™

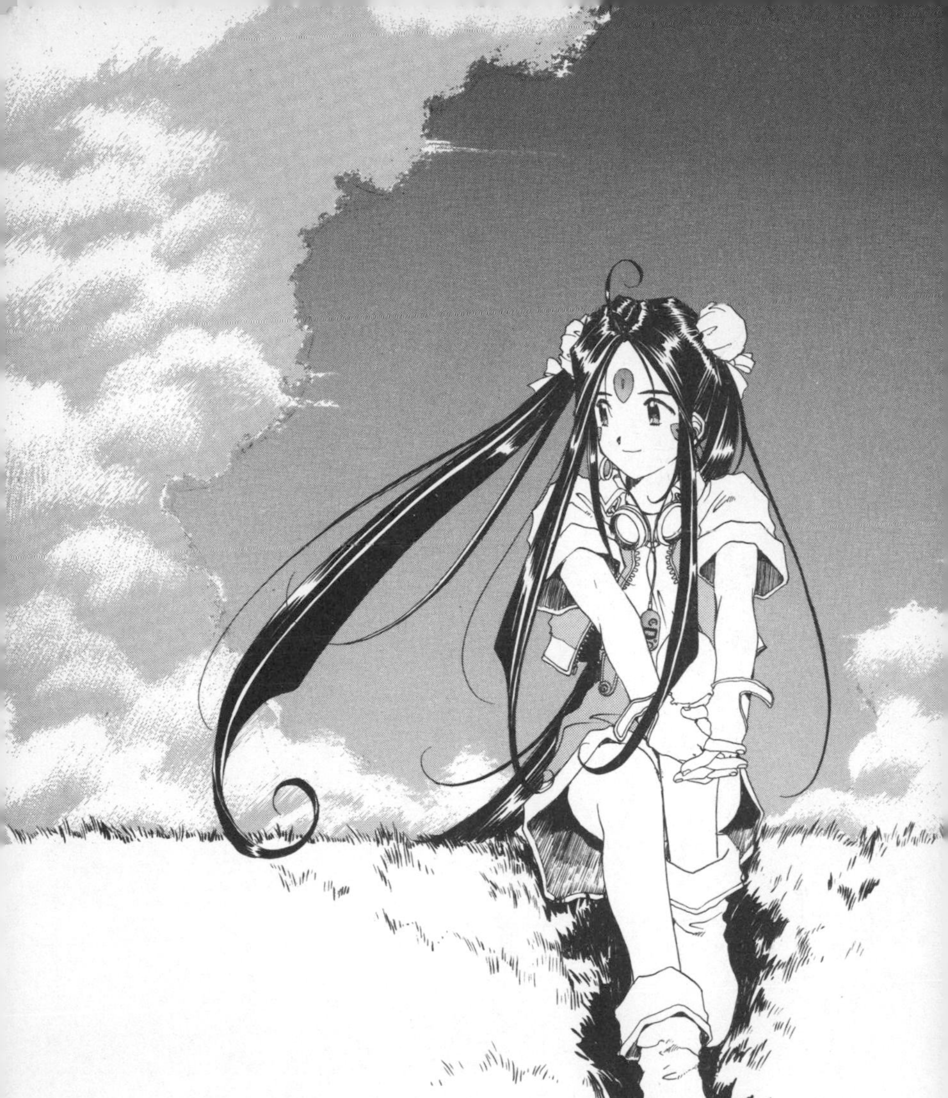

CHAPTER 73

Mean Sister

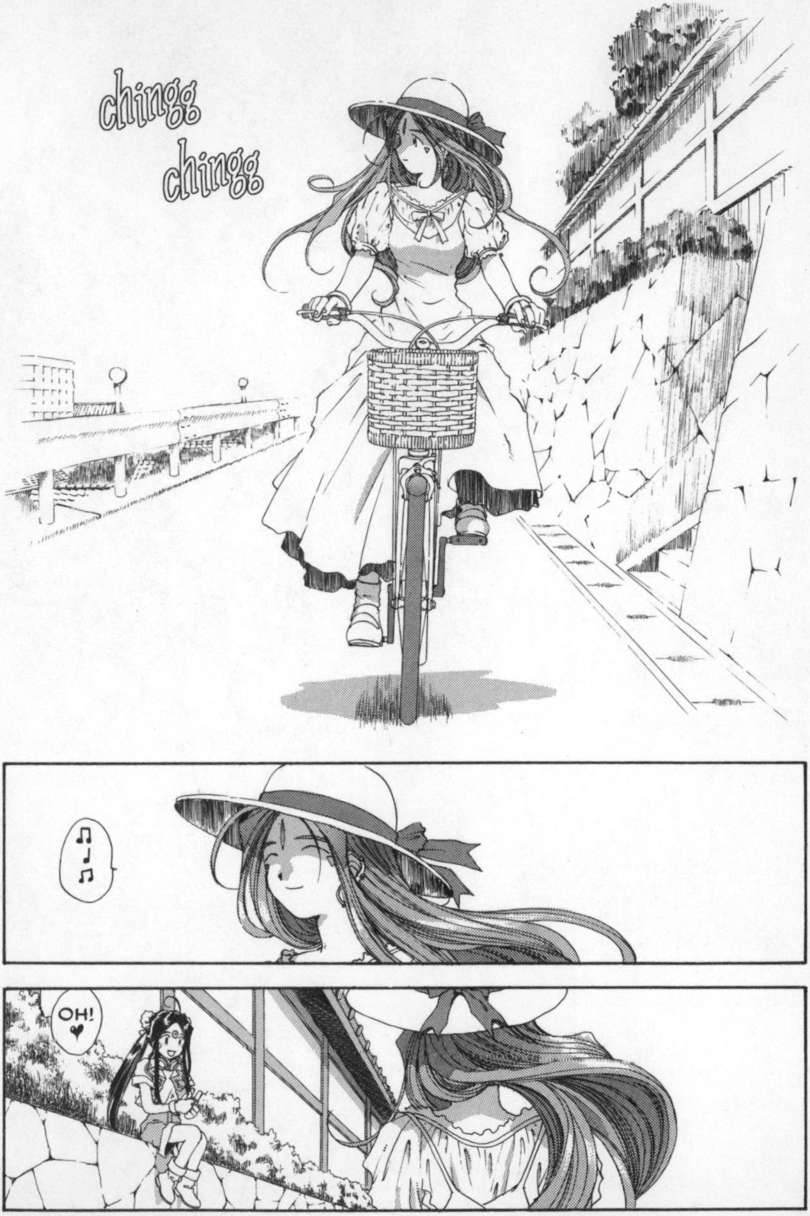
chingg
chingg
♫ ♩ ♫
OH! ♥

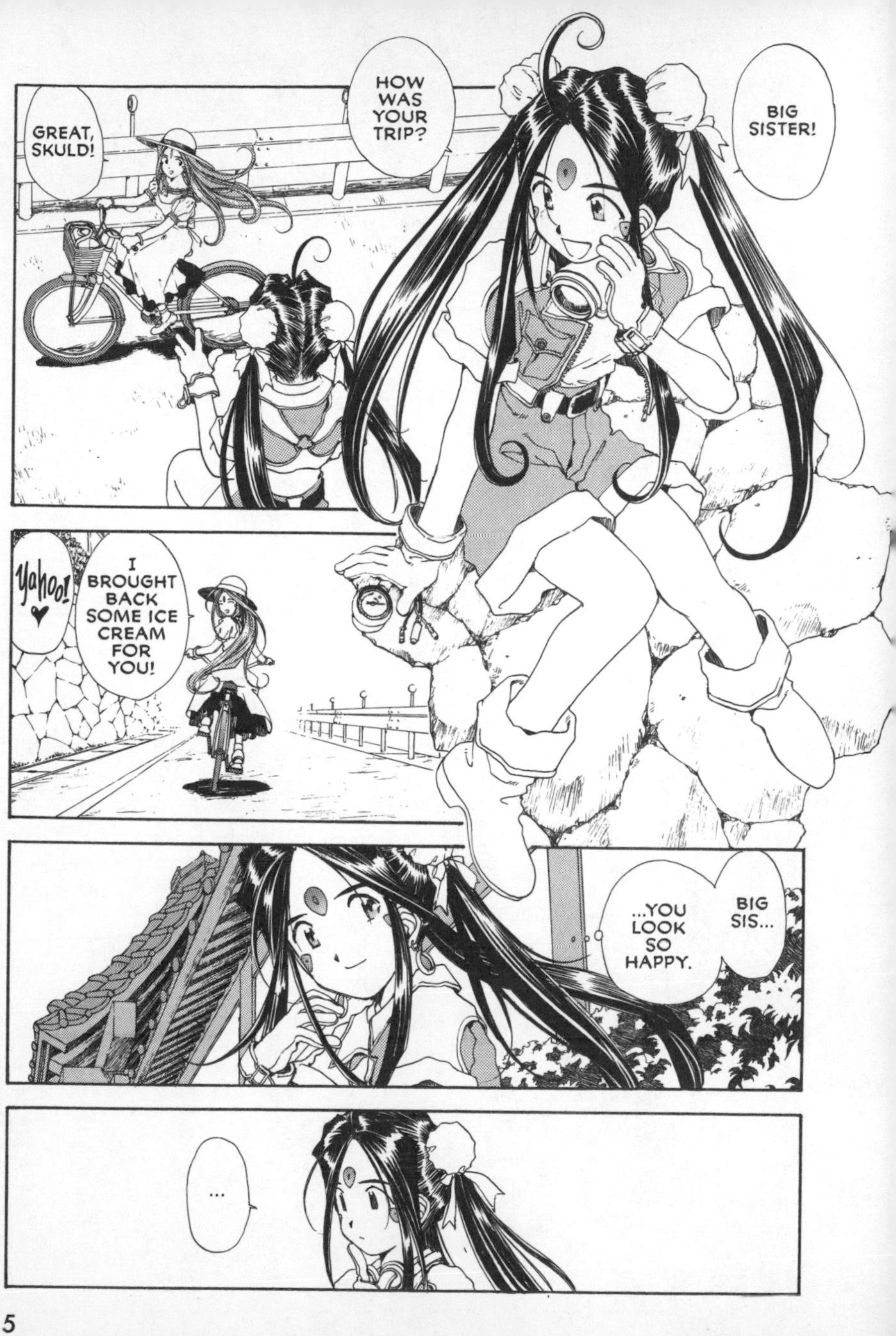
BIG SISTER!
HOW WAS YOUR TRIP?
GREAT, SKULD!
I BROUGHT BACK SOME ICE CREAM FOR YOU!
Yahoo! ♥
BIG SIS...
...YOU LOOK SO HAPPY.
...

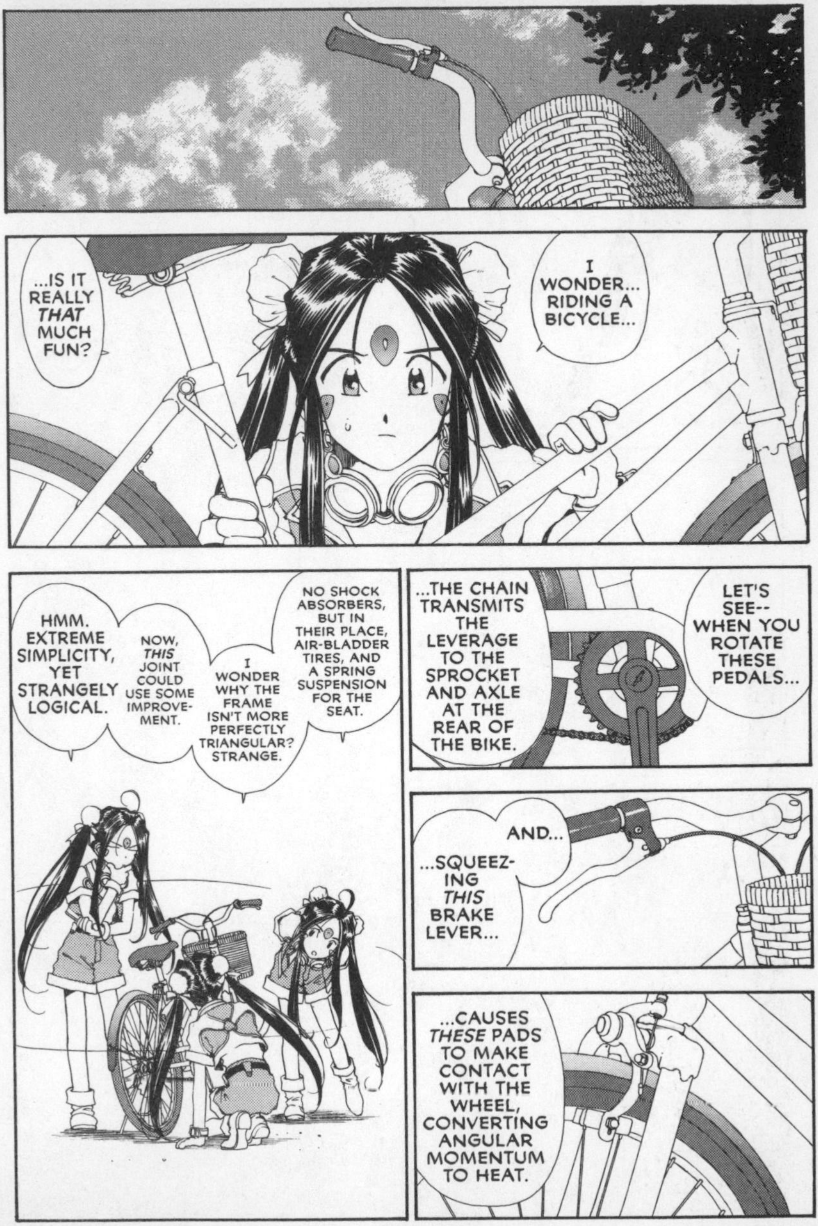
I WONDER... RIDING A BICYCLE...
...IS IT REALLY *THAT* MUCH FUN?
LET'S SEE-- WHEN YOU ROTATE THESE PEDALS...
...THE CHAIN TRANSMITS THE LEVERAGE TO THE SPROCKET AND AXLE AT THE REAR OF THE BIKE.
AND...
...SQUEEZ-ING *THIS* BRAKE LEVER...
...CAUSES *THESE* PADS TO MAKE CONTACT WITH THE WHEEL, CONVERTING ANGULAR MOMENTUM TO HEAT.
NO SHOCK ABSORBERS, BUT IN THEIR PLACE, AIR-BLADDER TIRES, AND A SPRING SUSPENSION FOR THE SEAT.
I WONDER WHY THE FRAME ISN'T MORE PERFECTLY TRIANGULAR? STRANGE.
NOW, *THIS* JOINT COULD USE SOME IMPROVE-MENT.
HMM. EXTREME SIMPLICITY, YET STRANGELY LOGICAL.

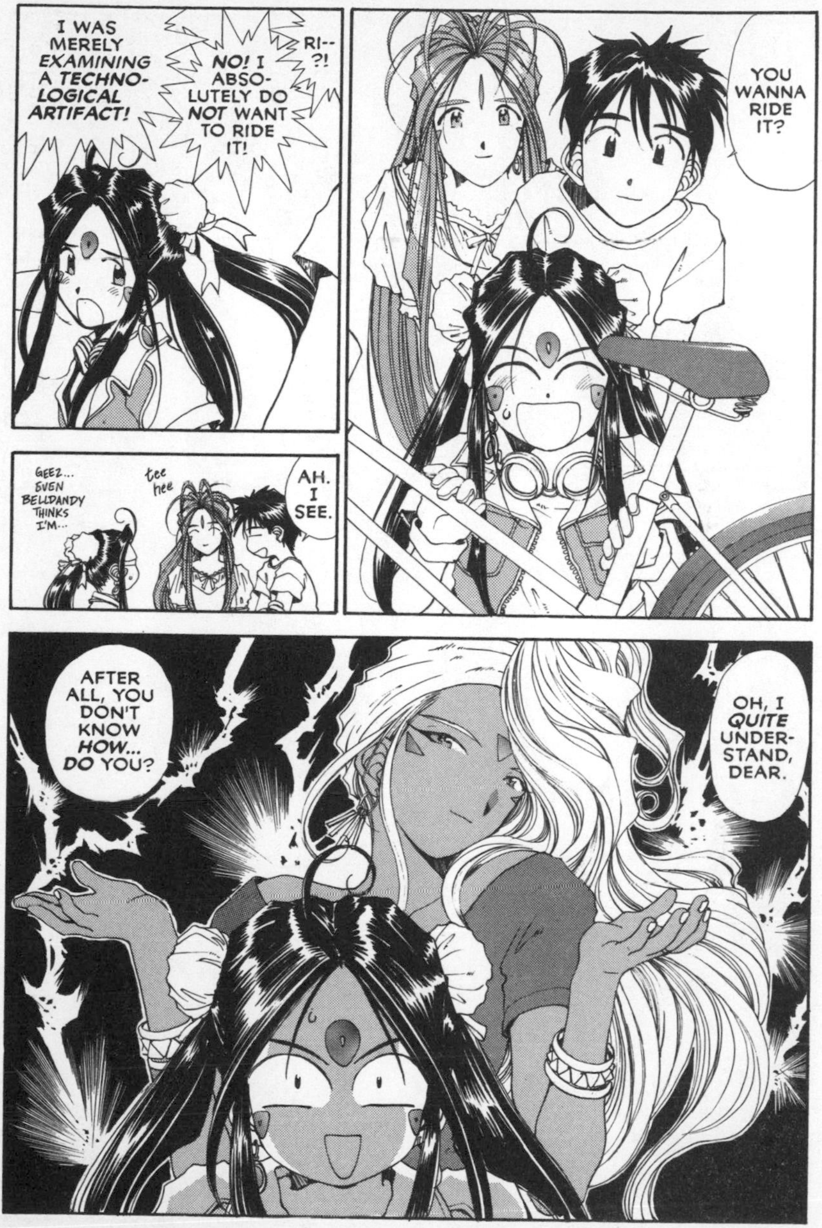
YOU WANNA RIDE IT?
RI-- ?!
NO! I ABSOLUTELY DO NOT WANT TO RIDE IT!
I WAS MERELY EXAMINING A TECHNOLOGICAL ARTIFACT!
AH. I SEE.
tee hee
GEEZ... EVEN BELLDANDY THINKS I'M...
OH, I QUITE UNDERSTAND, DEAR.
AFTER ALL, YOU DON'T KNOW HOW... DO YOU?

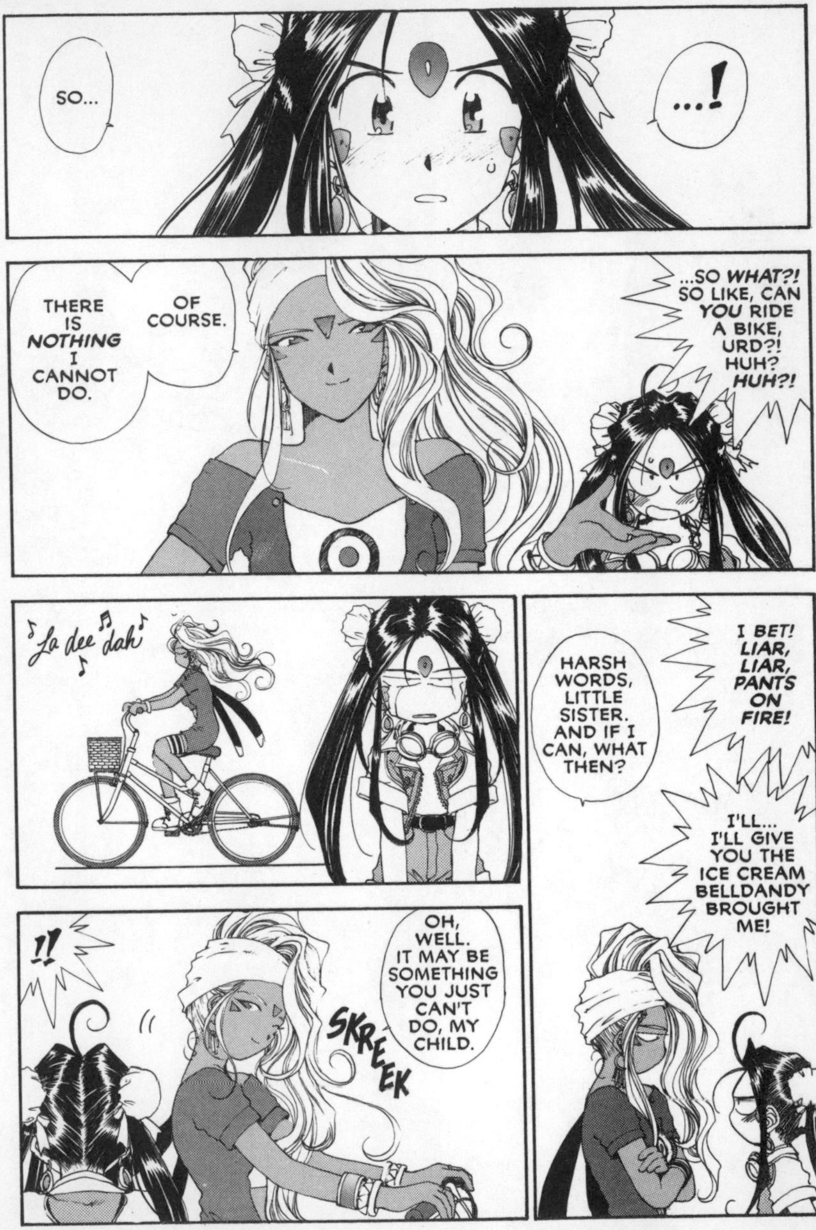
...!
SO...
...SO WHAT?! SO LIKE, CAN YOU RIDE A BIKE, URD?! HUH? HUH?!
OF COURSE.
THERE IS NOTHING I CANNOT DO.
I BET! LIAR, LIAR, PANTS ON FIRE!
HARSH WORDS, LITTLE SISTER. AND IF I CAN, WHAT THEN?
I'LL... I'LL GIVE YOU THE ICE CREAM BELLDANDY BROUGHT ME!
La dee dah
OH, WELL. IT MAY BE SOMETHING YOU JUST CAN'T DO, MY CHILD.
SKREEEK
!!

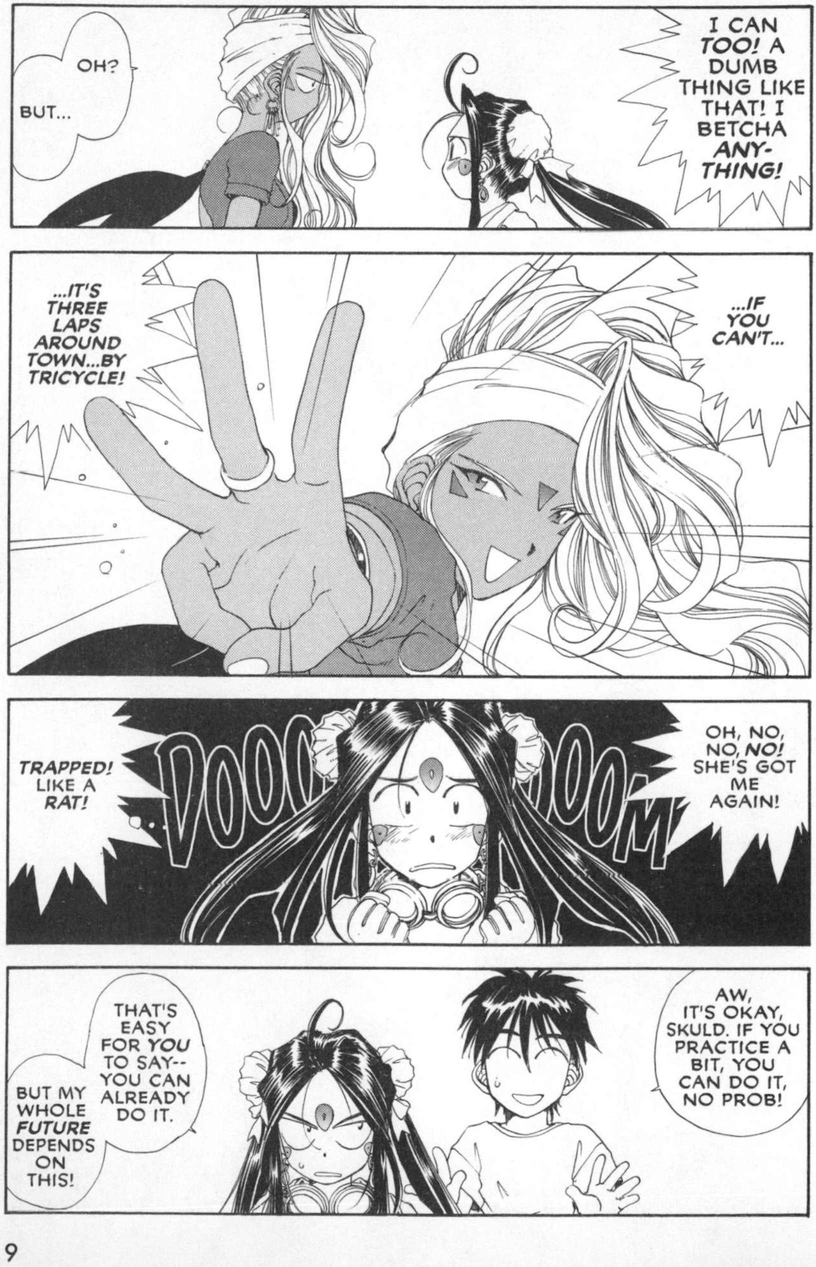
I CAN *TOO!* A DUMB THING LIKE THAT! I BETCHA *ANYTHING!*
OH?
BUT...
...IF YOU CAN'T...
...IT'S THREE LAPS AROUND TOWN...BY TRICYCLE!
OH, NO, NO, *NO!* SHE'S GOT ME AGAIN!
DOOO
OOOM
TRAPPED! LIKE A *RAT!*
AW, IT'S OKAY, SKULD. IF YOU PRACTICE A BIT, YOU CAN DO IT, NO PROB!
THAT'S EASY FOR *YOU* TO SAY-- YOU CAN ALREADY DO IT.
BUT MY WHOLE *FUTURE* DEPENDS ON THIS!

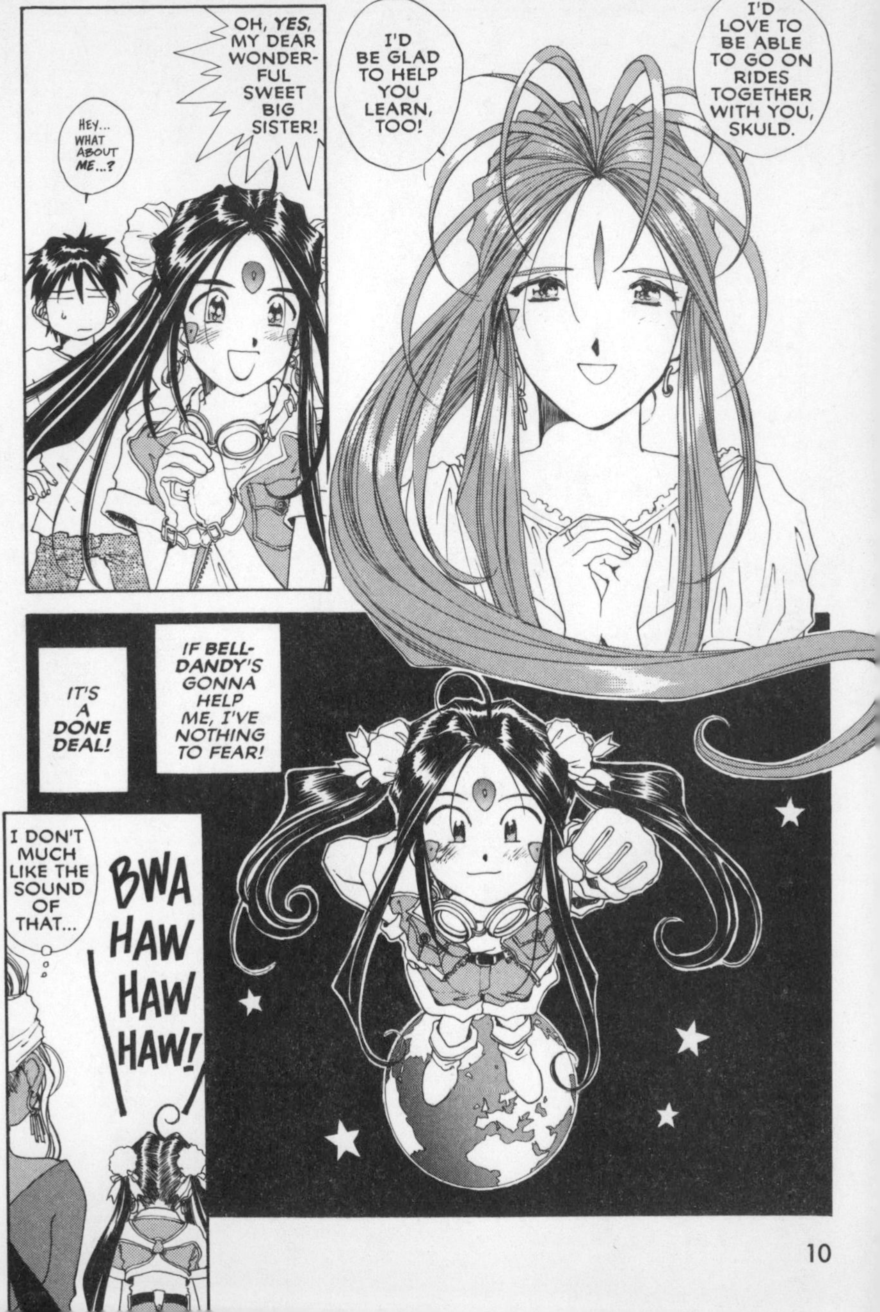
I'D LOVE TO BE ABLE TO GO ON RIDES TOGETHER WITH YOU, SKULD.
I'D BE GLAD TO HELP YOU LEARN, TOO!
OH, *YES*, MY DEAR WONDERFUL SWEET BIG SISTER!
HEY... WHAT ABOUT *ME*...?
IF BELL-DANDY'S GONNA HELP ME, I'VE NOTHING TO FEAR!
IT'S A DONE DEAL!
BWA HAW HAW HAW!
I DON'T MUCH LIKE THE SOUND OF THAT...

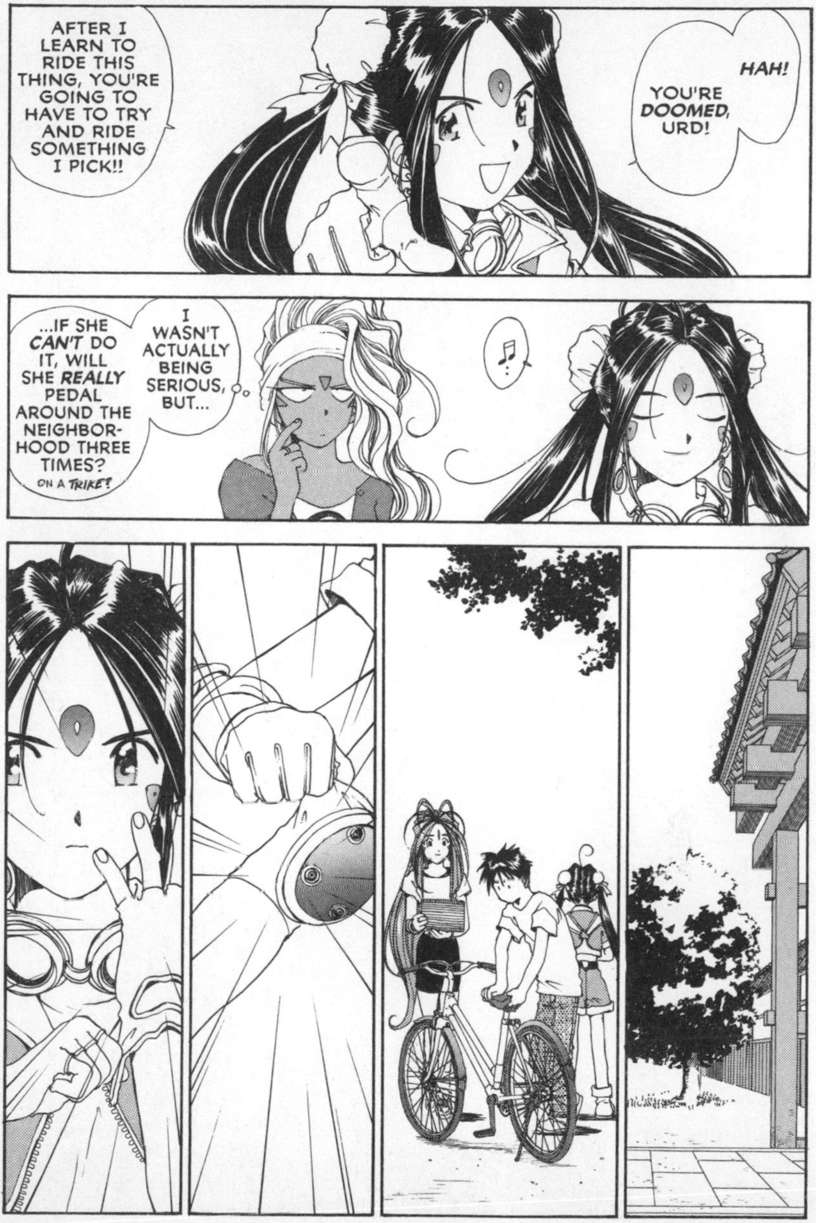
HAH!
YOU'RE *DOOMED*, URD!
AFTER I LEARN TO RIDE THIS THING, YOU'RE GOING TO HAVE TO TRY AND RIDE SOMETHING I PICK!!
I WASN'T ACTUALLY BEING SERIOUS, BUT...
...IF SHE *CAN'T* DO IT, WILL SHE *REALLY* PEDAL AROUND THE NEIGHBOR-HOOD THREE TIMES?
ON A *TRIKE?*

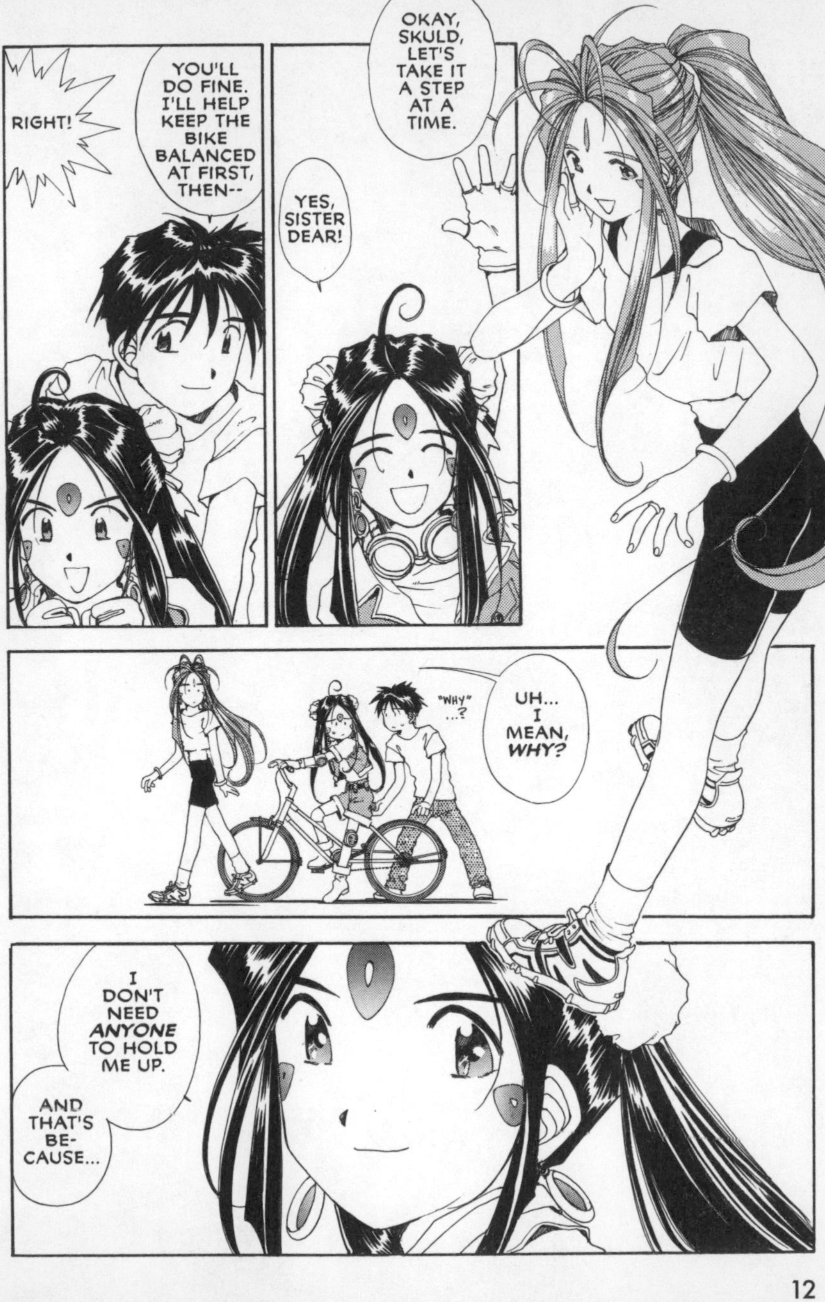
OKAY, SKULD, LET'S TAKE IT A STEP AT A TIME.
YES, SISTER DEAR!
YOU'LL DO FINE. I'LL HELP KEEP THE BIKE BALANCED AT FIRST, THEN--
RIGHT!
UH... I MEAN, *WHY?*
"WHY" ...?
I DON'T NEED *ANYONE* TO HOLD ME UP.
AND THAT'S BE-CAUSE...

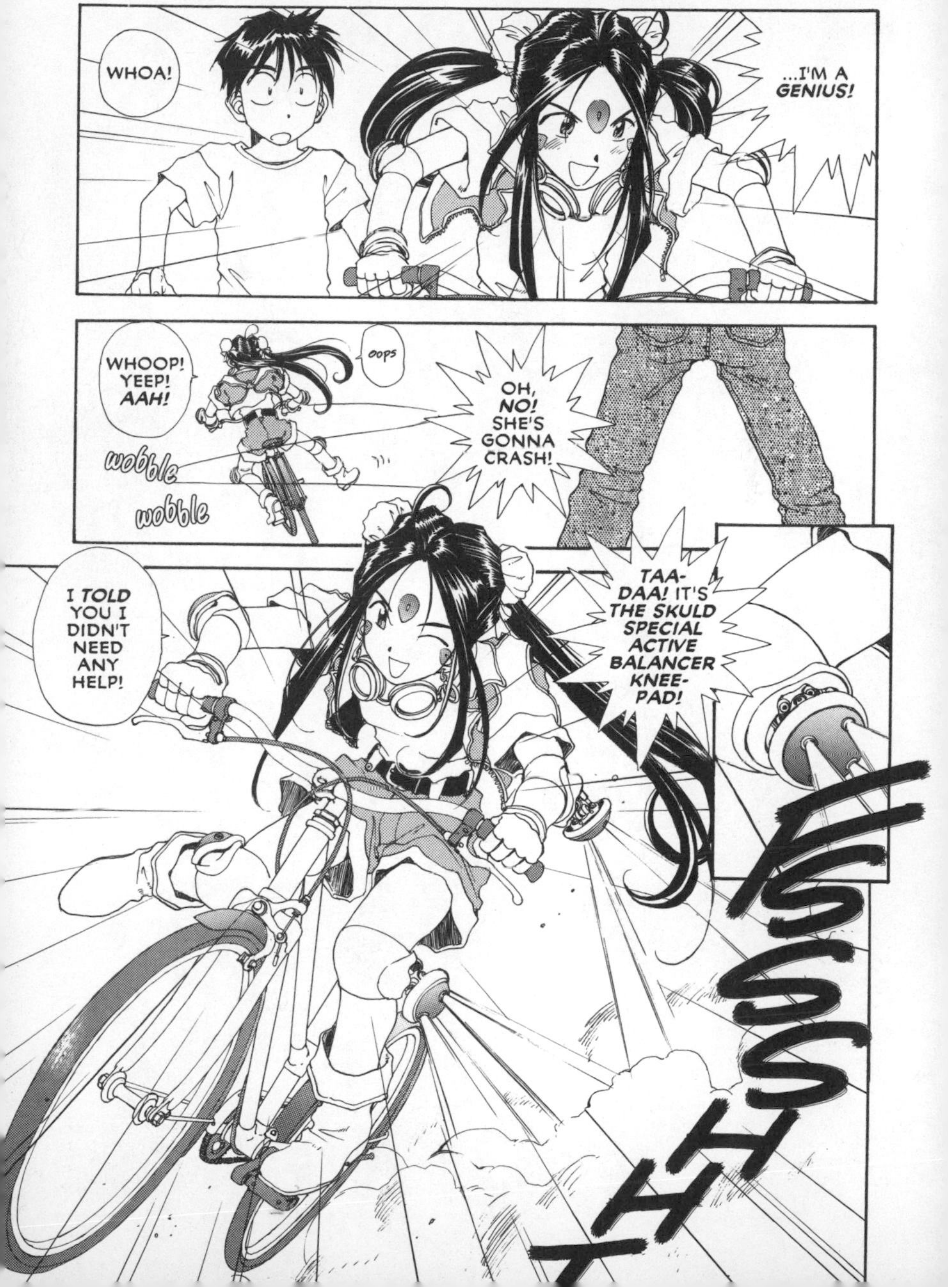
...I'M A GENIUS!
WHOA!
OH, NO! SHE'S GONNA CRASH!
oops
WHOOP! YEEP! AAH!
wobble
wobble
TAA-DAA! IT'S THE SKULD SPECIAL ACTIVE BALANCER KNEE-PAD!
I TOLD YOU I DIDN'T NEED ANY HELP!
FSSSHHH

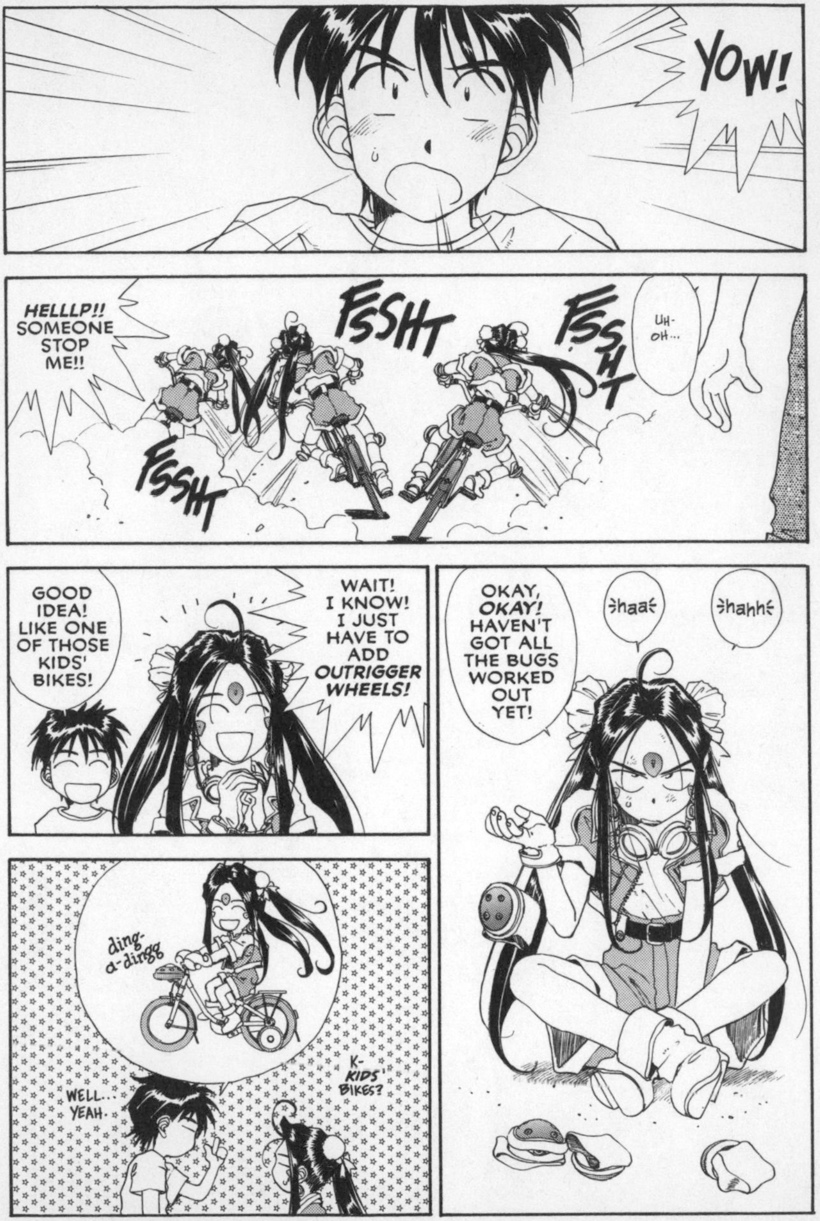
YOW!
UH-OH...
FSSHT
FSSHT
HELLLP!! SOMEONE STOP ME!!
FSSHT
hahh
haa
OKAY, OKAY! HAVEN'T GOT ALL THE BUGS WORKED OUT YET!
WAIT! I KNOW! I JUST HAVE TO ADD OUTRIGGER WHEELS!
GOOD IDEA! LIKE ONE OF THOSE KIDS' BIKES!
ding-a-dingg
K-KIDS' BIKES?
WELL... YEAH.

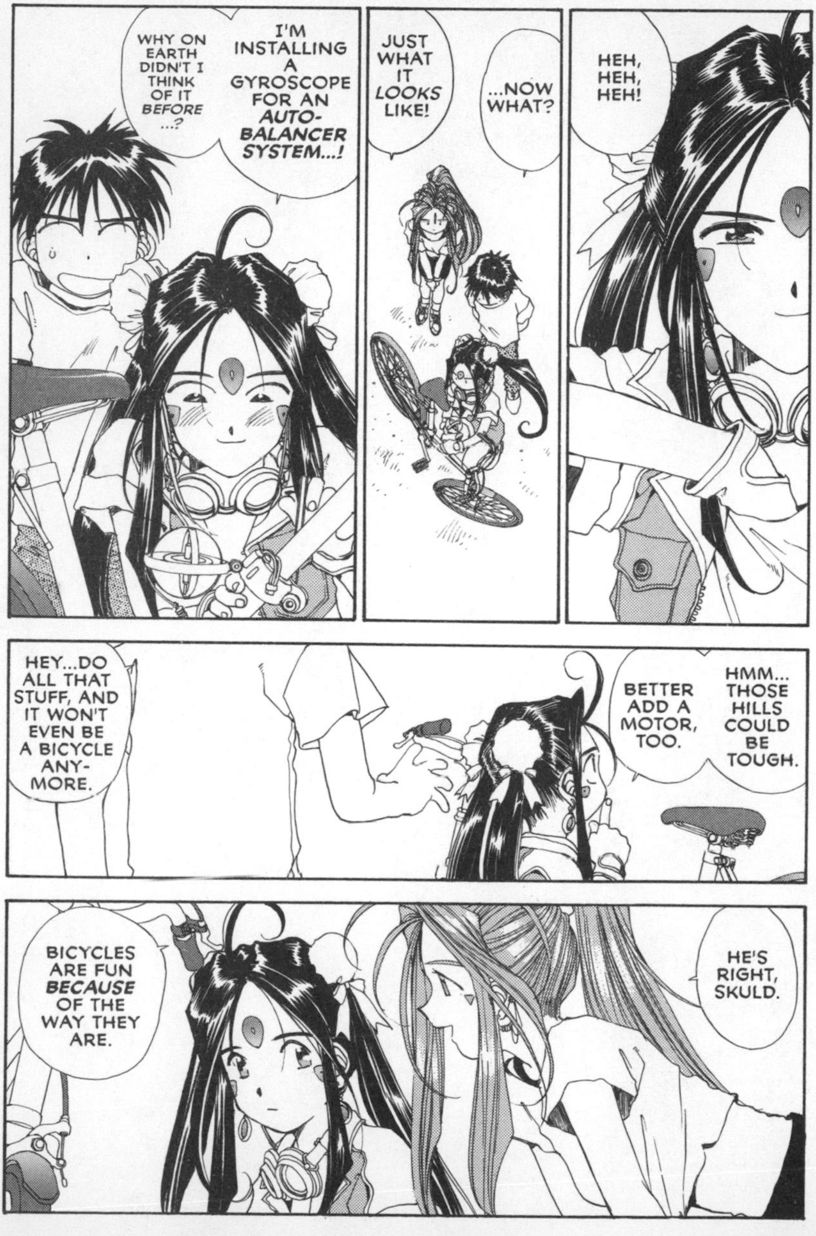
HEH, HEH, HEH!
...NOW WHAT?
JUST WHAT IT *LOOKS* LIKE!
I'M INSTALLING A GYROSCOPE FOR AN ***AUTO-BALANCER SYSTEM...!***
WHY ON EARTH DIDN'T I THINK OF IT *BEFORE* ...?
HMM... THOSE HILLS COULD BE TOUGH.
BETTER ADD A MOTOR, TOO.
HEY...DO ALL THAT STUFF, AND IT WON'T EVEN BE A BICYCLE ANY-MORE.
HE'S RIGHT, SKULD.
BICYCLES ARE FUN ***BECAUSE*** OF THE WAY THEY ARE.

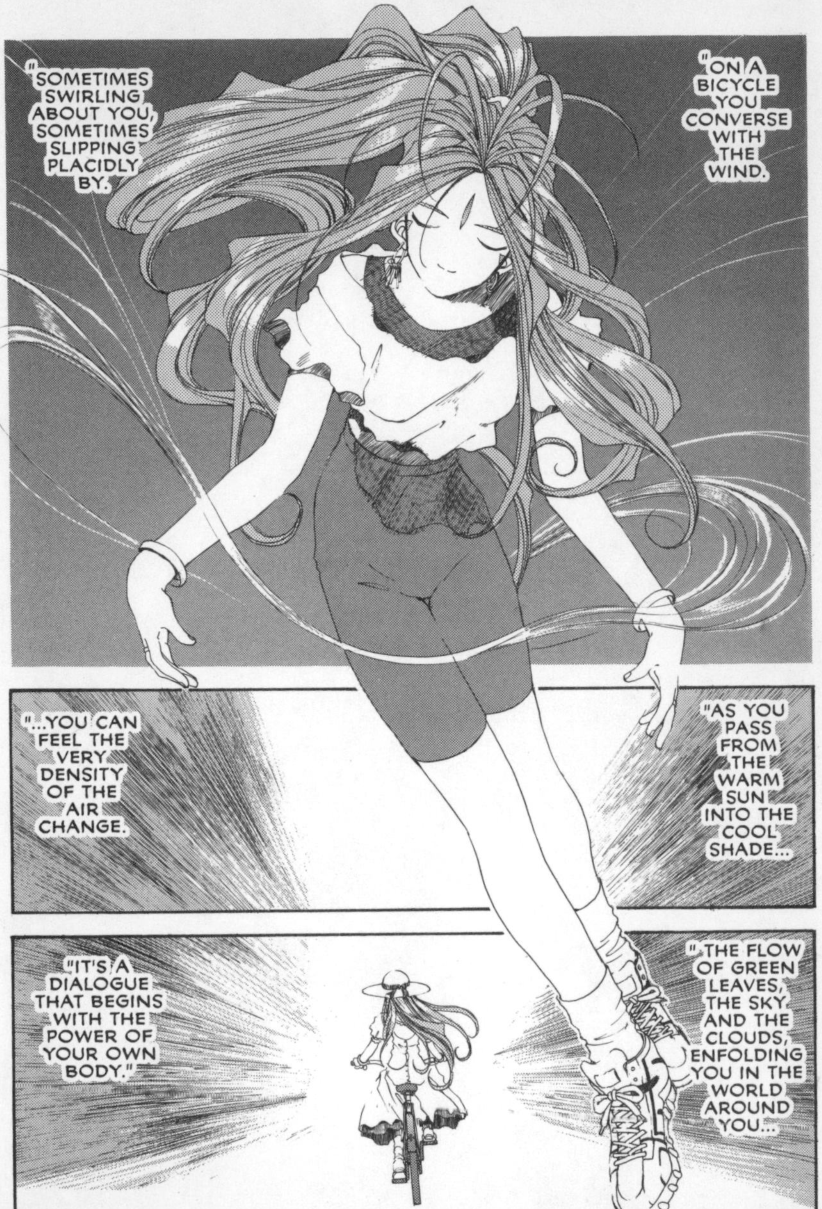
"ON A BICYCLE YOU CONVERSE WITH THE WIND.
"SOMETIMES SWIRLING ABOUT YOU, SOMETIMES SLIPPING PLACIDLY BY.
"AS YOU PASS FROM THE WARM SUN INTO THE COOL SHADE...
"...YOU CAN FEEL THE VERY DENSITY OF THE AIR CHANGE.
"THE FLOW OF GREEN LEAVES, THE SKY AND THE CLOUDS, ENFOLDING YOU IN THE WORLD AROUND YOU...
"IT'S A DIALOGUE THAT BEGINS WITH THE POWER OF YOUR OWN BODY."

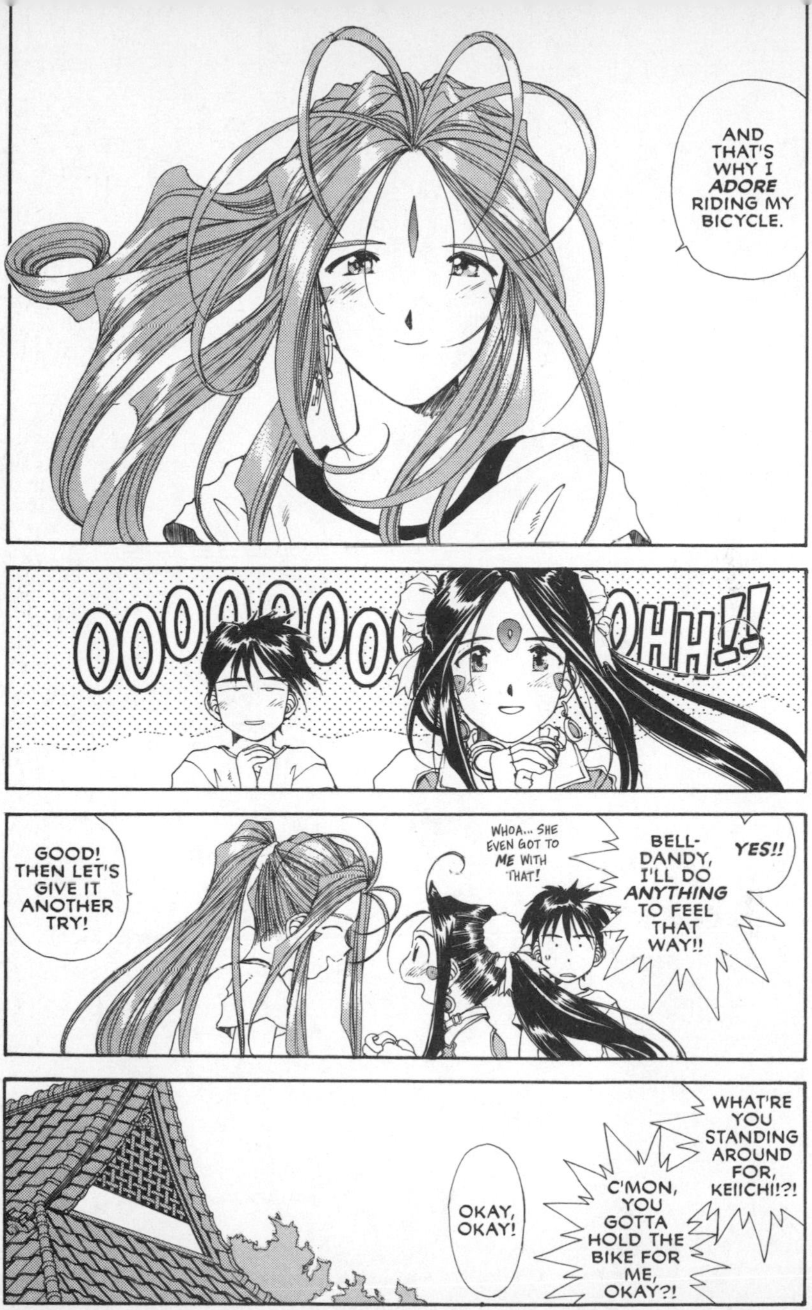
AND THAT'S WHY I ADORE RIDING MY BICYCLE.
OOOOOOOOOHH!!
YES!!
BELL-DANDY, I'LL DO ANYTHING TO FEEL THAT WAY!!
WHOA... SHE EVEN GOT TO ME WITH THAT!
GOOD! THEN LET'S GIVE IT ANOTHER TRY!
WHAT'RE YOU STANDING AROUND FOR, KEIICHI!?!
C'MON, YOU GOTTA HOLD THE BIKE FOR ME, OKAY?!
OKAY, OKAY!

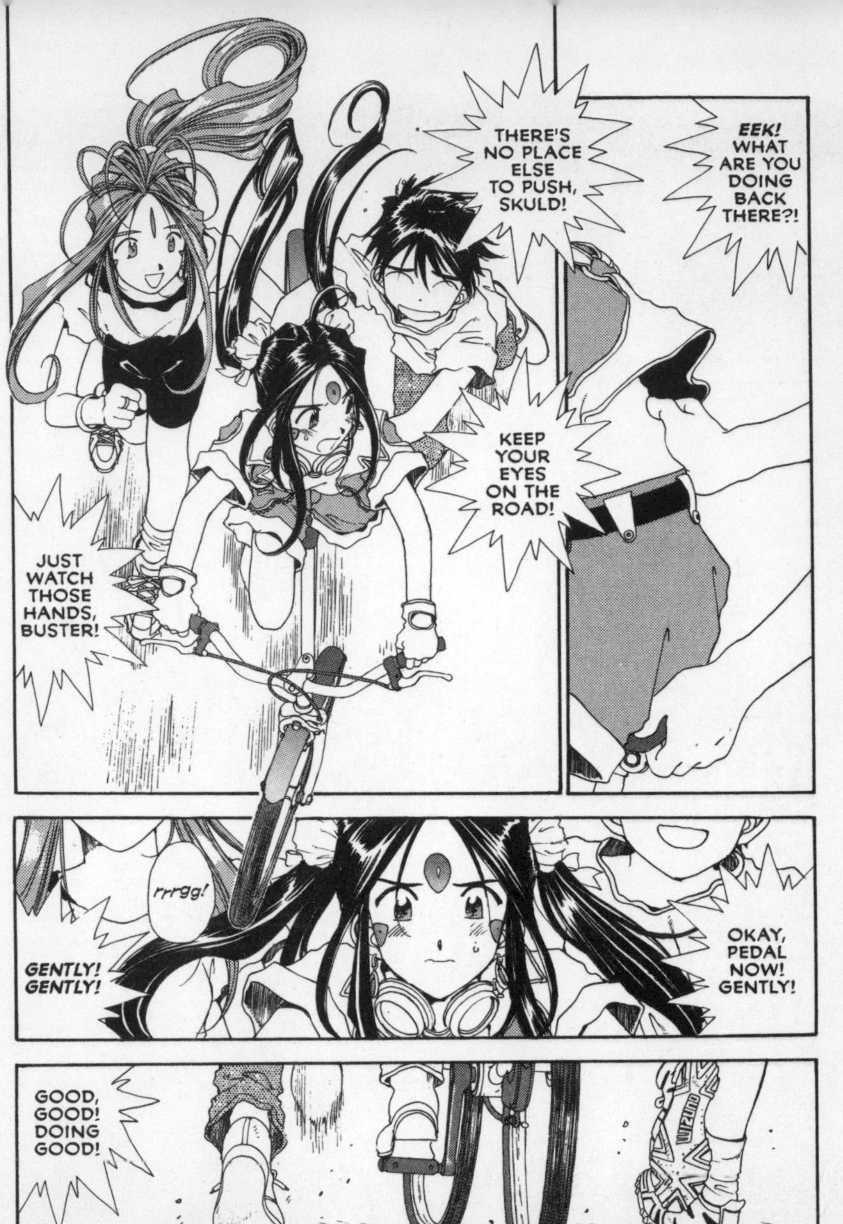
EEK! WHAT ARE YOU DOING BACK THERE?!
THERE'S NO PLACE ELSE TO PUSH, SKULD!
KEEP YOUR EYES ON THE ROAD!
JUST WATCH THOSE HANDS, BUSTER!
OKAY, PEDAL NOW! GENTLY!
rrrgg!
GENTLY! GENTLY!
GOOD, GOOD! DOING GOOD!

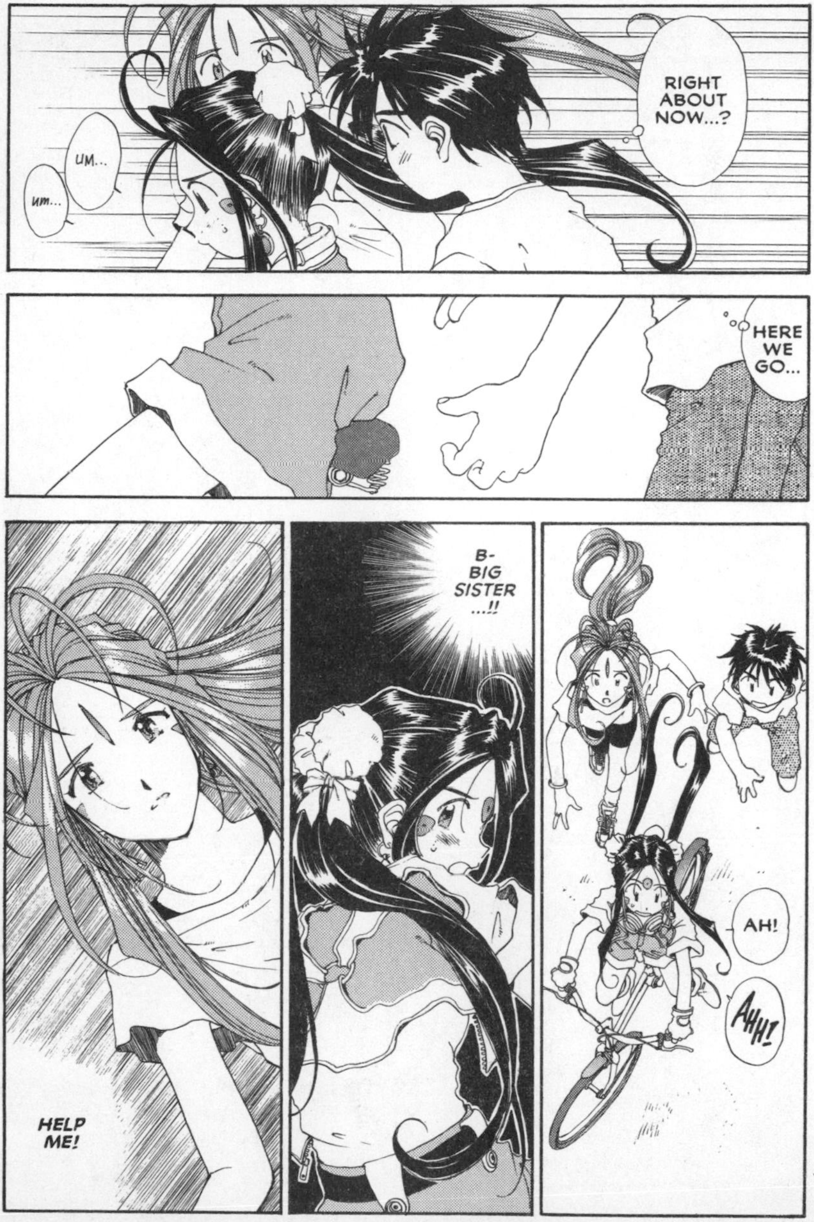
RIGHT ABOUT NOW...?
UM...
um...
HERE WE GO...
AH!
AHH!
B- BIG SISTER ...!!
HELP ME!

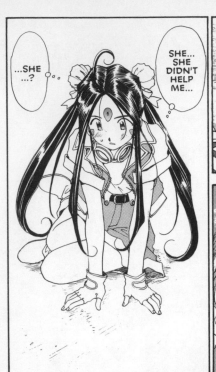

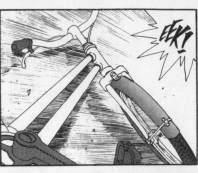

EEK!
SKULD! ARE YOU OKAY?!
SHE... SHE DIDN'T HELP ME...
...SHE ...?
OH, GOOD! YOU'RE NOT HURT.
HERE-- LET'S TRY IT ONE MORE TIME!

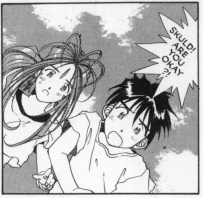

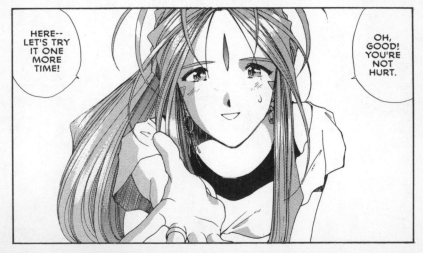

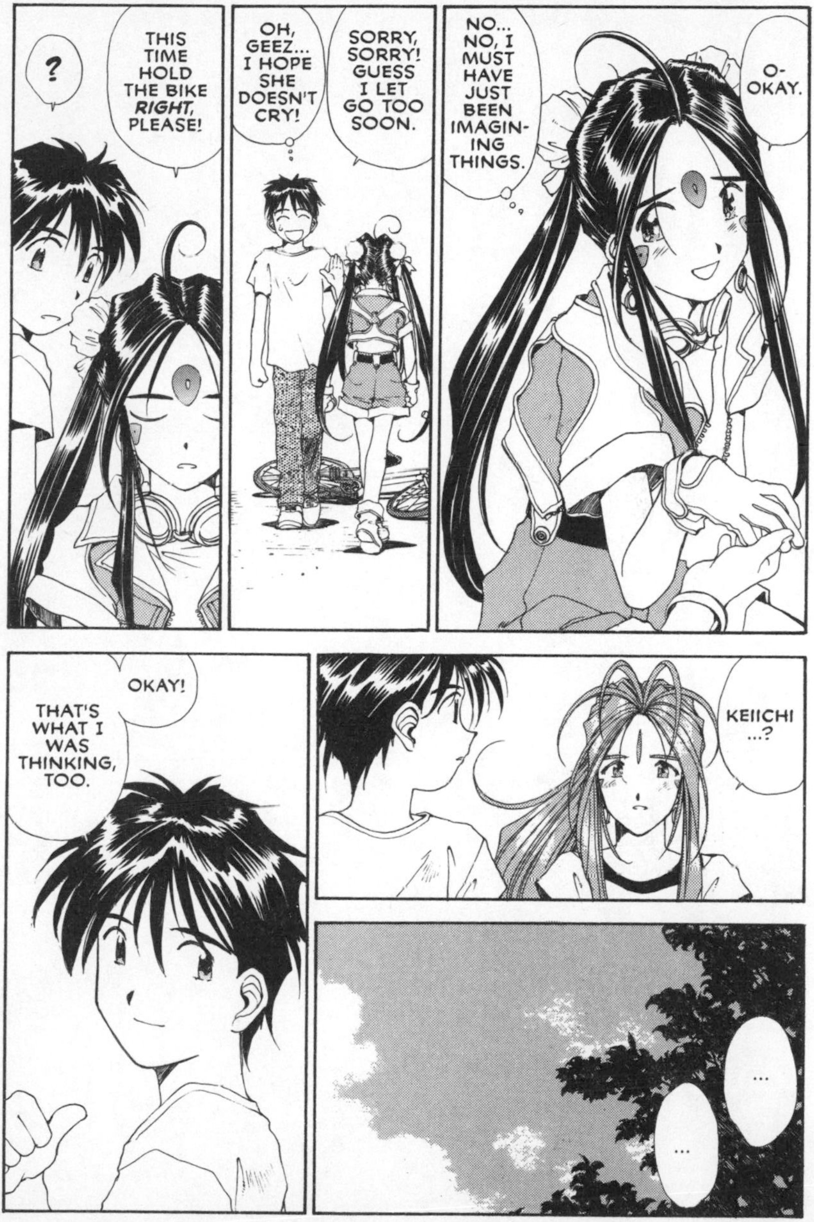
O-OKAY.
NO... NO, I MUST HAVE JUST BEEN IMAGINING THINGS.
SORRY, SORRY! GUESS I LET GO TOO SOON.
OH, GEEZ... I HOPE SHE DOESN'T CRY!
THIS TIME HOLD THE BIKE *RIGHT*, PLEASE!
?
KEIICHI ...?
...
...
OKAY!
THAT'S WHAT I WAS THINKING, TOO.

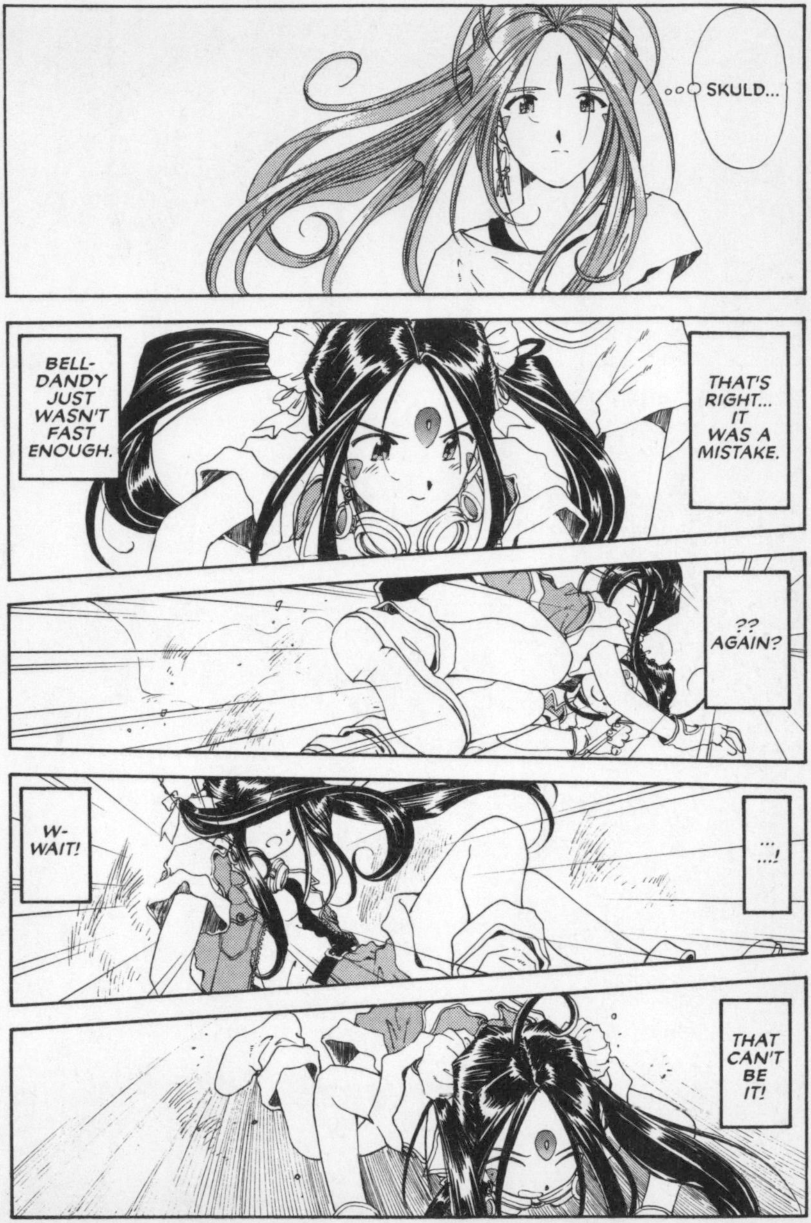
...SKULD...
THAT'S RIGHT... IT WAS A MISTAKE.
BELL-DANDY JUST WASN'T FAST ENOUGH.
?? AGAIN?
..., ...!
W-WAIT!
THAT CAN'T BE IT!

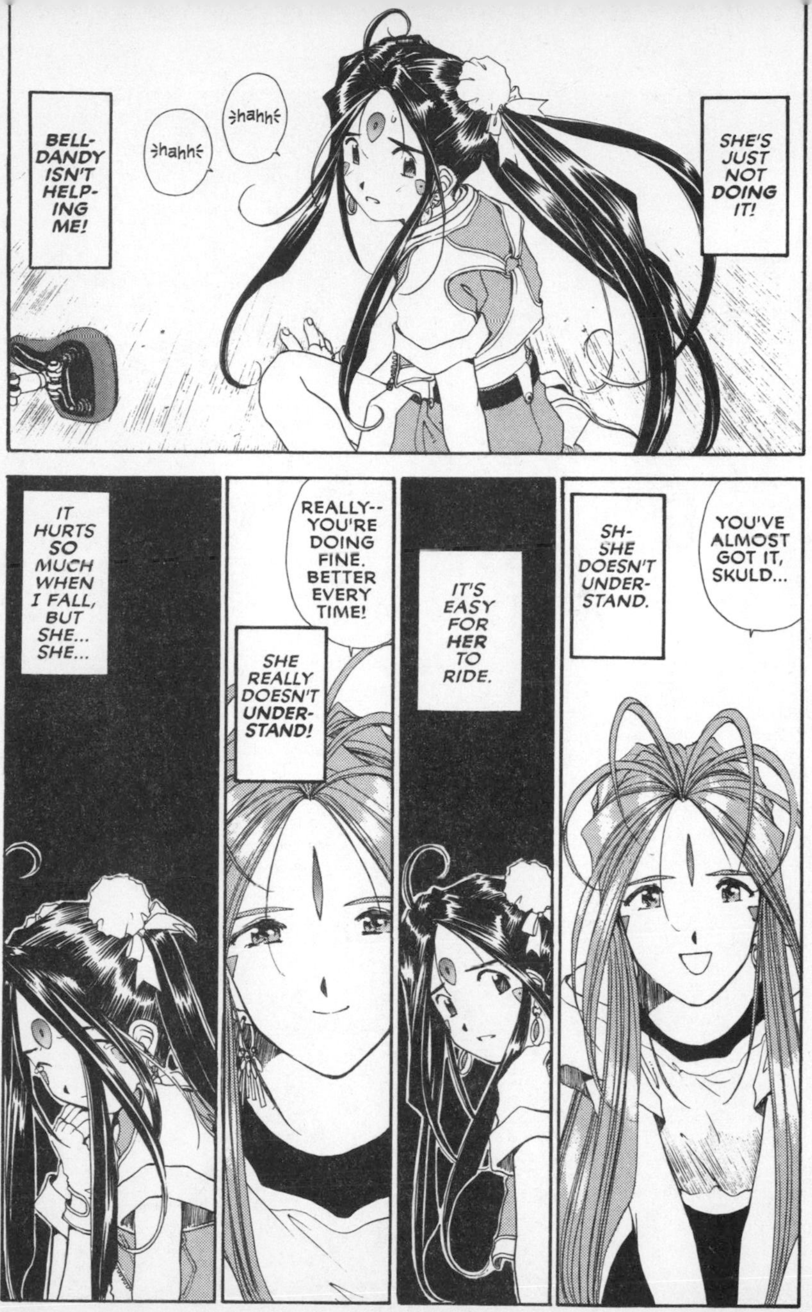
SHE'S JUST NOT DOING IT!
hahh
hahh
BELL-DANDY ISN'T HELPING ME!
YOU'VE ALMOST GOT IT, SKULD...
SH- SHE DOESN'T UNDER-STAND.
IT'S EASY FOR HER TO RIDE.
REALLY-- YOU'RE DOING FINE. BETTER EVERY TIME!
SHE REALLY DOESN'T UNDER-STAND!
IT HURTS SO MUCH WHEN I FALL, BUT SHE... SHE...

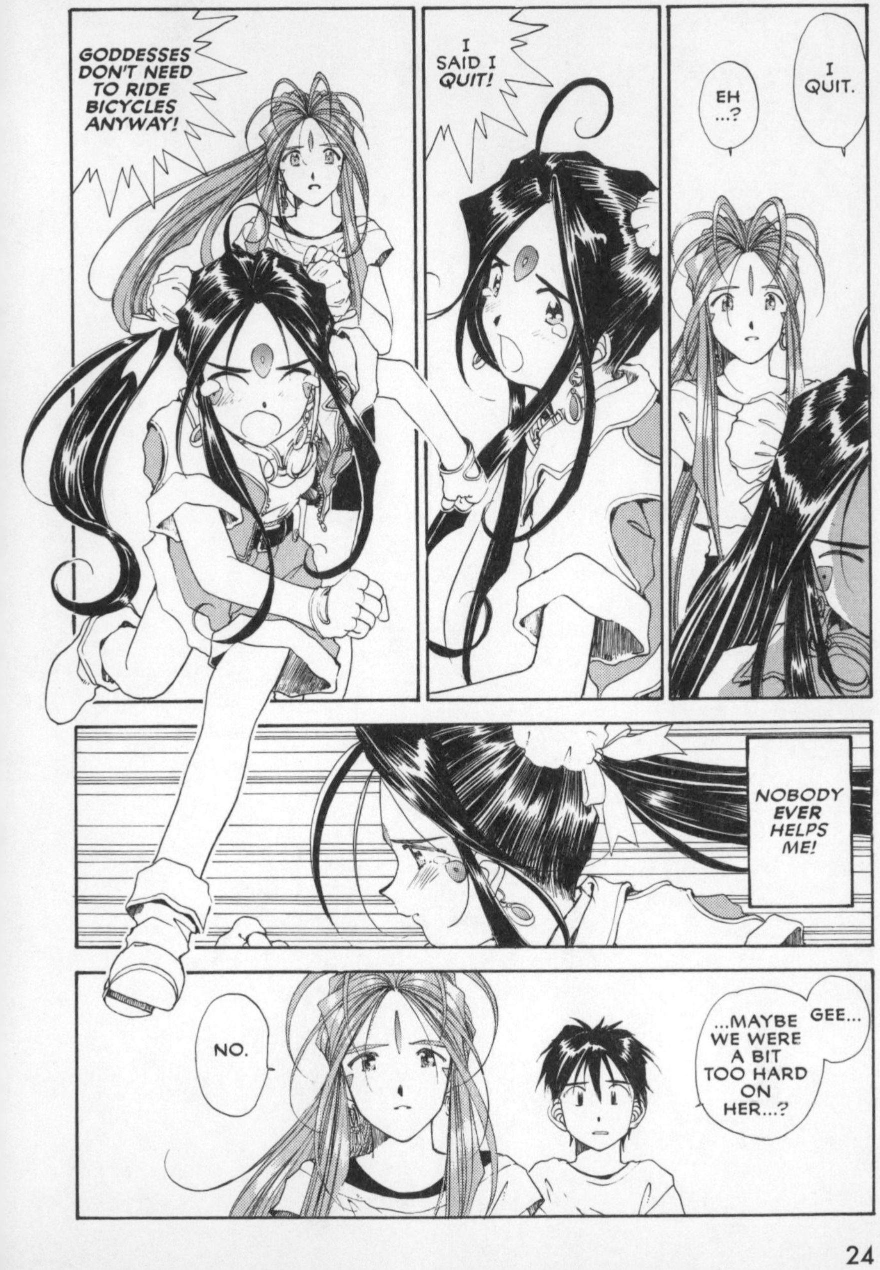
I QUIT.
EH ...?
I SAID I QUIT!
GODDESSES DON'T NEED TO RIDE BICYCLES ANYWAY!
NOBODY EVER HELPS ME!
GEE... ...MAYBE WE WERE A BIT TOO HARD ON HER...?
NO.

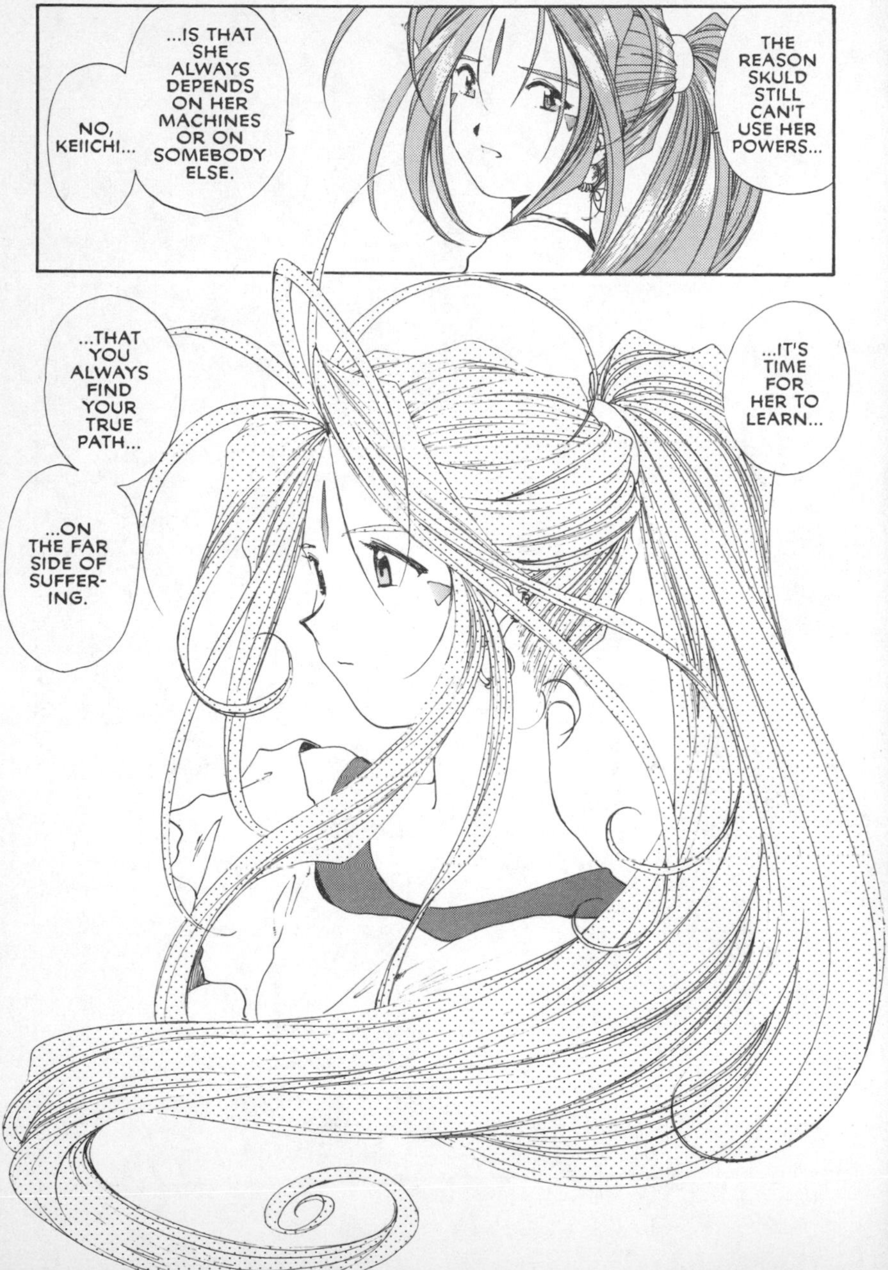
THE REASON SKULD STILL CAN'T USE HER POWERS...
...IS THAT SHE ALWAYS DEPENDS ON HER MACHINES OR ON SOMEBODY ELSE.
NO, KEIICHI...
...IT'S TIME FOR HER TO LEARN...
...THAT YOU ALWAYS FIND YOUR TRUE PATH...
...ON THE FAR SIDE OF SUFFER-ING.

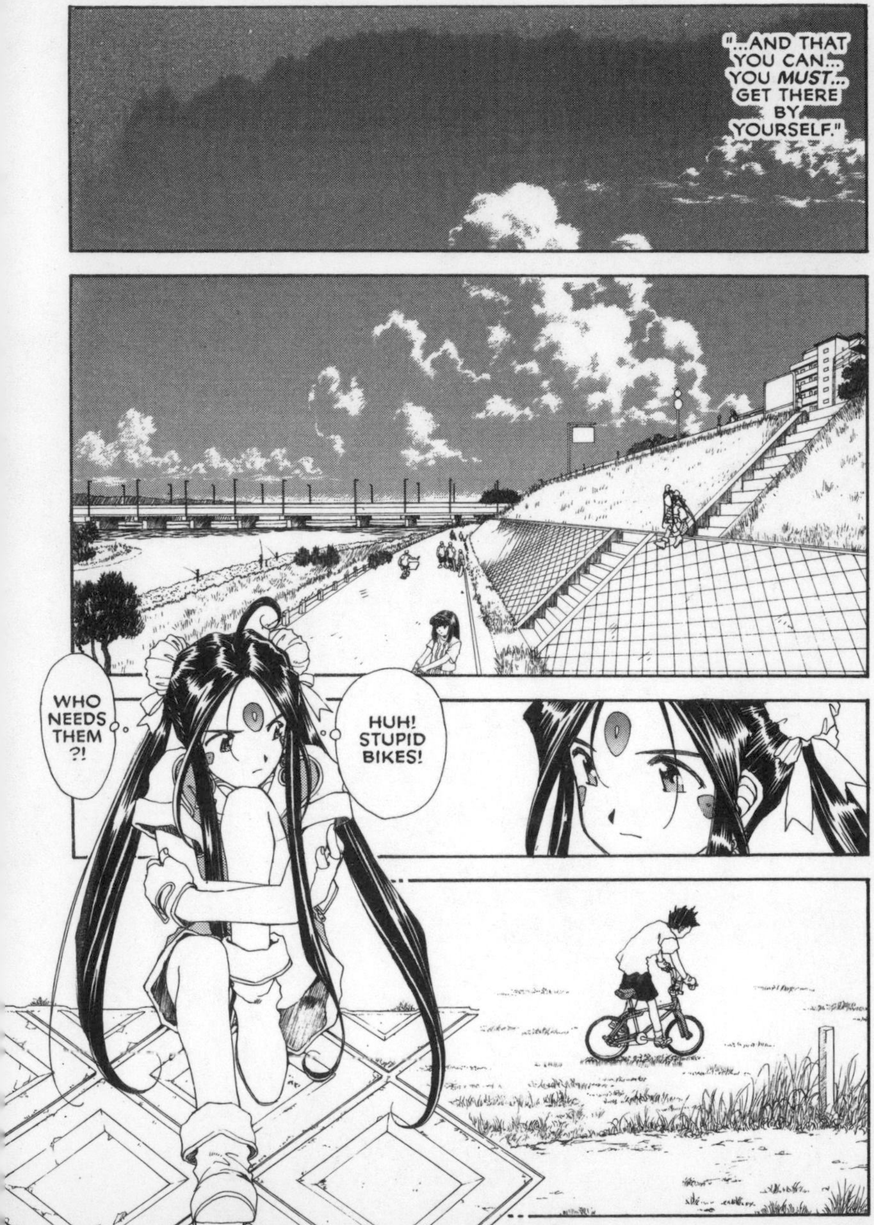
"...AND THAT YOU CAN... YOU *MUST*... GET THERE BY YOURSELF."
HUH! STUPID BIKES!
WHO NEEDS THEM ?!

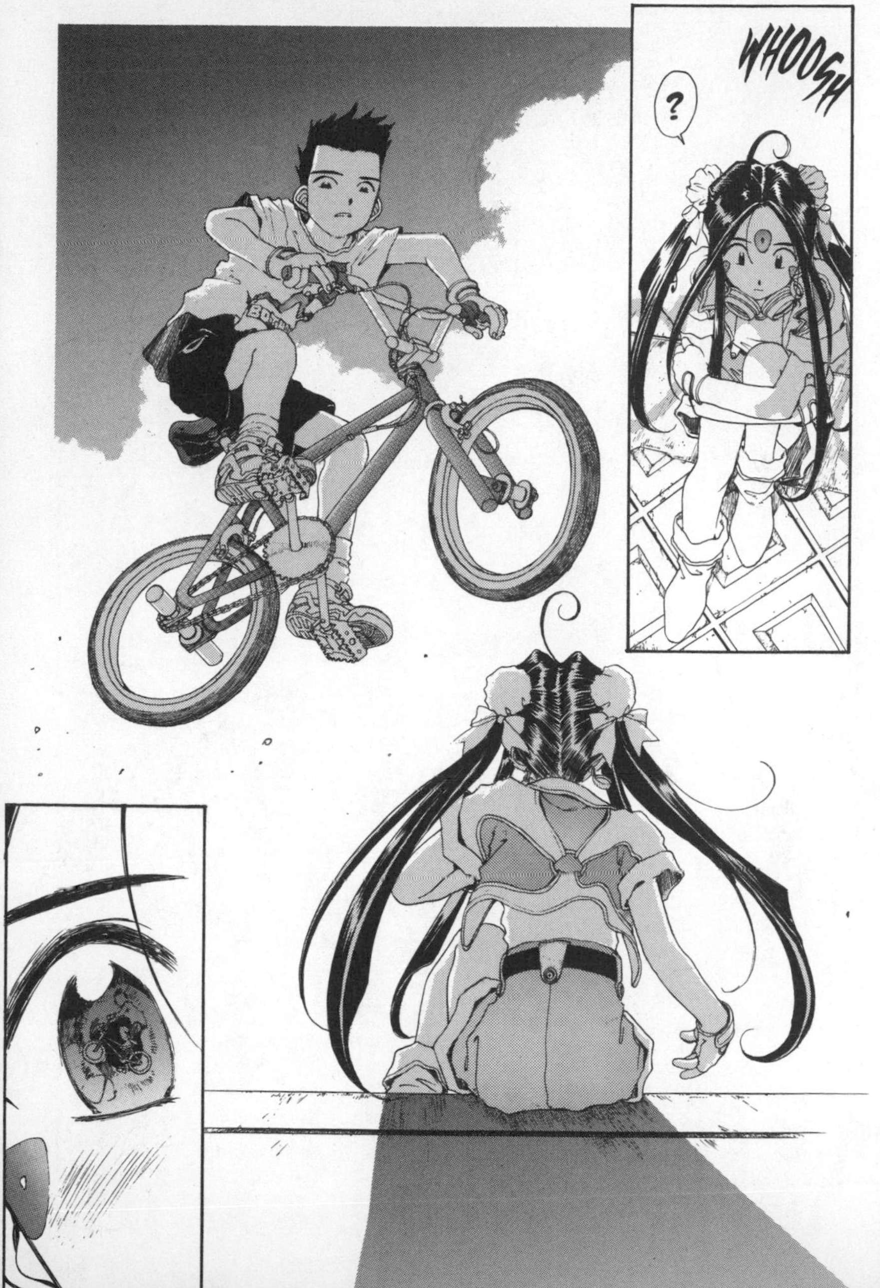
WHOOSH
?

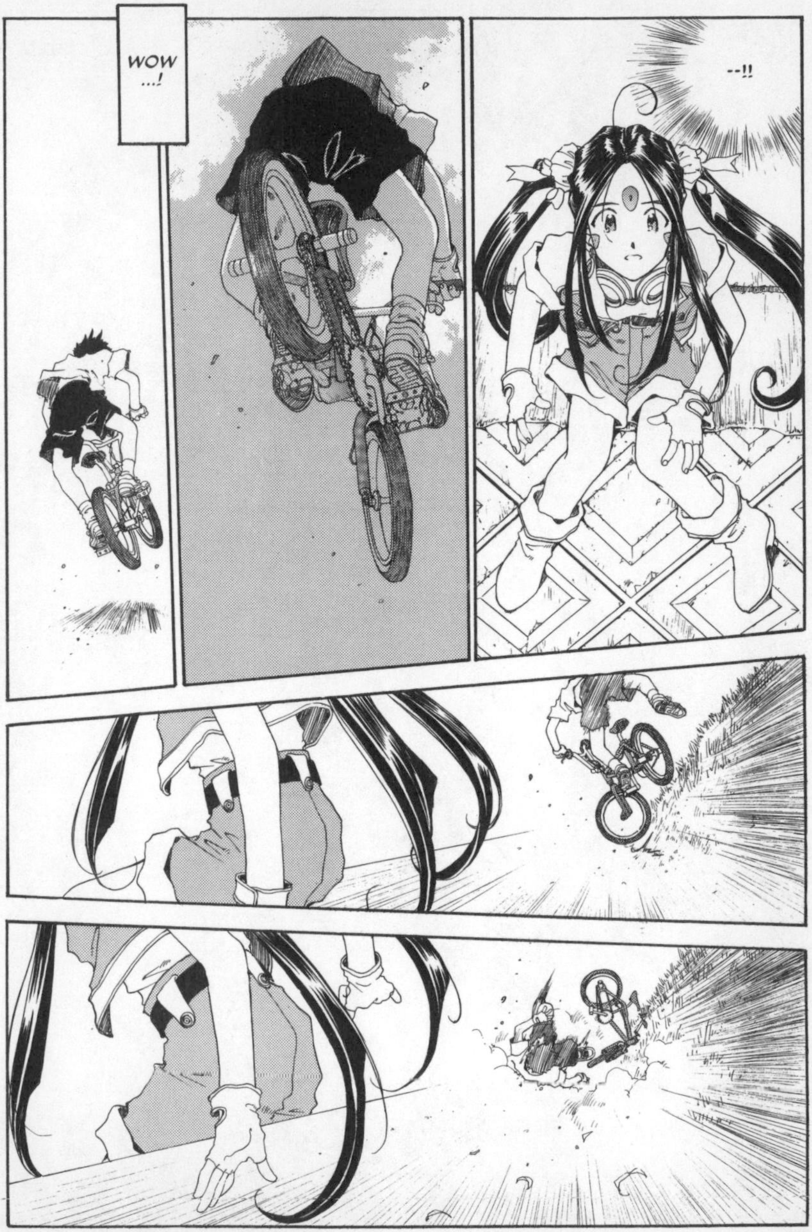
--!!
WOW ...!

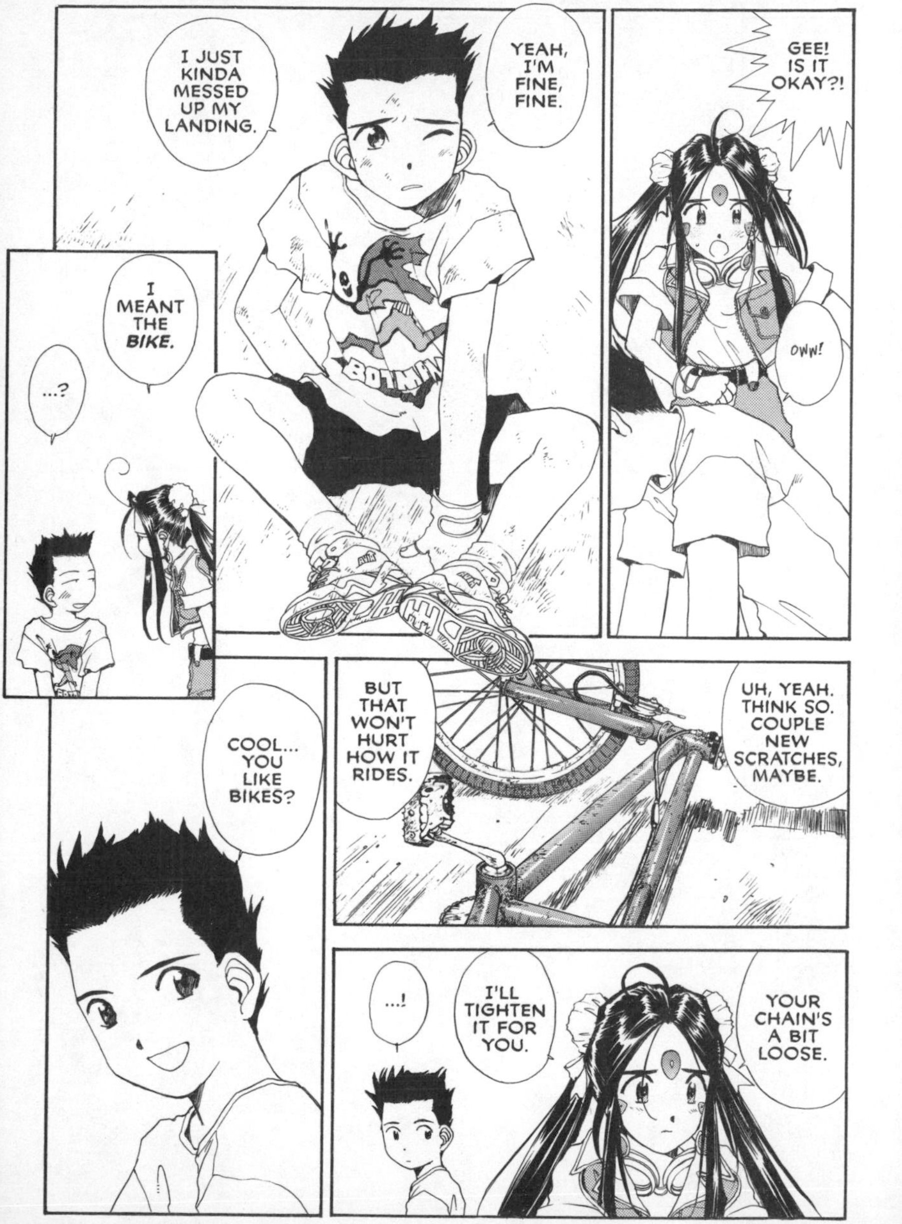
GEE! IS IT OKAY?!
OWW!
YEAH, I'M FINE, FINE.
I JUST KINDA MESSED UP MY LANDING.
I MEANT THE *BIKE.*
...?
UH, YEAH. THINK SO. COUPLE NEW SCRATCHES, MAYBE.
BUT THAT WON'T HURT HOW IT RIDES.
YOUR CHAIN'S A BIT LOOSE.
I'LL TIGHTEN IT FOR YOU.
...!
COOL... YOU LIKE BIKES?

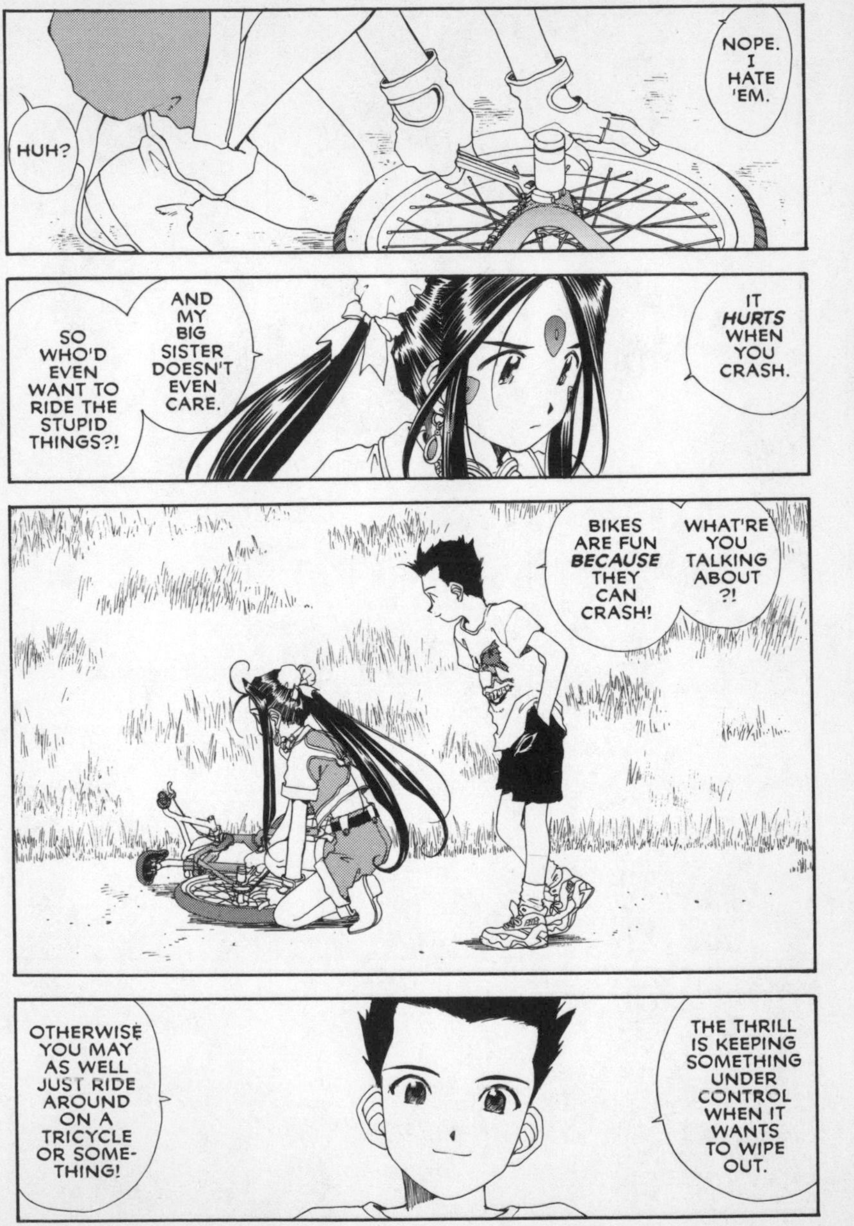
NOPE. I HATE 'EM.
HUH?
IT HURTS WHEN YOU CRASH.
AND MY BIG SISTER DOESN'T EVEN CARE.
SO WHO'D EVEN WANT TO RIDE THE STUPID THINGS?!
WHAT'RE YOU TALKING ABOUT?!
BIKES ARE FUN BECAUSE THEY CAN CRASH!
THE THRILL IS KEEPING SOMETHING UNDER CONTROL WHEN IT WANTS TO WIPE OUT.
OTHERWISE YOU MAY AS WELL JUST RIDE AROUND ON A TRICYCLE OR SOME-THING!

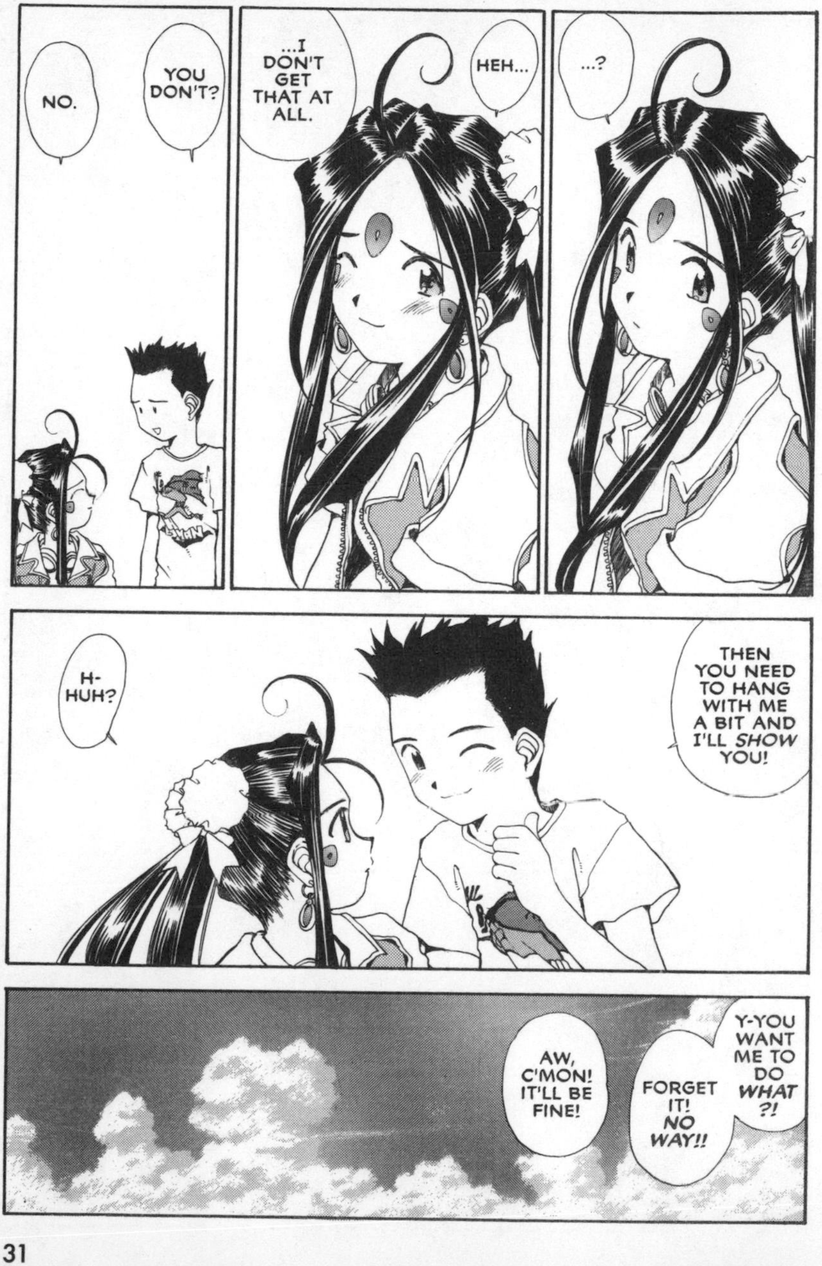
...?
HEH...
...I DON'T GET THAT AT ALL.
YOU DON'T?
NO.
THEN YOU NEED TO HANG WITH ME A BIT AND I'LL *SHOW* YOU!
H-HUH?
Y-YOU WANT ME TO DO *WHAT?!*
FORGET IT! *NO WAY!!*
AW, C'MON! IT'LL BE FINE!

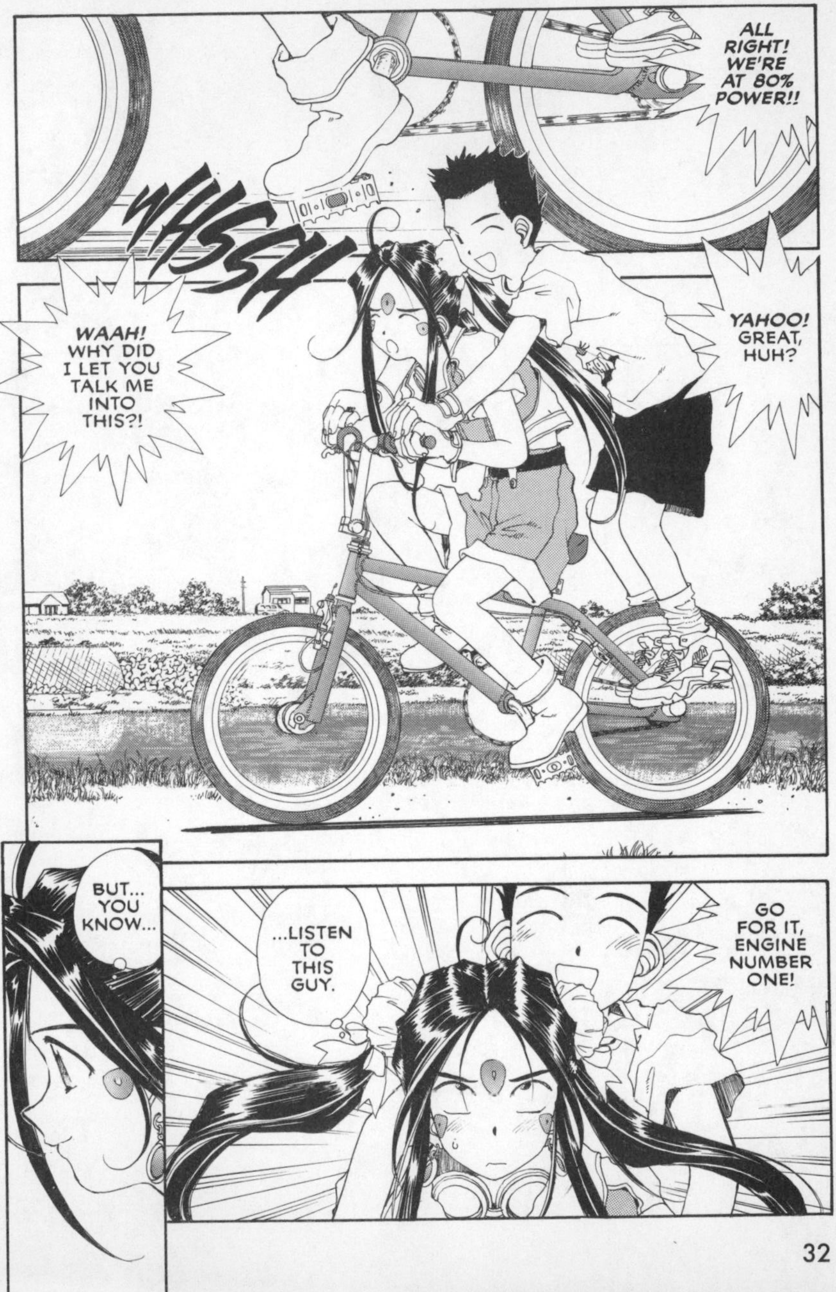
ALL RIGHT! WE'RE AT 80% POWER!!
WHSSH
YAHOO! GREAT, HUH?
WAAH! WHY DID I LET YOU TALK ME INTO THIS?!
GO FOR IT, ENGINE NUMBER ONE!
...LISTEN TO THIS GUY.
BUT... YOU KNOW...

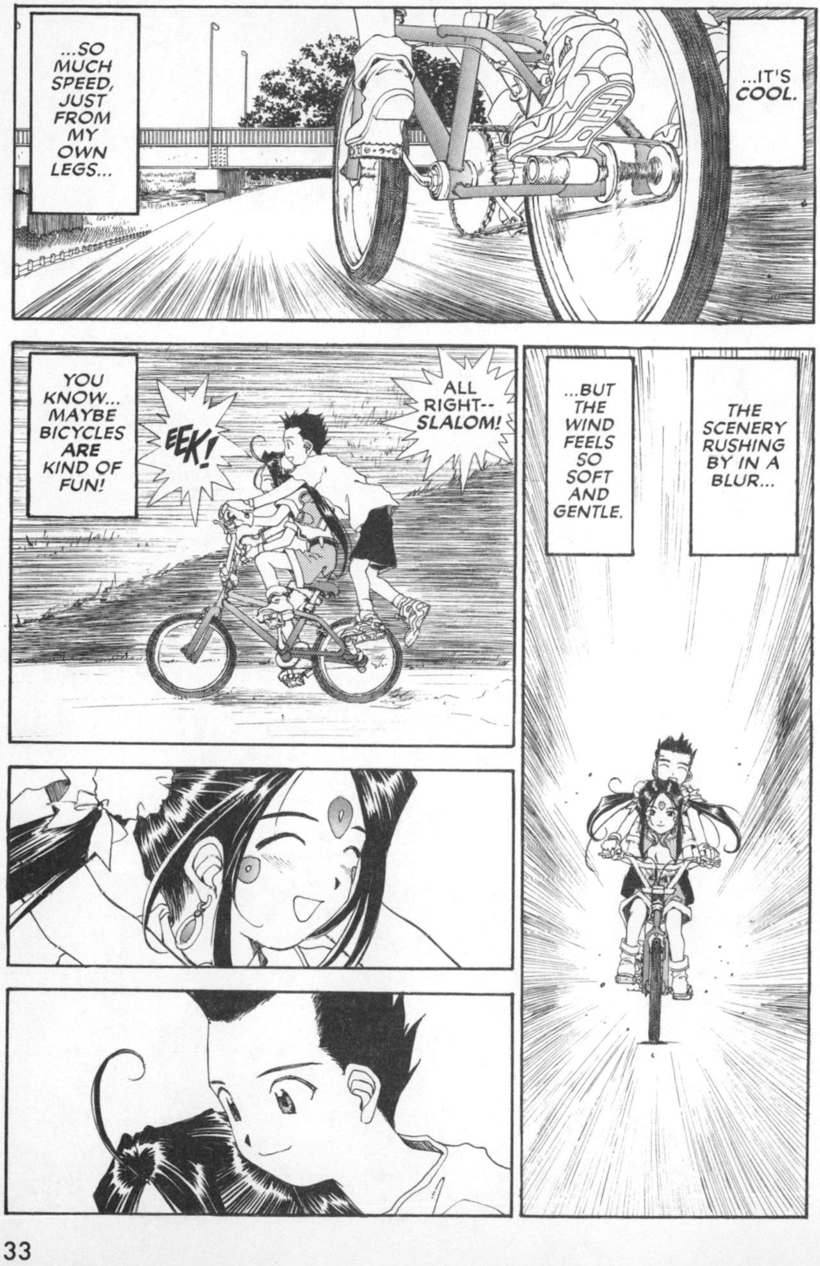
...IT'S COOL.
...SO MUCH SPEED, JUST FROM MY OWN LEGS...
THE SCENERY RUSHING BY IN A BLUR...
...BUT THE WIND FEELS SO SOFT AND GENTLE.
ALL RIGHT-- SLALOM!
EEK!
YOU KNOW... MAYBE BICYCLES ARE KIND OF FUN!

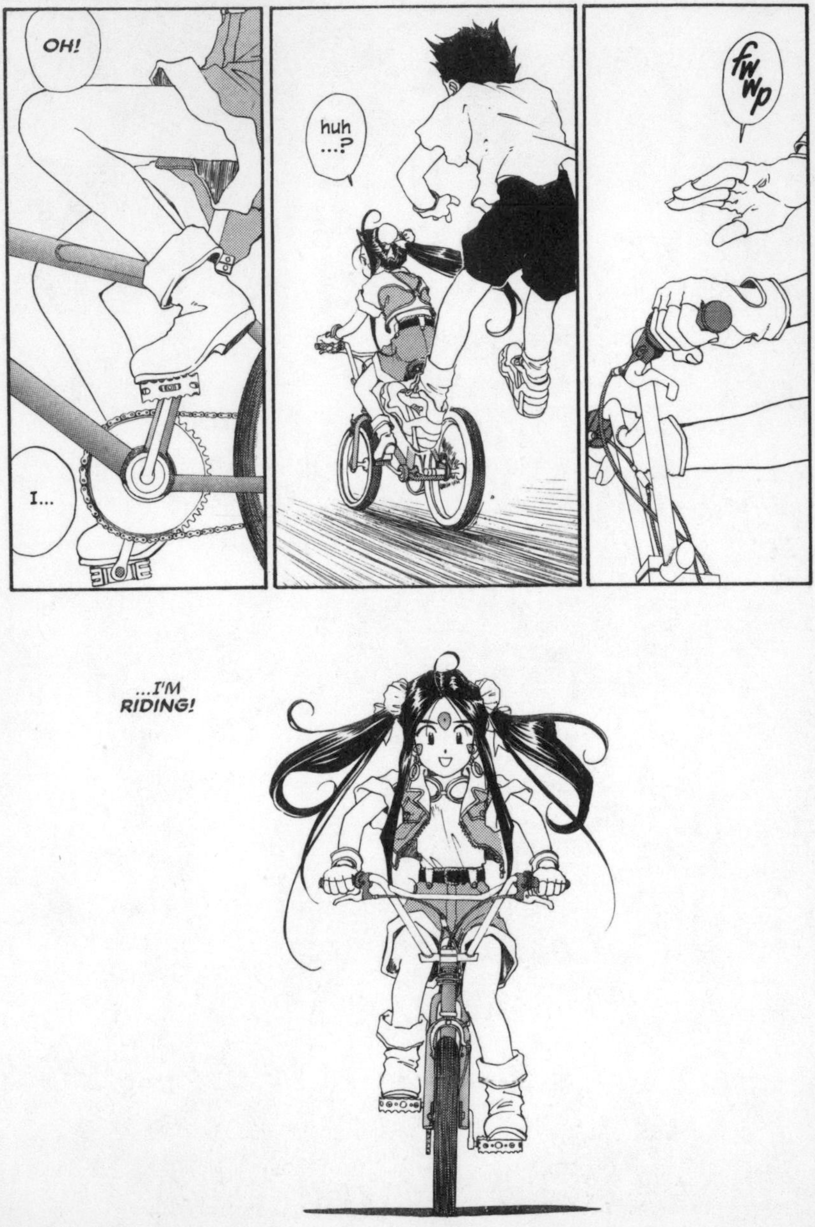
fwwp
huh ...?
OH!
I...
...I'M RIDING!

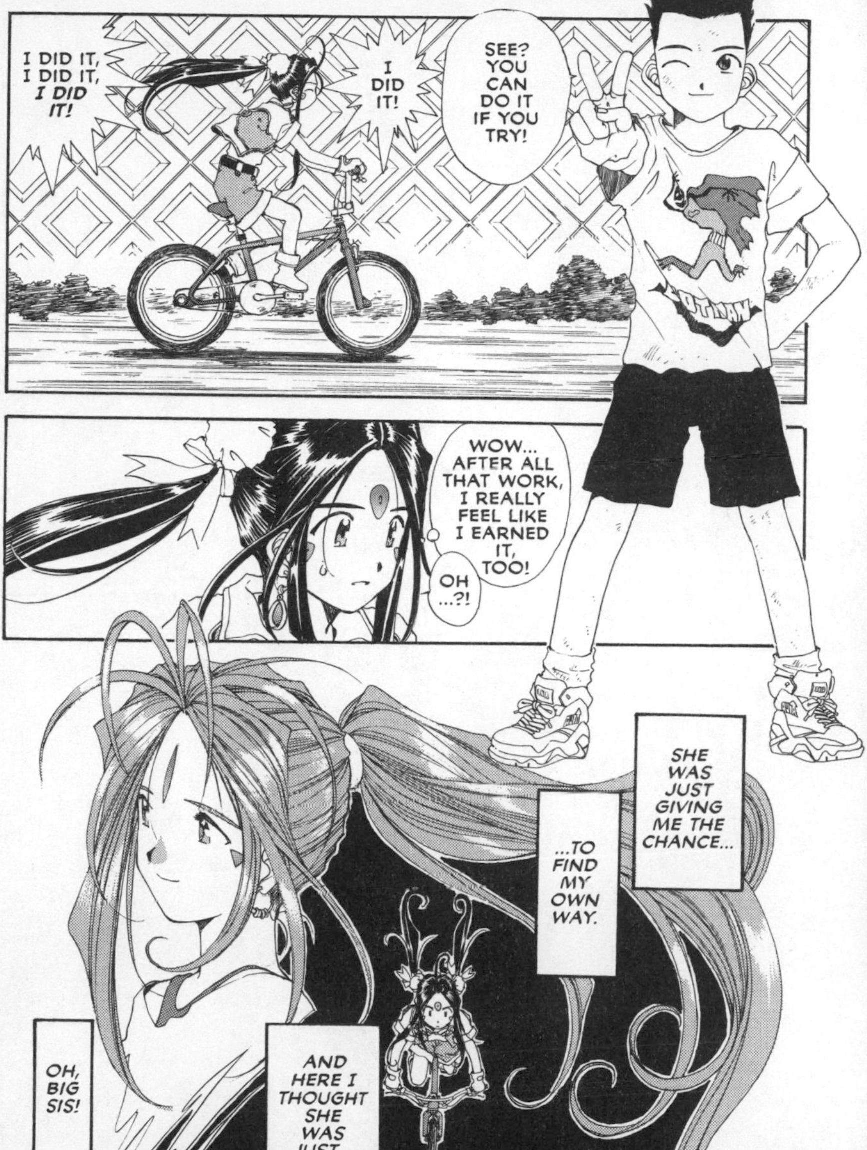
SEE? YOU CAN DO IT IF YOU TRY!
I DID IT!
I DID IT, I DID IT, *I DID IT!*
WOW... AFTER ALL THAT WORK, I REALLY FEEL LIKE I EARNED IT, TOO!
OH ...?!
SHE WAS JUST GIVING ME THE CHANCE...
...TO FIND MY OWN WAY.
AND HERE I THOUGHT SHE WAS JUST...
OH, BIG SIS!

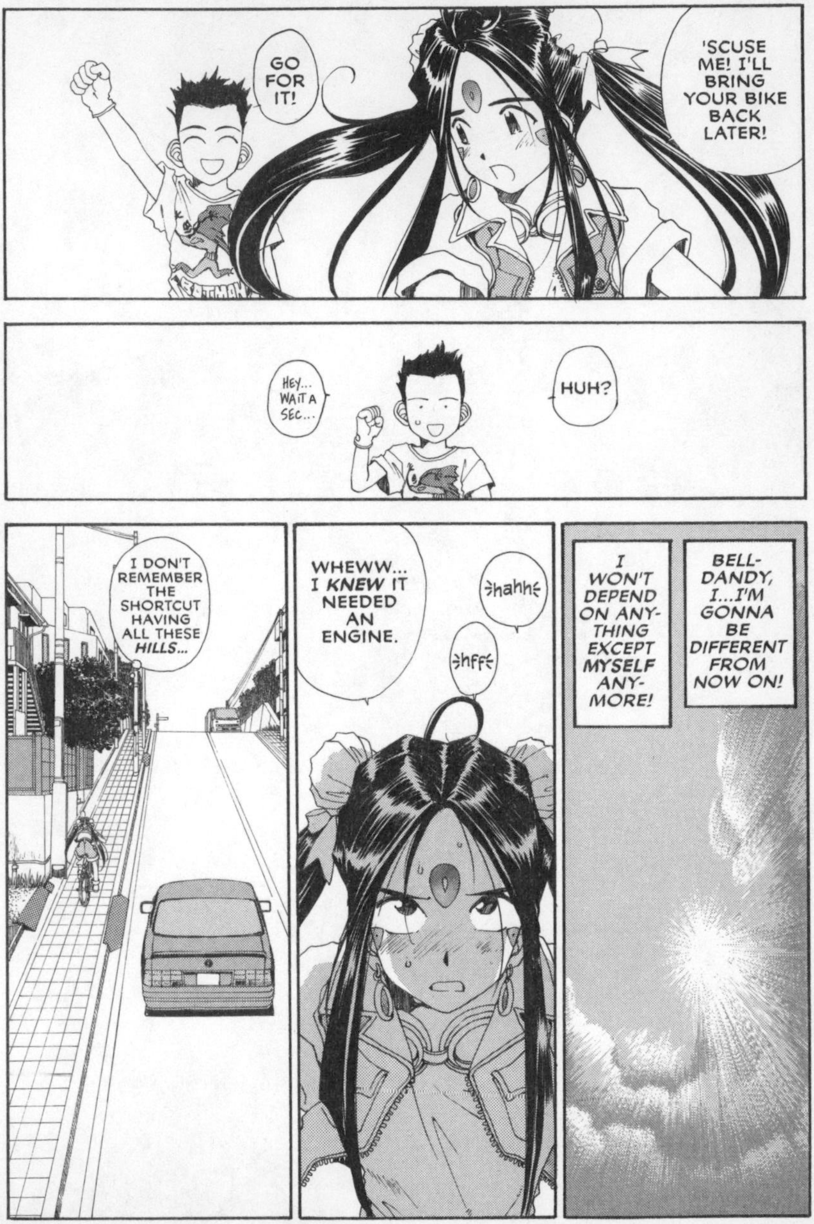
'SCUSE ME! I'LL BRING YOUR BIKE BACK LATER!
GO FOR IT!
HUH?
HEY... WAIT A SEC...
BELL-DANDY, I...I'M GONNA BE DIFFERENT FROM NOW ON!
I WON'T DEPEND ON ANY-THING EXCEPT MYSELF ANY-MORE!
hahh
hff
WHEWW... I KNEW IT NEEDED AN ENGINE.
I DON'T REMEMBER THE SHORTCUT HAVING ALL THESE HILLS...

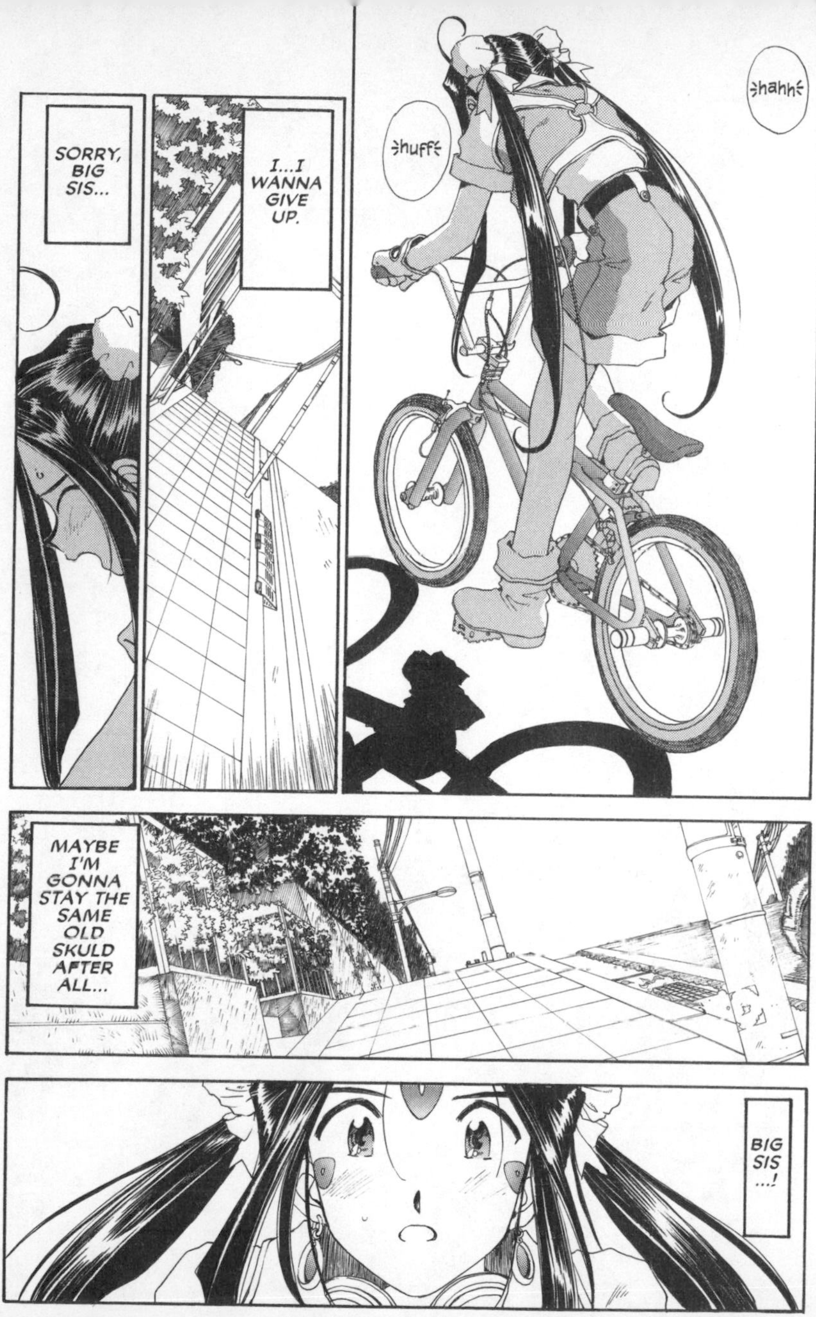

hahn
huff
I...I WANNA GIVE UP.
SORRY, BIG SIS...
MAYBE I'M GONNA STAY THE SAME OLD SKULD AFTER ALL...
BIG SIS ...!

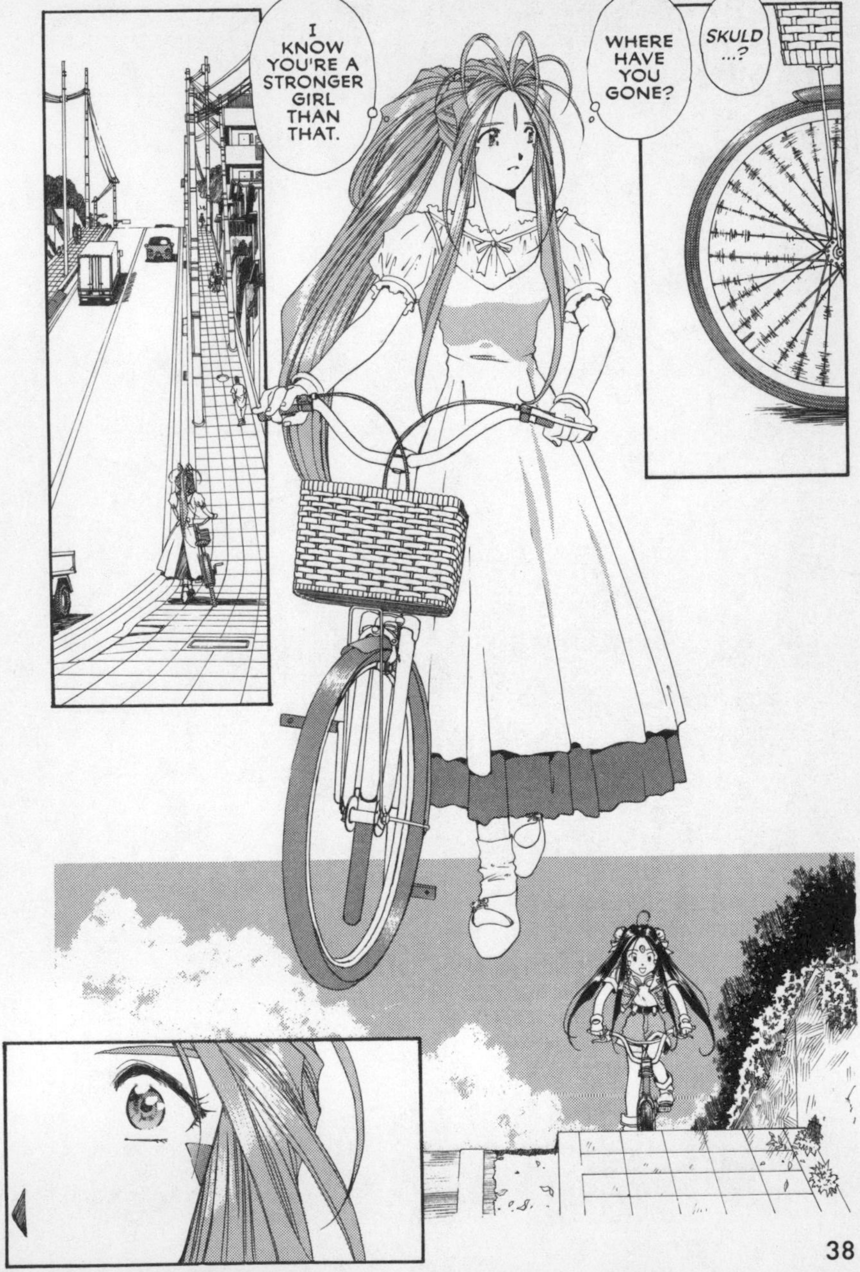
SKULD ...?
WHERE HAVE YOU GONE?
I KNOW YOU'RE A STRONGER GIRL THAN THAT.

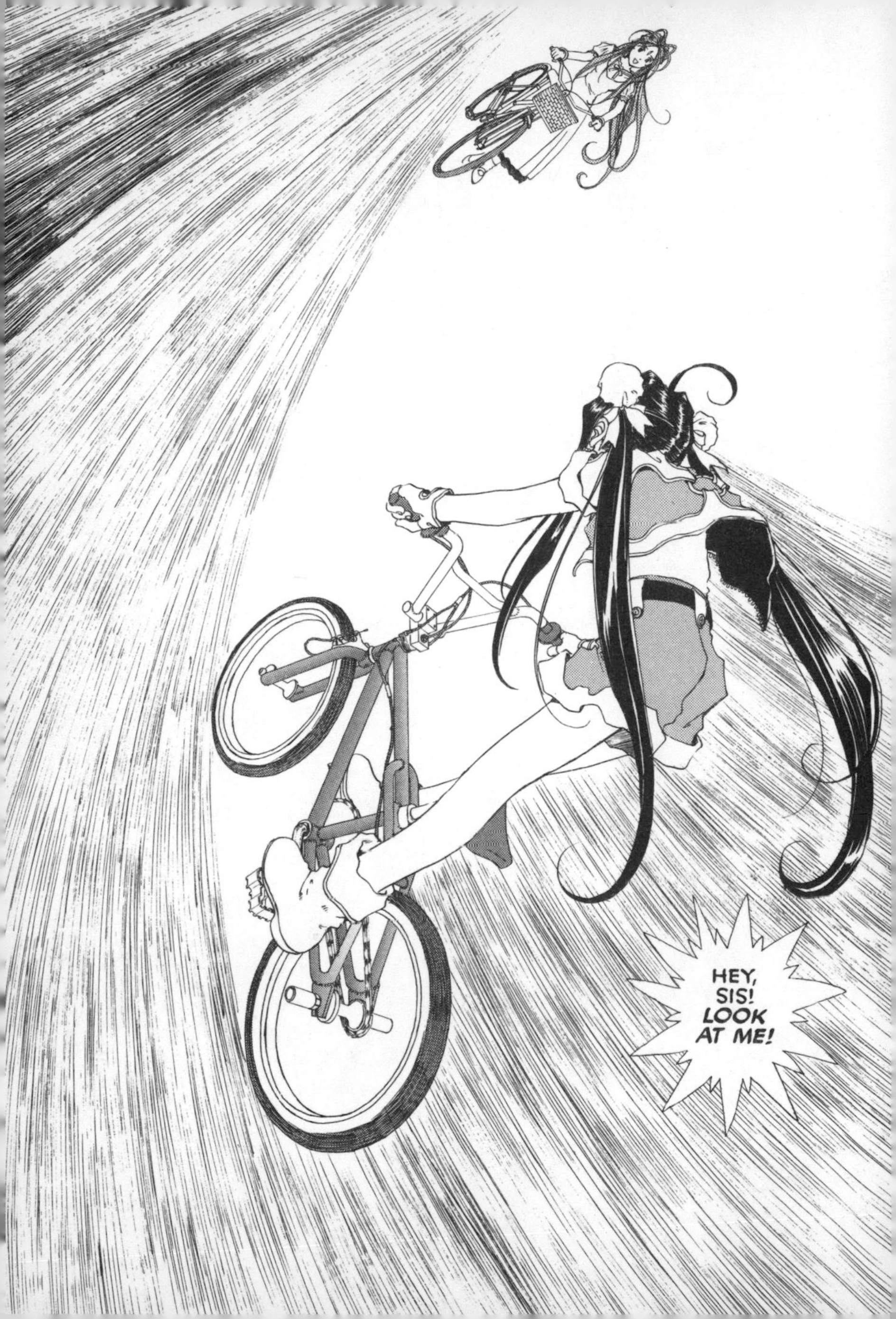
HEY, SIS! LOOK AT ME!

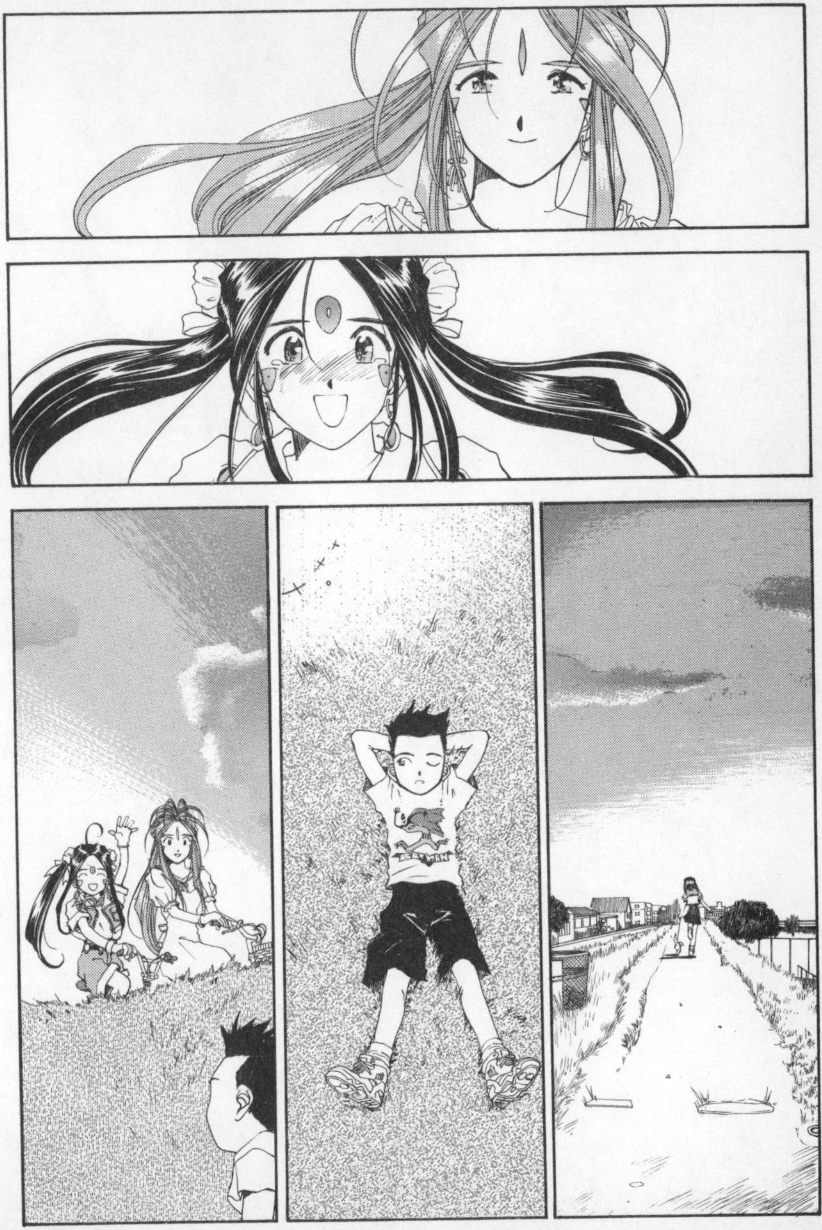

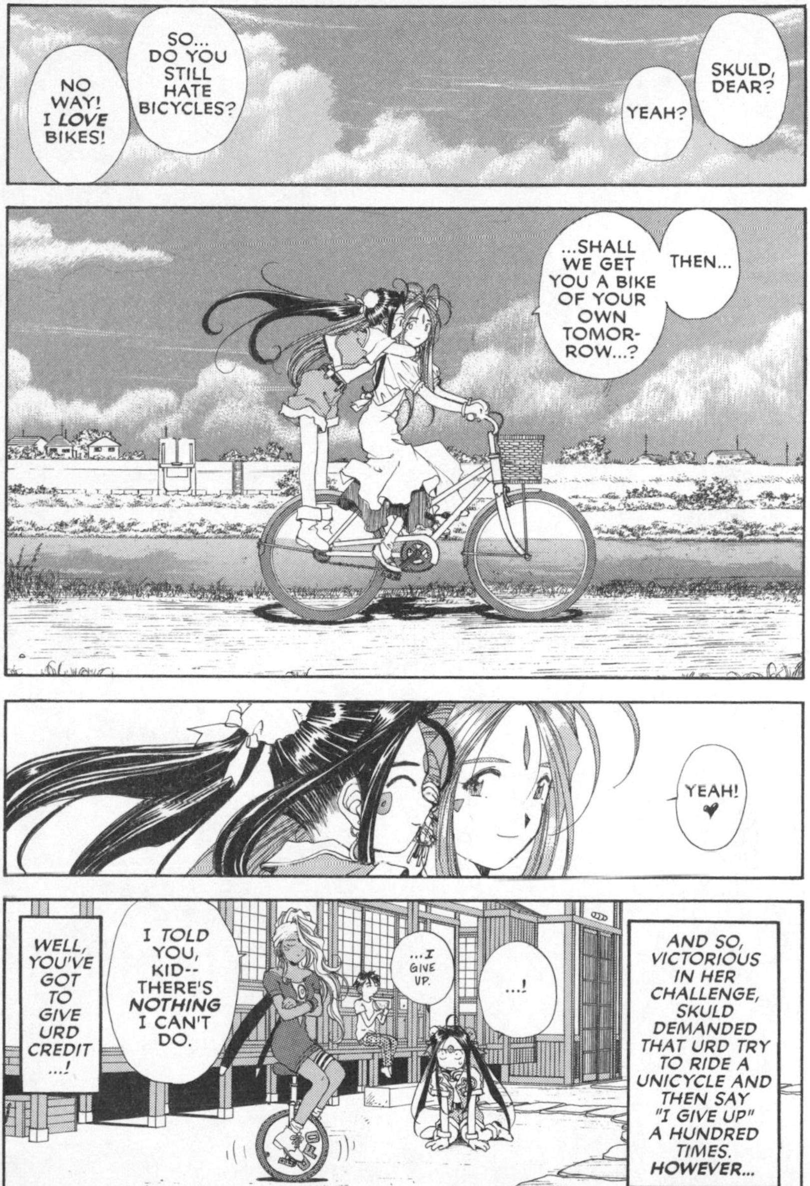
SKULD, DEAR?
YEAH?
SO... DO YOU STILL HATE BICYCLES?
NO WAY! I LOVE BIKES!
THEN...
...SHALL WE GET YOU A BIKE OF YOUR OWN TOMORROW...?
YEAH! ♥
AND SO, VICTORIOUS IN HER CHALLENGE, SKULD DEMANDED THAT URD TRY TO RIDE A UNICYCLE AND THEN SAY "I GIVE UP" A HUNDRED TIMES. HOWEVER...
...!
...I GIVE UP.
I TOLD YOU, KID-- THERE'S NOTHING I CAN'T DO.
WELL, YOU'VE GOT TO GIVE URD CREDIT ...!

THE *GODDESS!* GARAGE

A look at the vehicles owned by each character

女神用語の基礎知識 ガレージ拝見

SPECIAL BONUS ARTICLE!

Honda CT50 Motra

Toraichi Tamiya bestrides this four-stroke, air-cooled, single-cylinder, 49cc bike like a colossus, and whereas one horse might have difficulty carrying Tamiya, the Motra's 4.5 horsepower can cart him around with ease. For that matter, Tamiya can cart around the Motra, as it only weighs 76 kilograms. The Motra had a very brief production run during 1982–83. A tough, and tough-looking, minibike, it provides two different levels on its three gear speeds. One level is designed for off-road, steep conditions, where the Motra can climb grades of up to 23 degrees.

Kosuke Fujishima comments, "They're not making them now, and that's something sad. It has a militaristic design, and fits Tamiya's *doboku* [hard-hat worker—*ed.*] style very well. It only came in two colors: Motra-Green, and Motra-Yellow, which seems a little militaristic, too. Tamiya prefers the green, but I had thought originally that yellow was the more industrial, utilitarian look, and perhaps that would have been better. When I was drawing his Motra, I didn't have many references on hand, so I worked really hard on getting it right. And, wouldn't you know it, just as soon as I had finished, some Motra club came roaring down the street—dozens of them. Now, that's something *really* sad."

HONDA

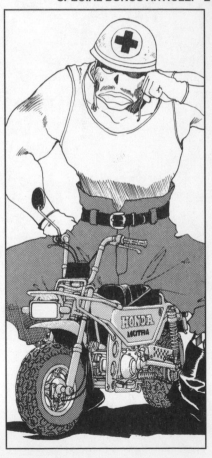

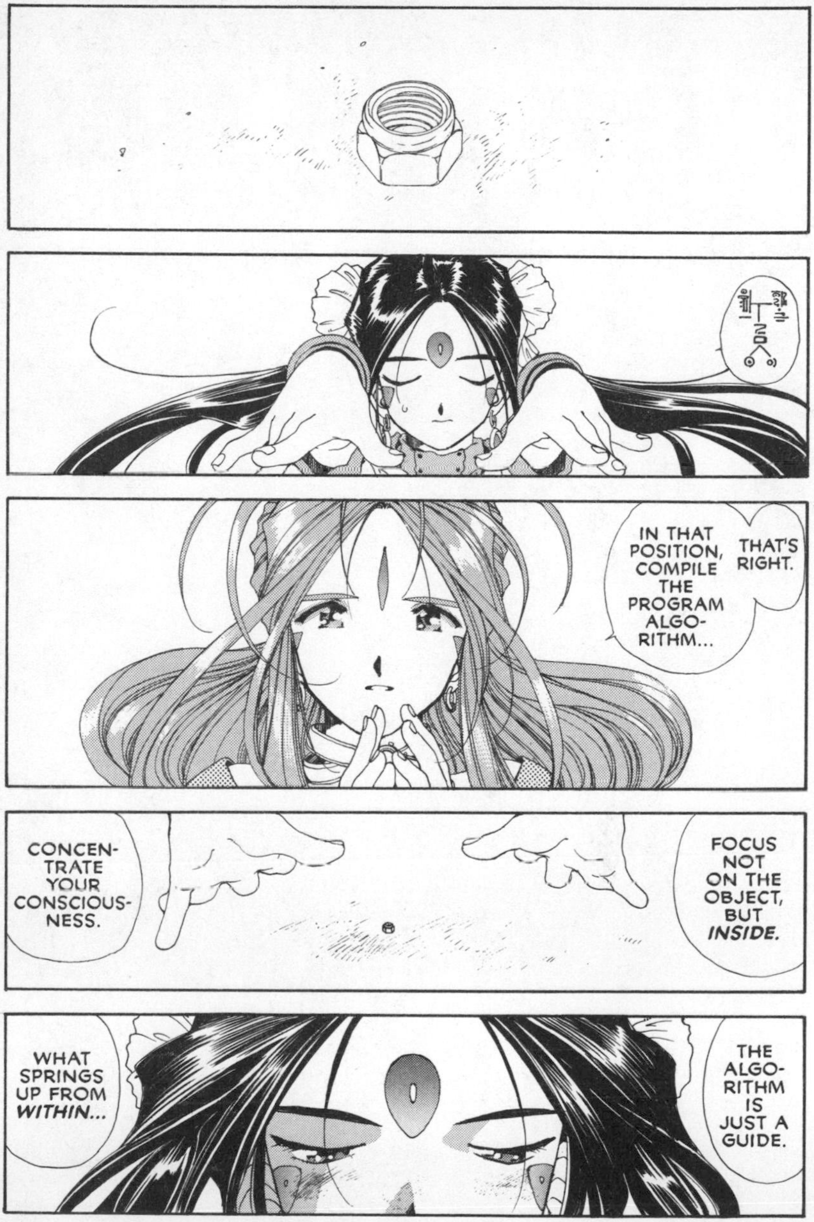
THAT'S RIGHT.
IN THAT POSITION, COMPILE THE PROGRAM ALGO-RITHM...
FOCUS NOT ON THE OBJECT, BUT *INSIDE.*
CONCEN-TRATE YOUR CONSCIOUS-NESS.
THE ALGO-RITHM IS JUST A GUIDE.
WHAT SPRINGS UP FROM *WITHIN...*

CHAPTER 74

Crazy Little Thing Called Love

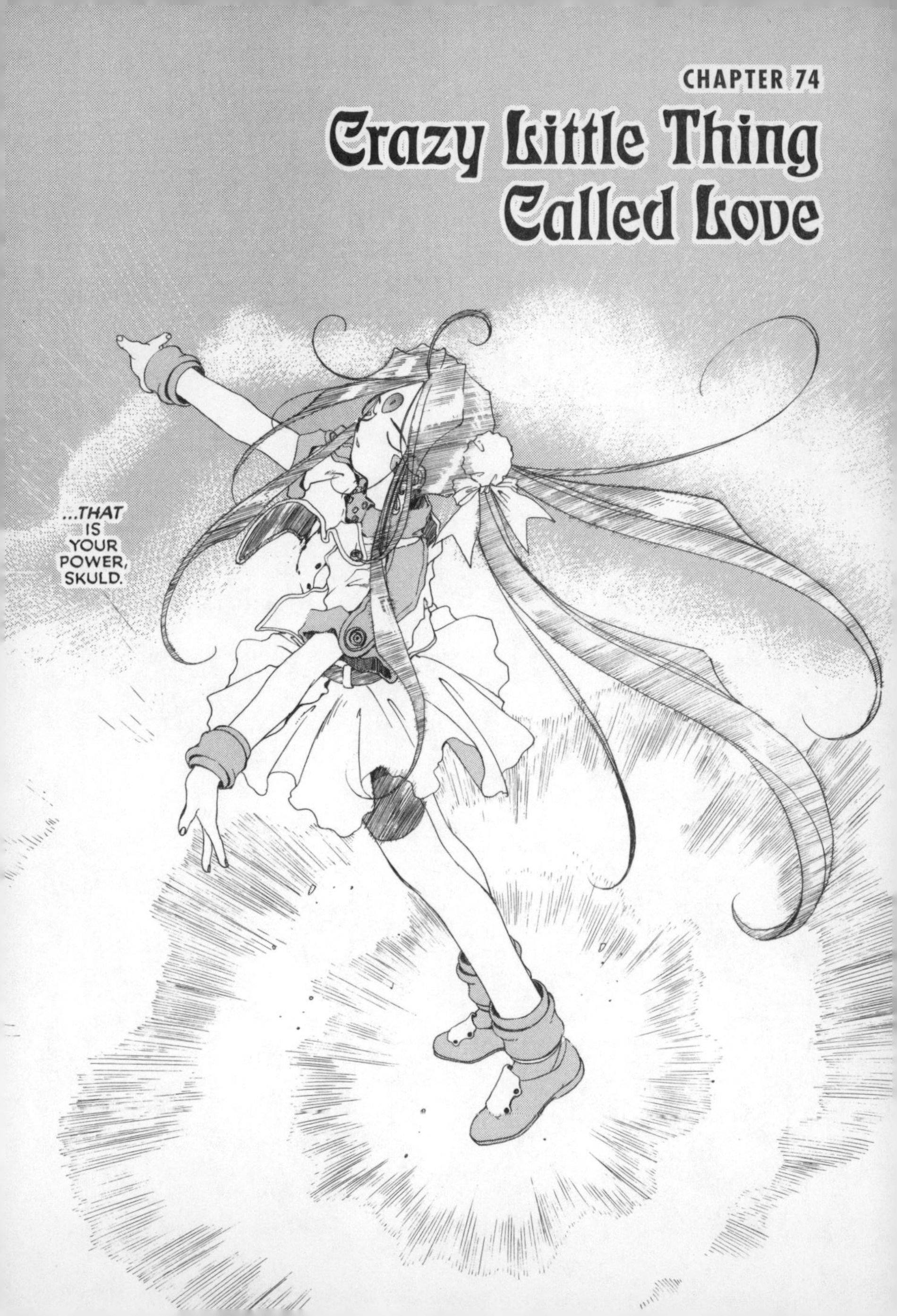
...THAT IS YOUR POWER, SKULD.

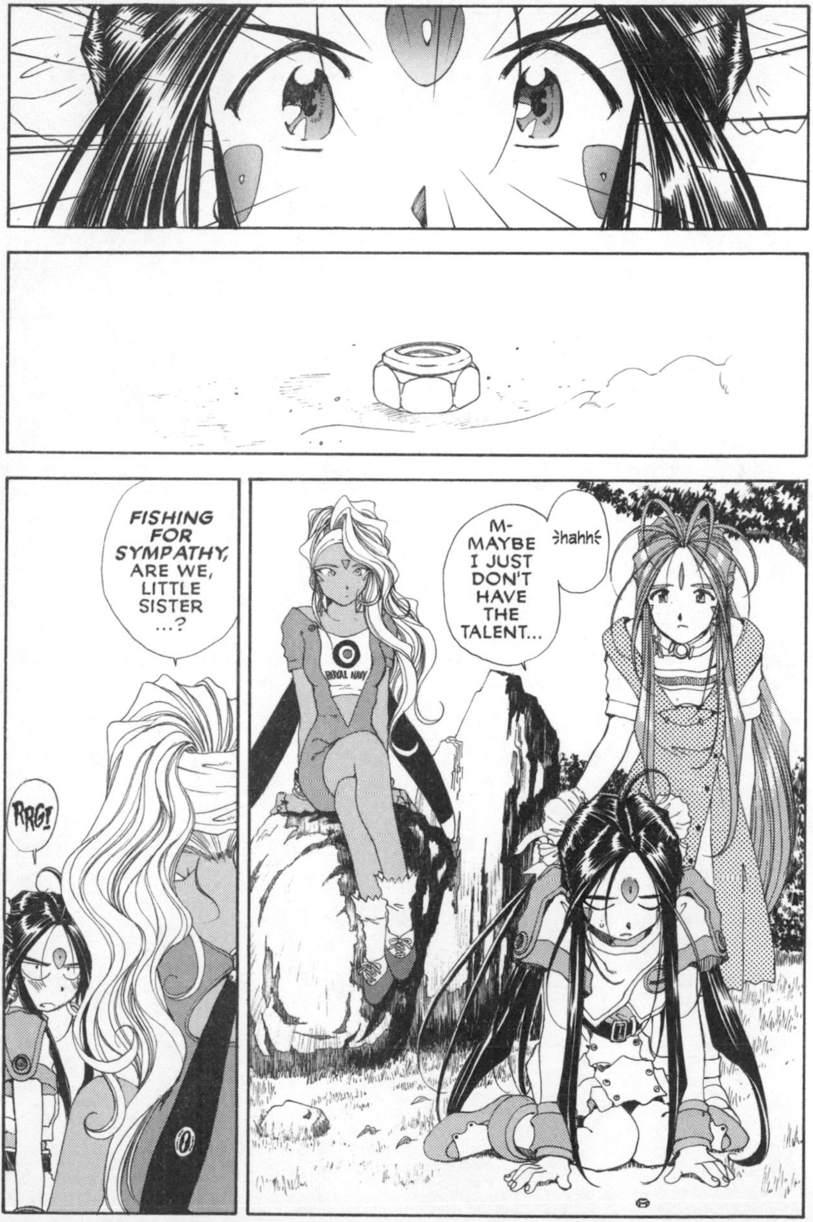

hahh
M-MAYBE I JUST DON'T HAVE THE TALENT...
FISHING FOR SYMPATHY, ARE WE, LITTLE SISTER ...?
RRG!

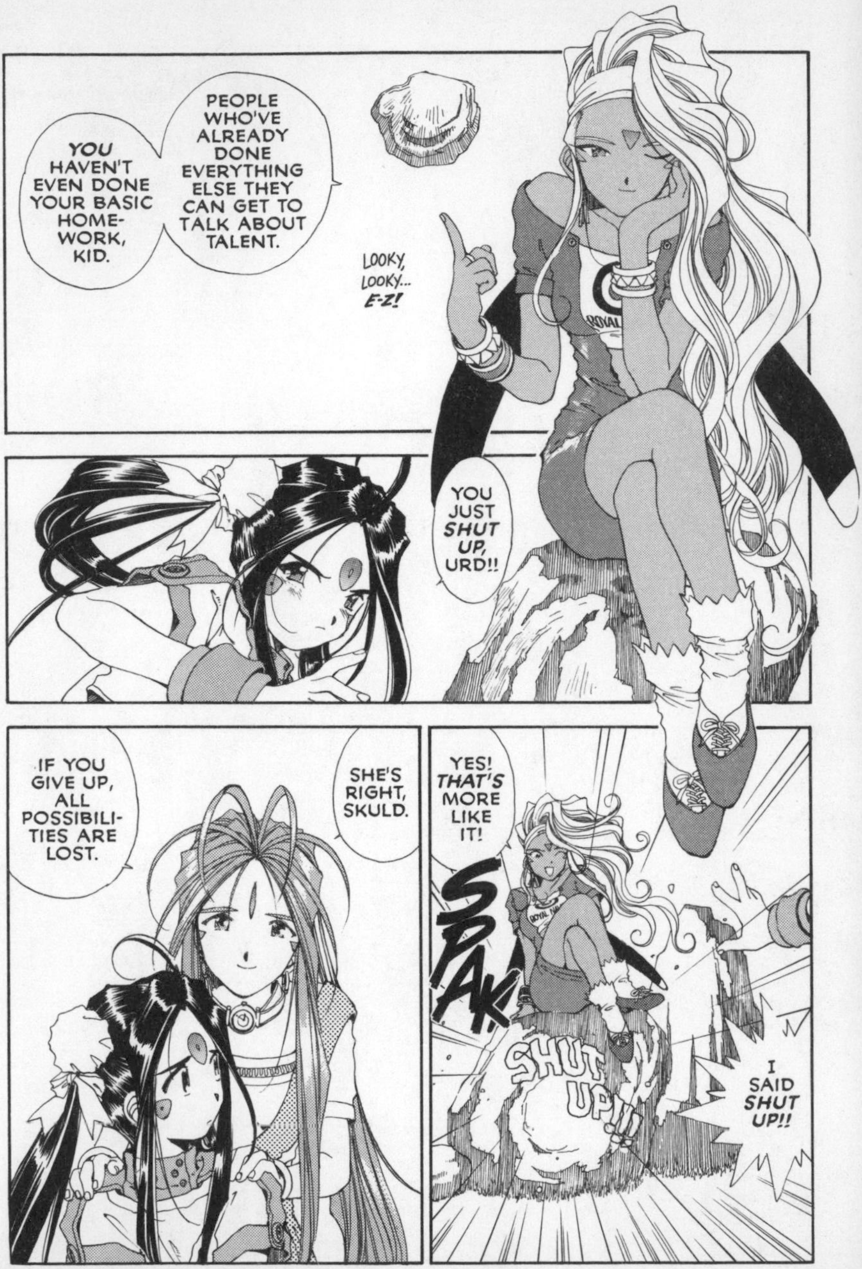
PEOPLE WHO'VE ALREADY DONE EVERYTHING ELSE THEY CAN GET TO TALK ABOUT TALENT.
YOU HAVEN'T EVEN DONE YOUR BASIC HOME-WORK, KID.
LOOKY, LOOKY... E-Z!
YOU JUST SHUT UP, URD!!
YES! THAT'S MORE LIKE IT!
SPAK
SHUT UP!!
I SAID SHUT UP!!
SHE'S RIGHT, SKULD.
IF YOU GIVE UP, ALL POSSIBILI-TIES ARE LOST.

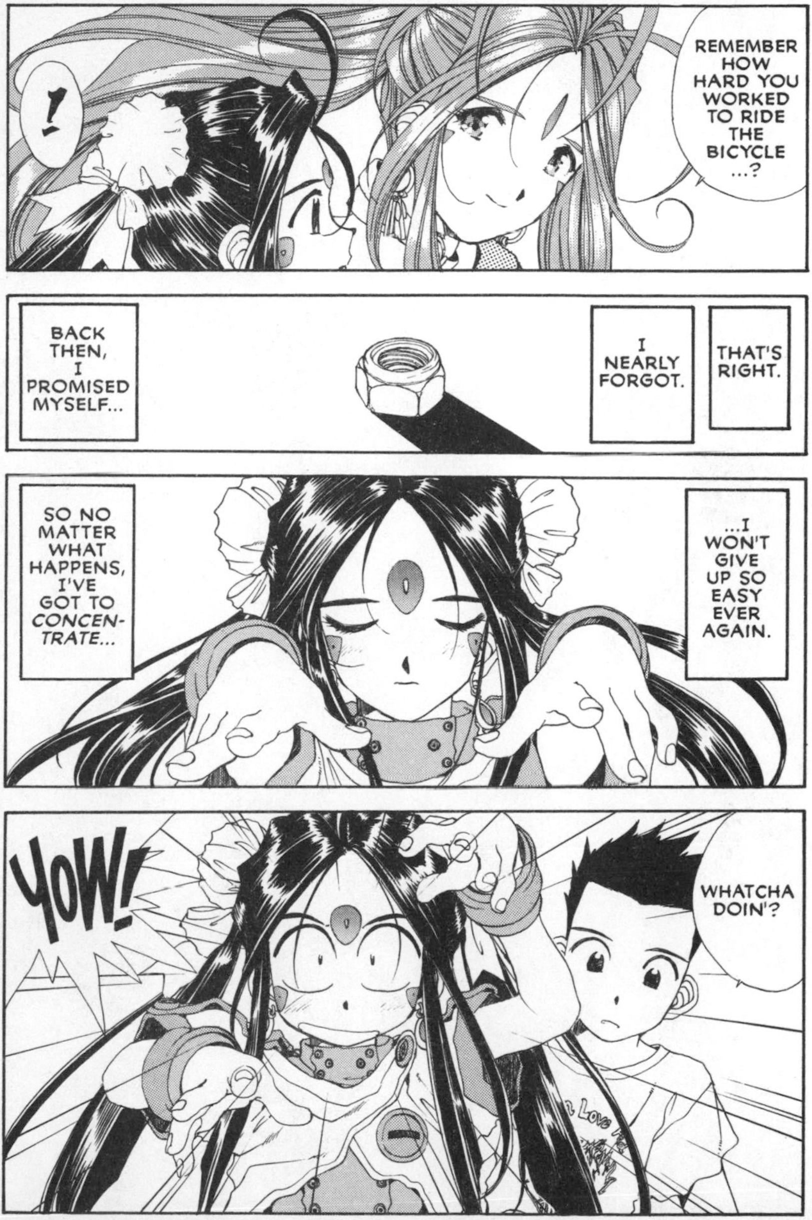
REMEMBER HOW HARD YOU WORKED TO RIDE THE BICYCLE ...?
!
THAT'S RIGHT.
I NEARLY FORGOT.
BACK THEN, I PROMISED MYSELF...
...I WON'T GIVE UP SO EASY EVER AGAIN.
SO NO MATTER WHAT HAPPENS, I'VE GOT TO *CONCENTRATE*...
WHATCHA DOIN'?
YOW!

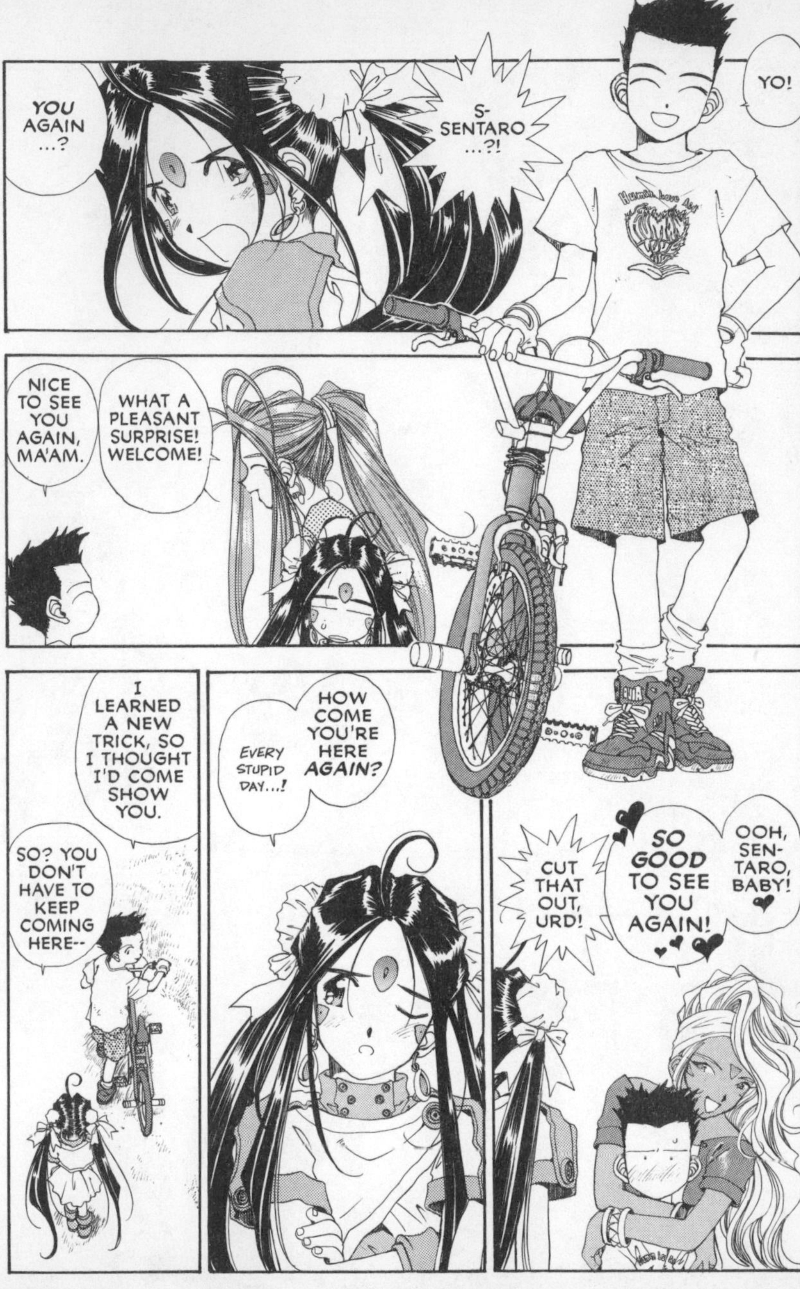
YO!
S-SENTARO ...?!
YOU AGAIN ...?
WHAT A PLEASANT SURPRISE! WELCOME!
NICE TO SEE YOU AGAIN, MA'AM.
OOH, SEN-TARO, BABY!
SO GOOD TO SEE YOU AGAIN!
CUT THAT OUT, URD!
HOW COME YOU'RE HERE AGAIN?
EVERY STUPID DAY...!
I LEARNED A NEW TRICK, SO I THOUGHT I'D COME SHOW YOU.
SO? YOU DON'T HAVE TO KEEP COMING HERE--

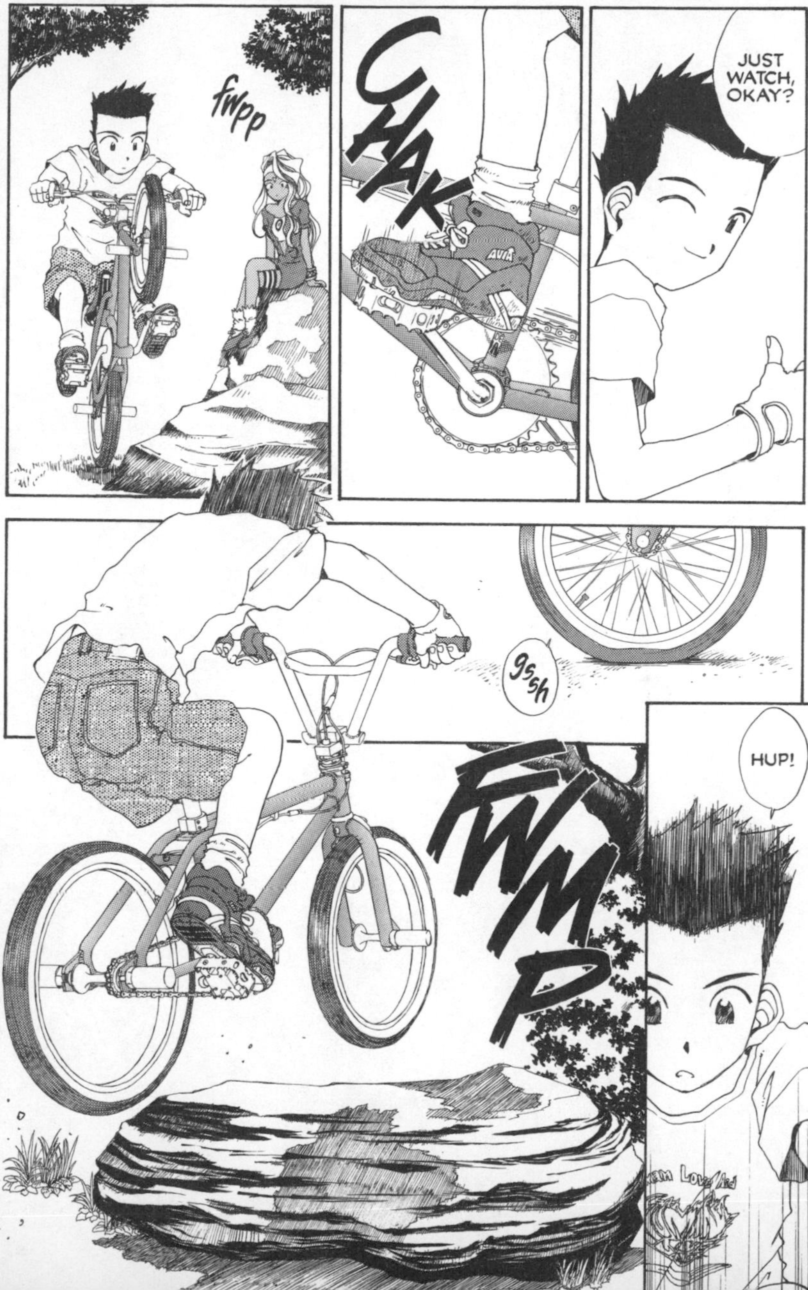
JUST WATCH, OKAY?
CHAK
fwpp
gssh
HUP!
FWMP

FWDD
CLAP CLAP
OOOOOOOOOOH!
TAA-DAA!
CLAP CLAP
WONDER-FUL!
THAT'S JUST *WONDER-FUL!*
HOW ON EARTH DO YOU LEARN TO *DO* THINGS LIKE THAT?!
EASY!
I *LOVE IT!*

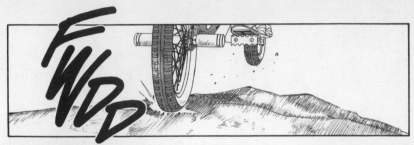

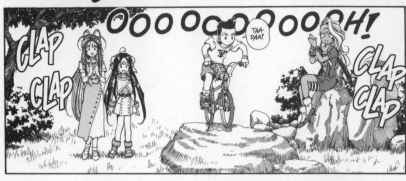

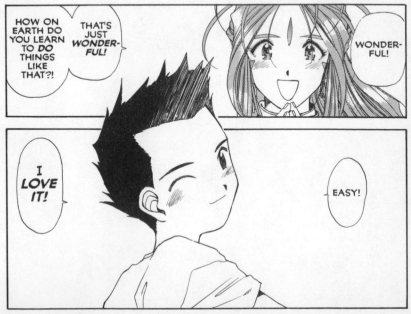

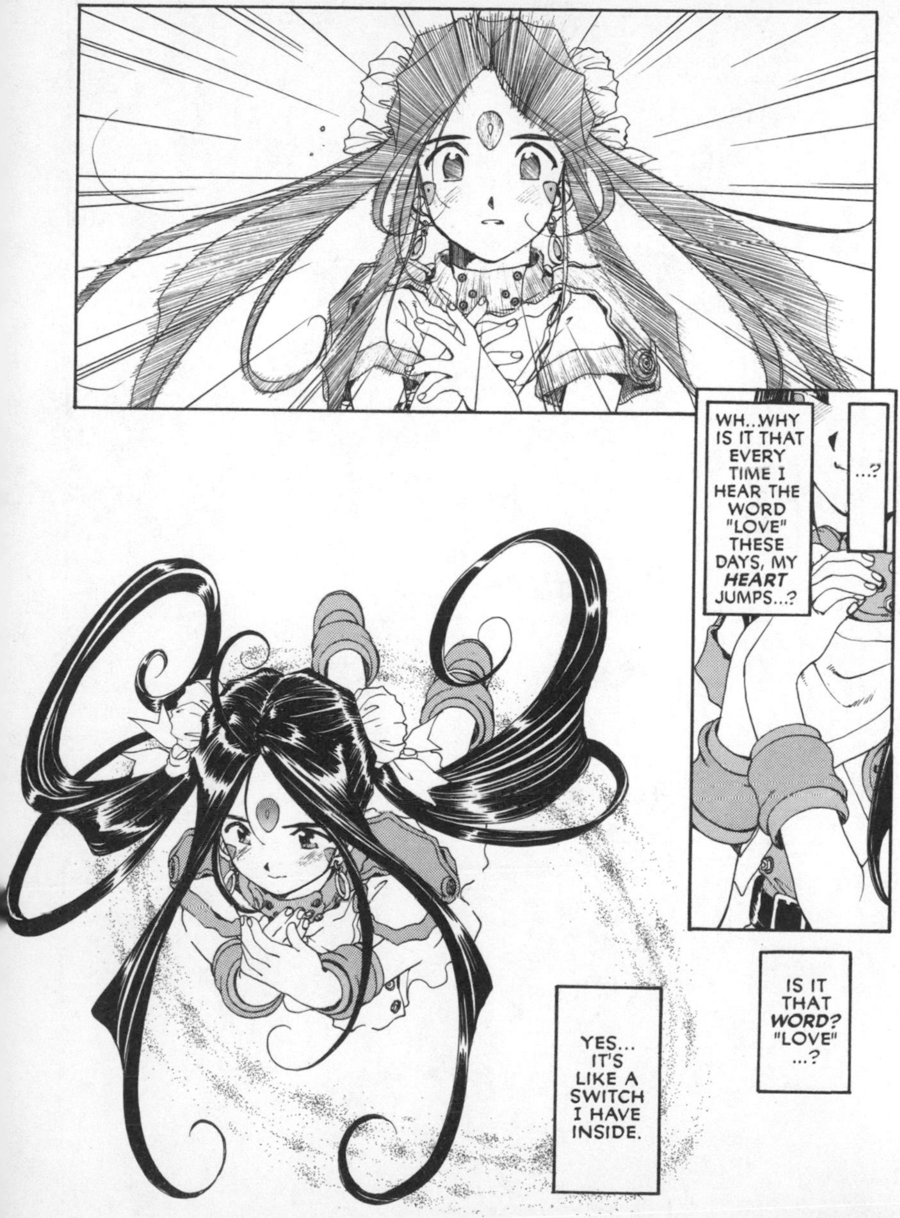
...?
WH...WHY IS IT THAT EVERY TIME I HEAR THE WORD "LOVE" THESE DAYS, MY ***HEART*** JUMPS...?
IS IT THAT ***WORD?*** "LOVE" ...?
YES... IT'S LIKE A SWITCH I HAVE INSIDE.

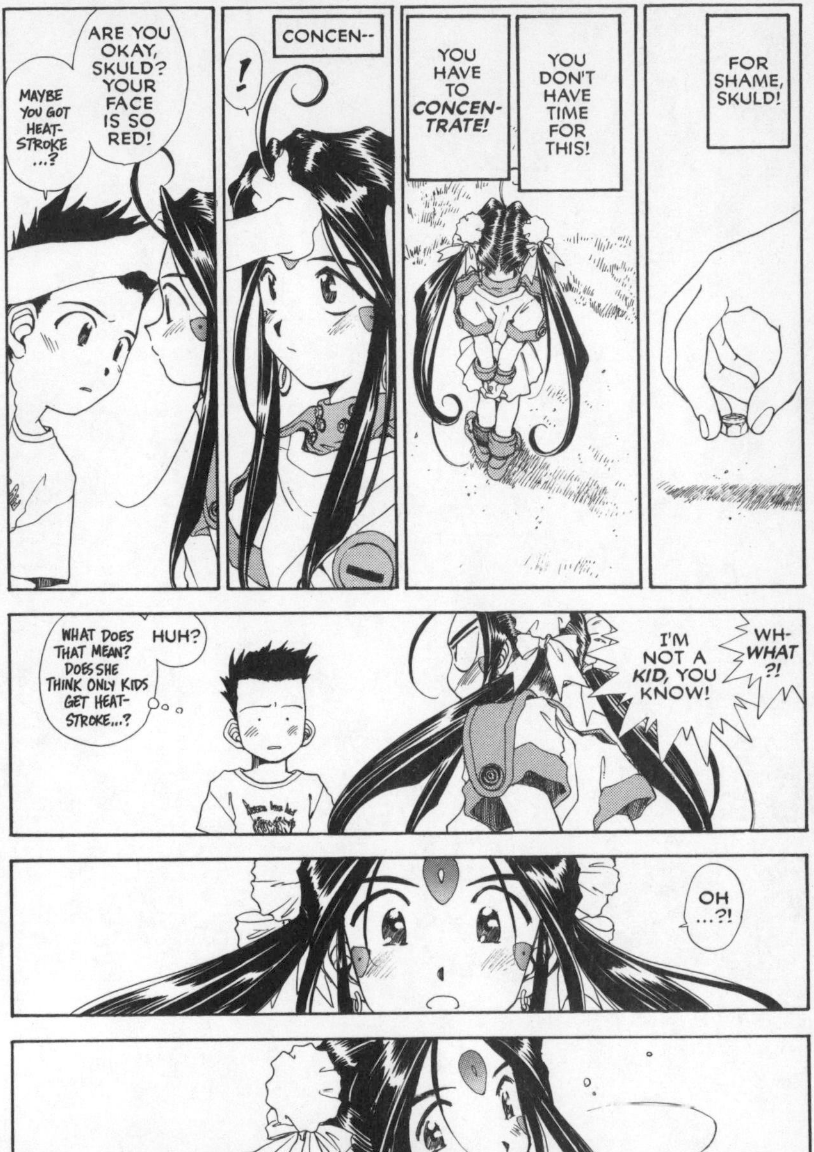
FOR SHAME, SKULD!
YOU DON'T HAVE TIME FOR THIS!
YOU HAVE TO CONCENTRATE!
CONCEN--
!
ARE YOU OKAY, SKULD? YOUR FACE IS SO RED!
MAYBE YOU GOT HEAT-STROKE ...?
WH-WHAT?!
I'M NOT A KID, YOU KNOW!
HUH?
WHAT DOES THAT MEAN? DOES SHE THINK ONLY KIDS GET HEAT-STROKE...?
OH ...?!

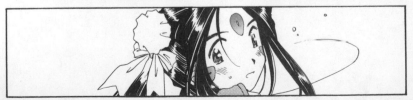

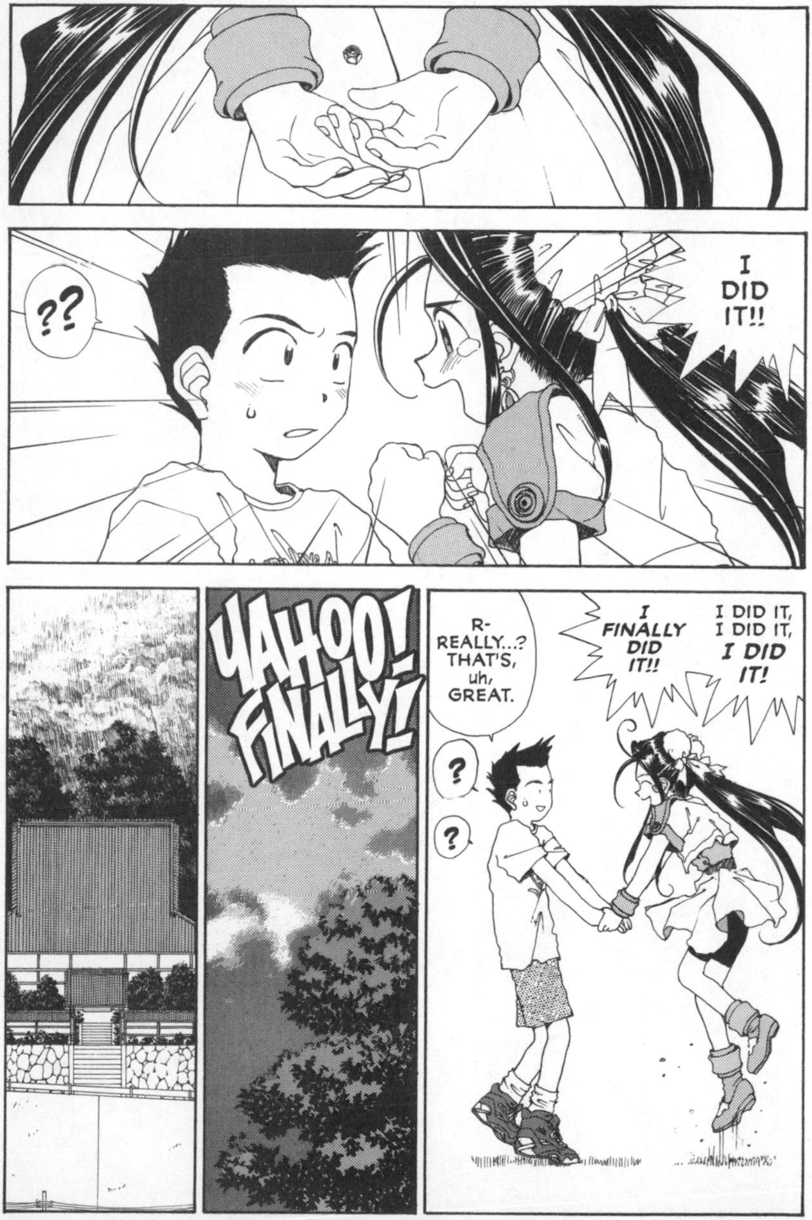
I DID IT!!
??
I DID IT, I DID IT, I DID IT!
I FINALLY DID IT!!
R-REALLY...? THAT'S, uh, GREAT.
?
?
YAHOO! FINALLY!!

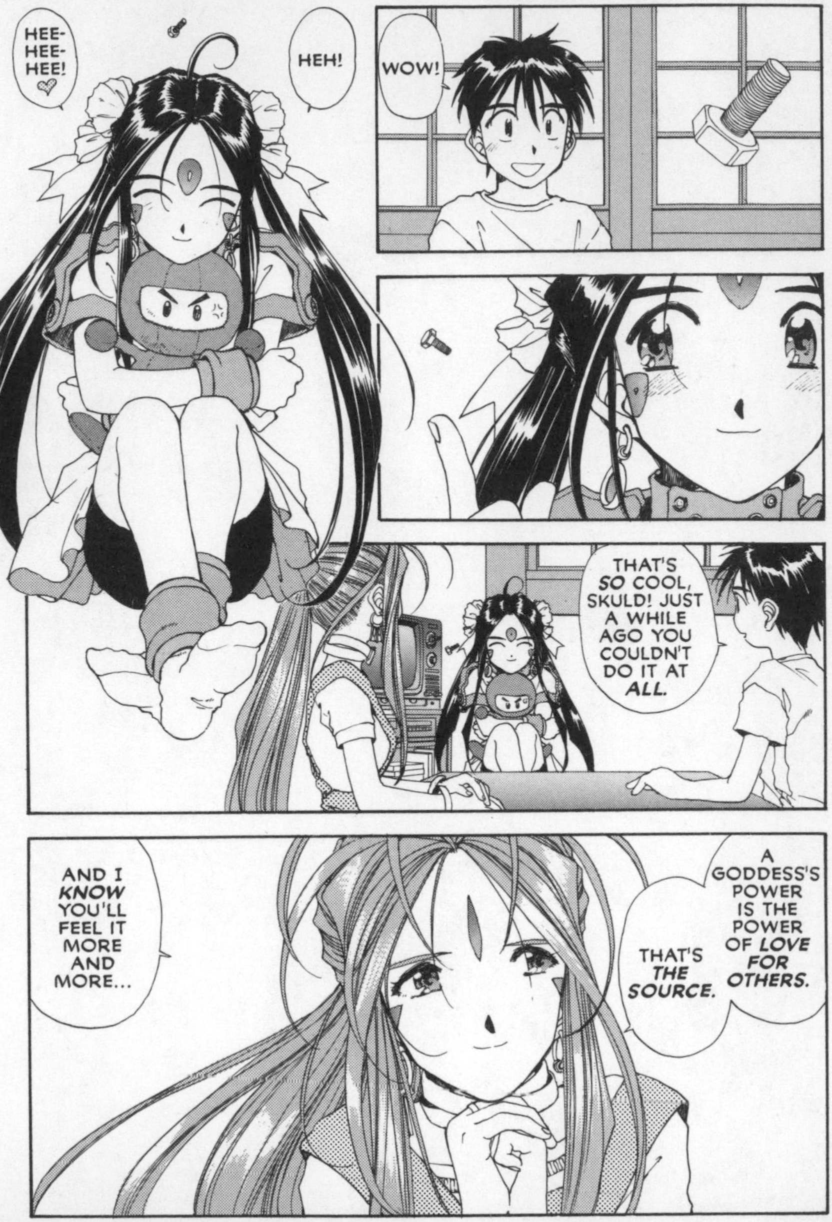
WOW!
HEH!
HEE-HEE-HEE! ♡
THAT'S *SO* COOL, SKULD! JUST A WHILE AGO YOU COULDN'T DO IT AT ***ALL.***
A GODDESS'S POWER IS THE POWER OF ***LOVE FOR OTHERS.***
THAT'S ***THE SOURCE.***
AND I ***KNOW*** YOU'LL FEEL IT MORE AND MORE...

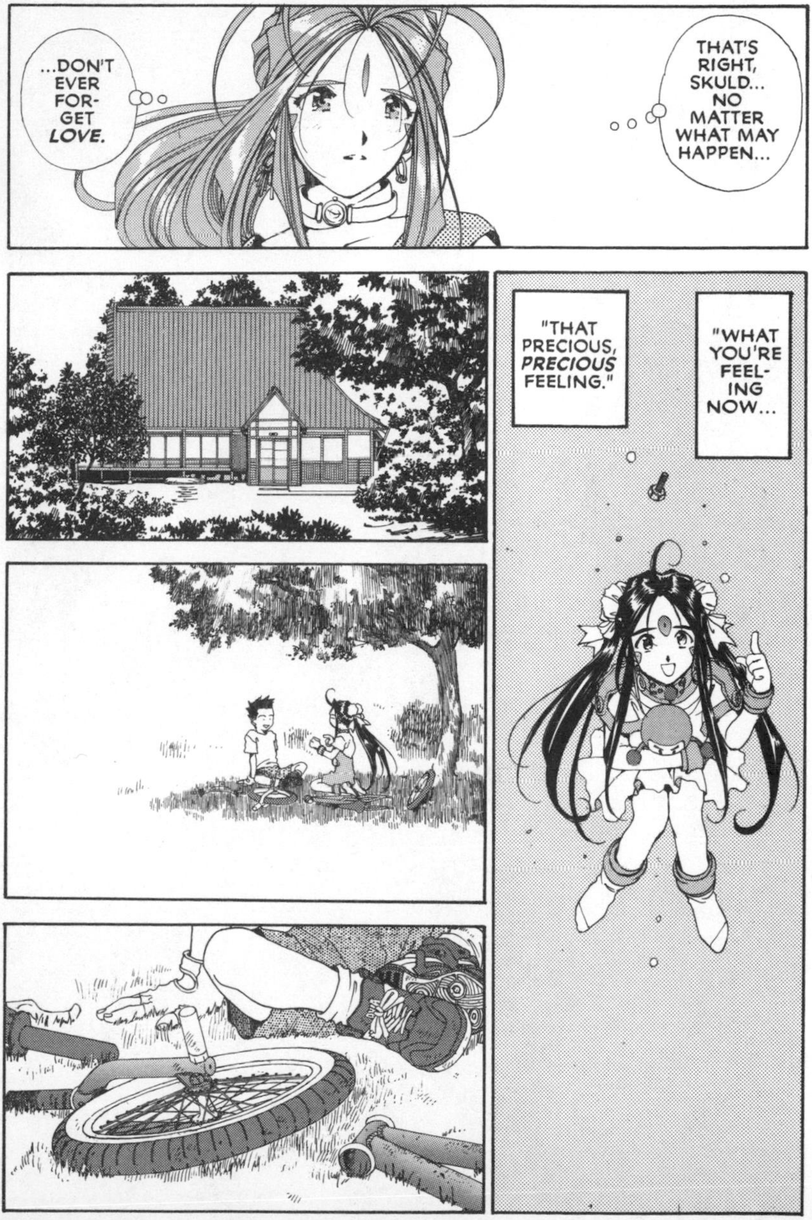
THAT'S RIGHT, SKULD... NO MATTER WHAT MAY HAPPEN...
...DON'T EVER FOR-GET *LOVE.*
"WHAT YOU'RE FEEL-ING NOW...
"THAT PRECIOUS, *PRECIOUS* FEELING."

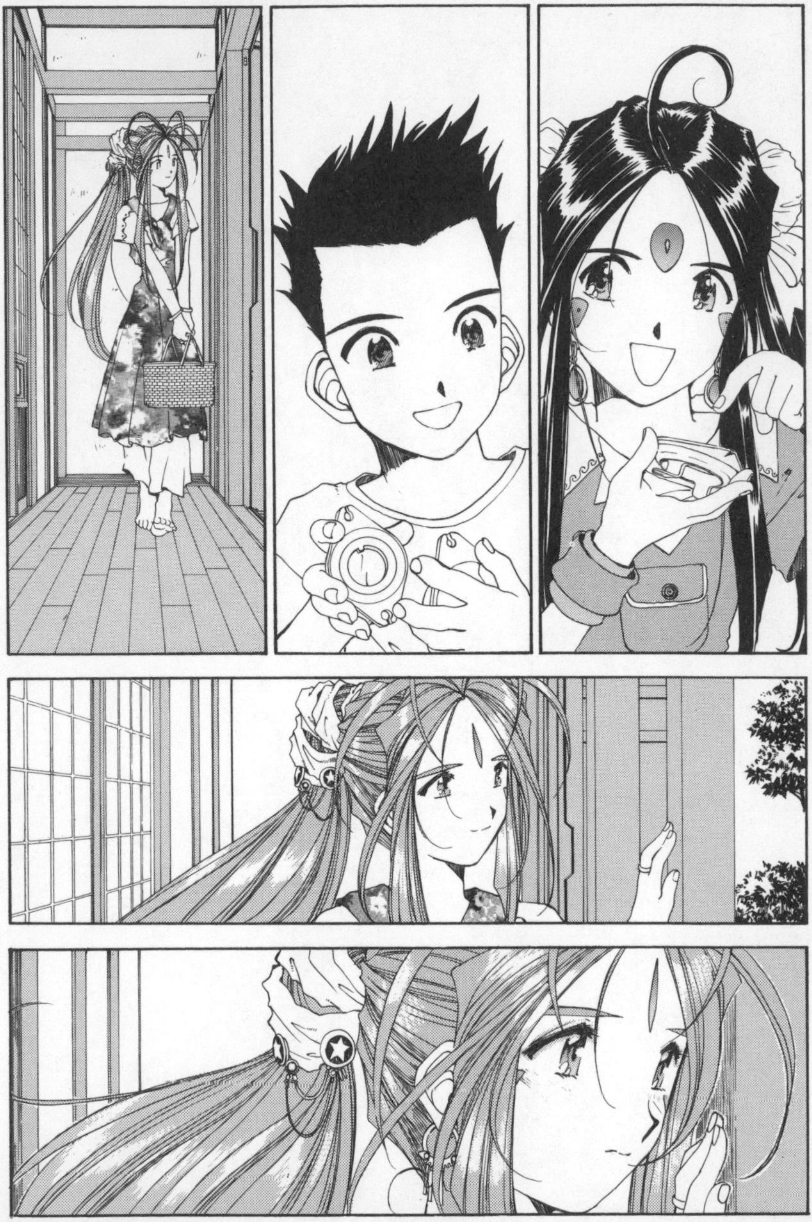

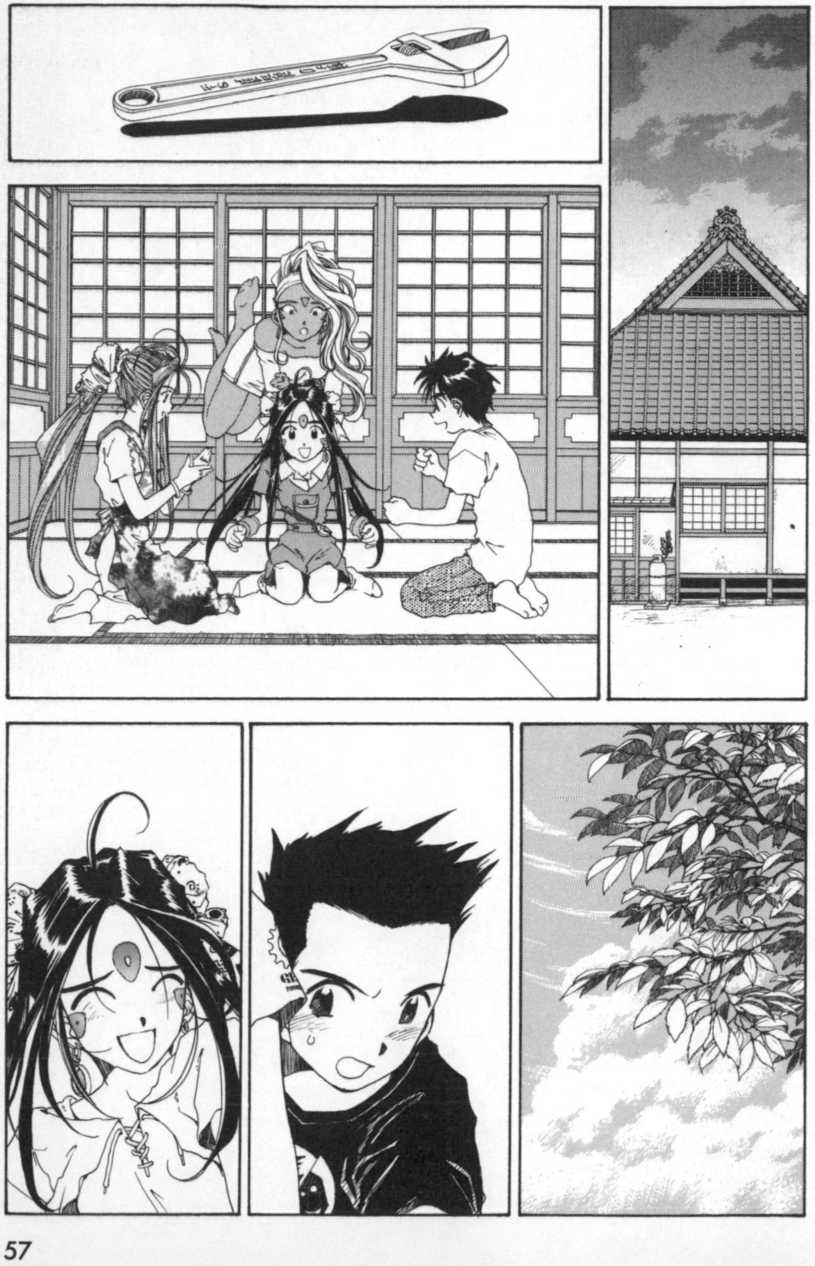

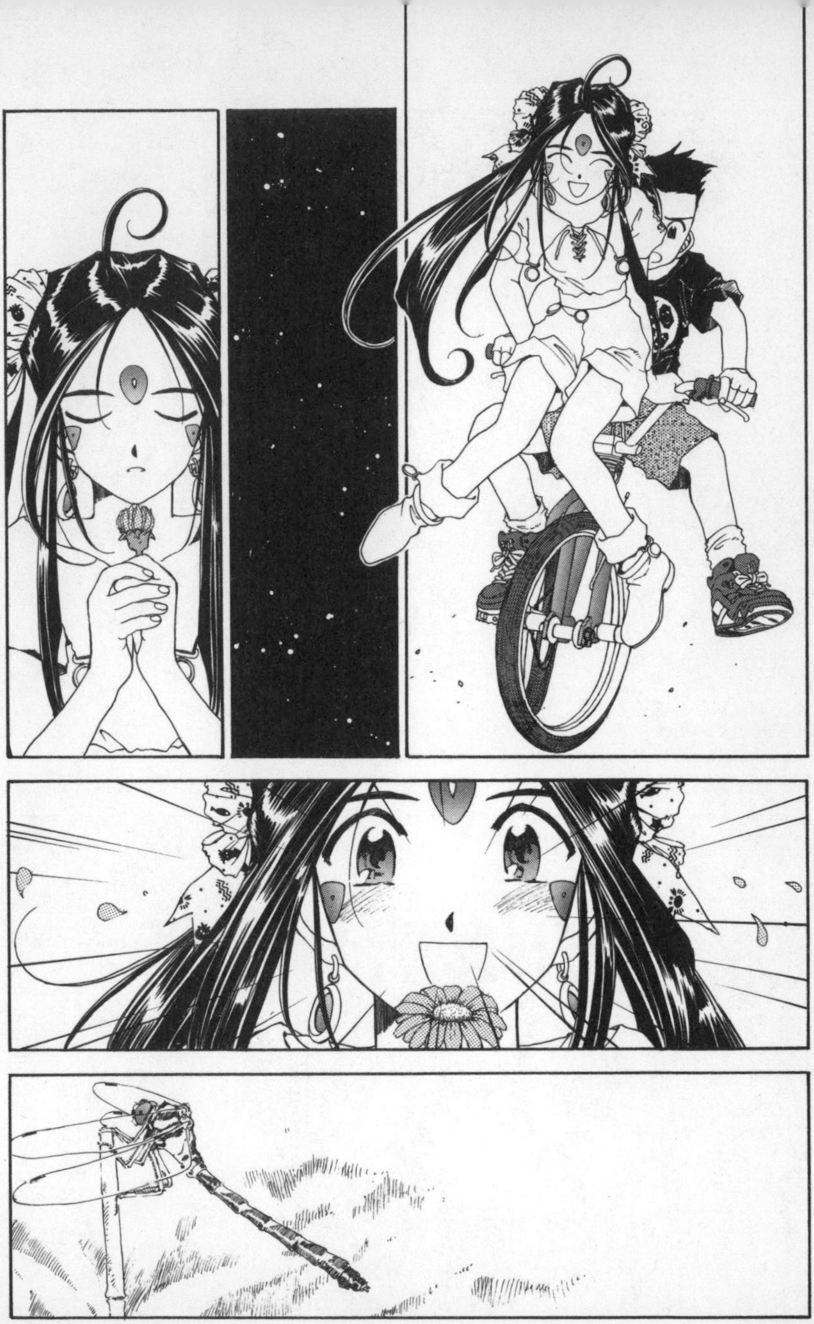

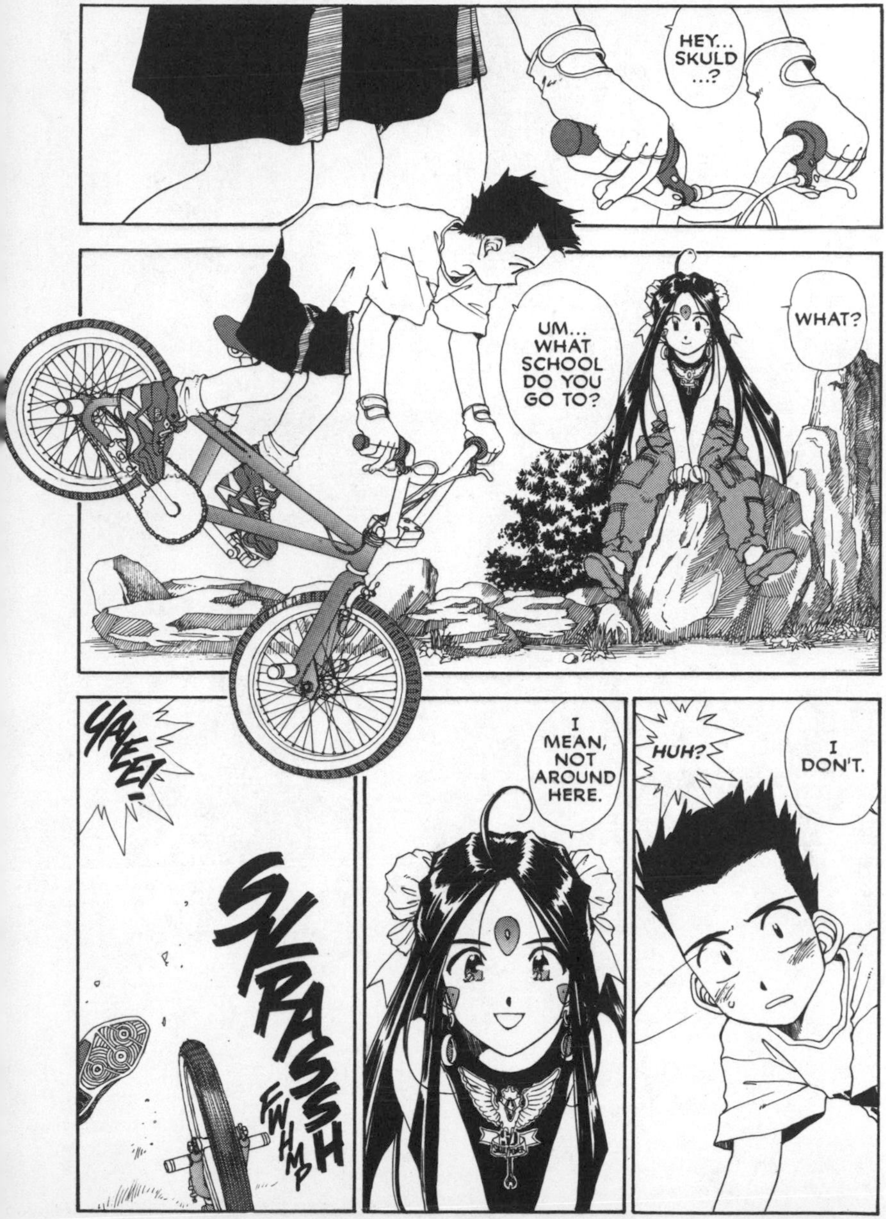
HEY... SKULD ...?
WHAT?
UM... WHAT SCHOOL DO YOU GO TO?
I DON'T.
HUH?
I MEAN, NOT AROUND HERE.
YAKEE!
SKRASSH
FWHMP

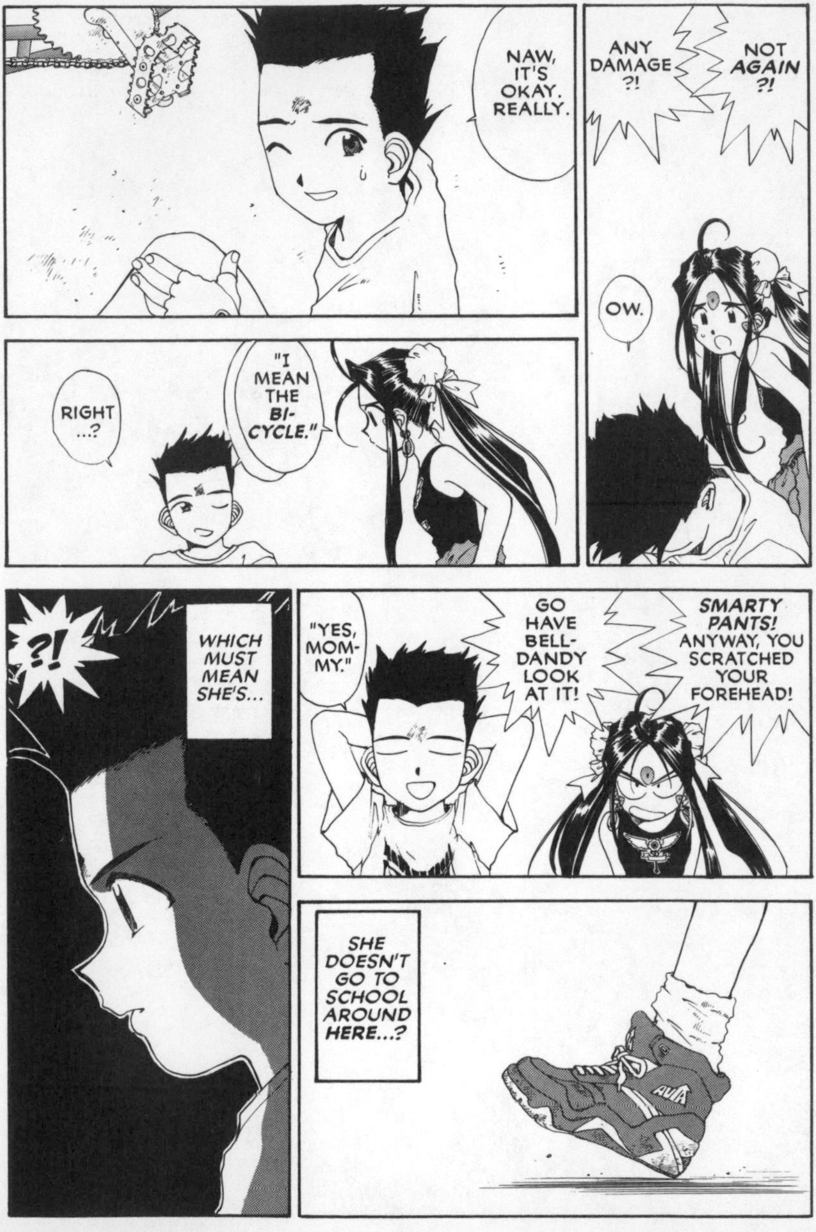
NOT AGAIN?!
ANY DAMAGE?!
OW.
NAW, IT'S OKAY. REALLY.
"I MEAN THE BI-CYCLE."
RIGHT ...?
SMARTY PANTS! ANYWAY, YOU SCRATCHED YOUR FOREHEAD!
GO HAVE BELL-DANDY LOOK AT IT!
"YES, MOM-MY."
SHE DOESN'T GO TO SCHOOL AROUND HERE...?
WHICH MUST MEAN SHE'S...
?!

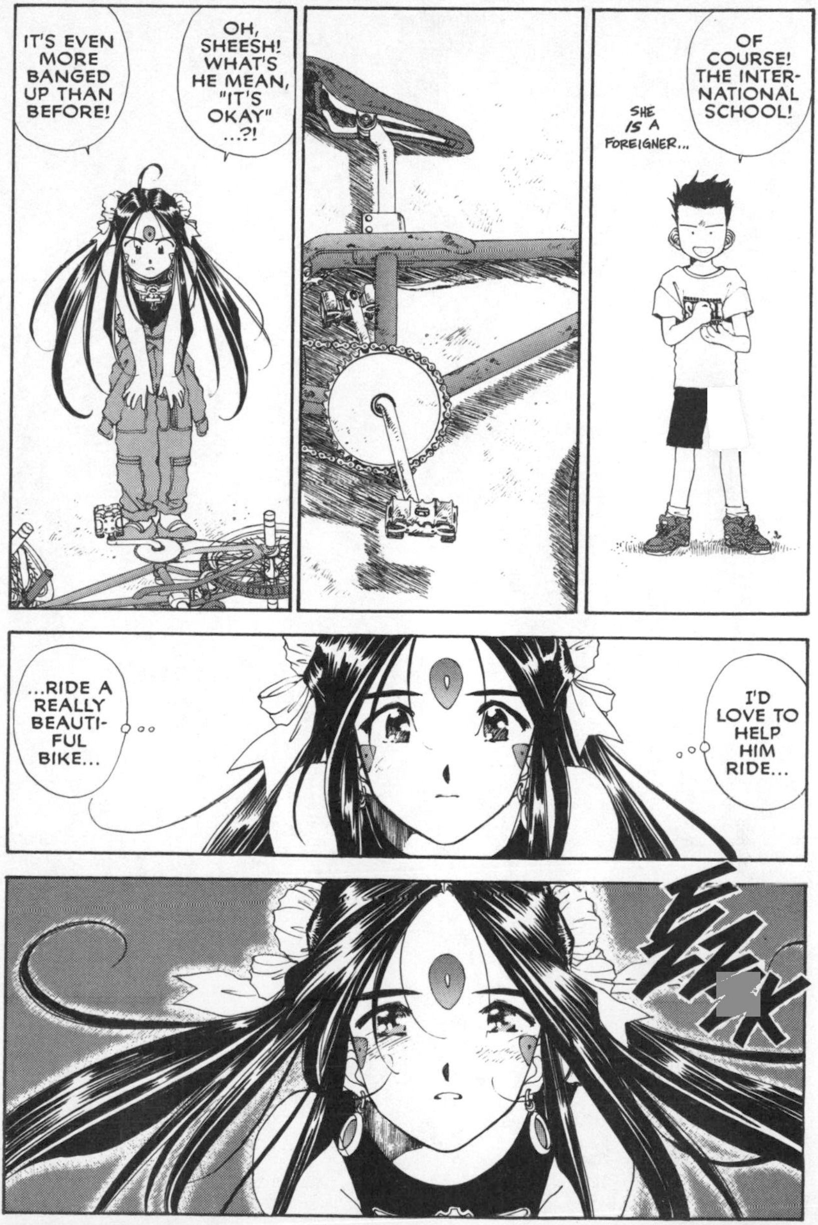
OF COURSE! THE INTER-NATIONAL SCHOOL!
SHE IS A FOREIGNER...
OH, SHEESH! WHAT'S HE MEAN, "IT'S OKAY" ...?!
IT'S EVEN MORE BANGED UP THAN BEFORE!
I'D LOVE TO HELP HIM RIDE...
...RIDE A REALLY BEAUTI-FUL BIKE...

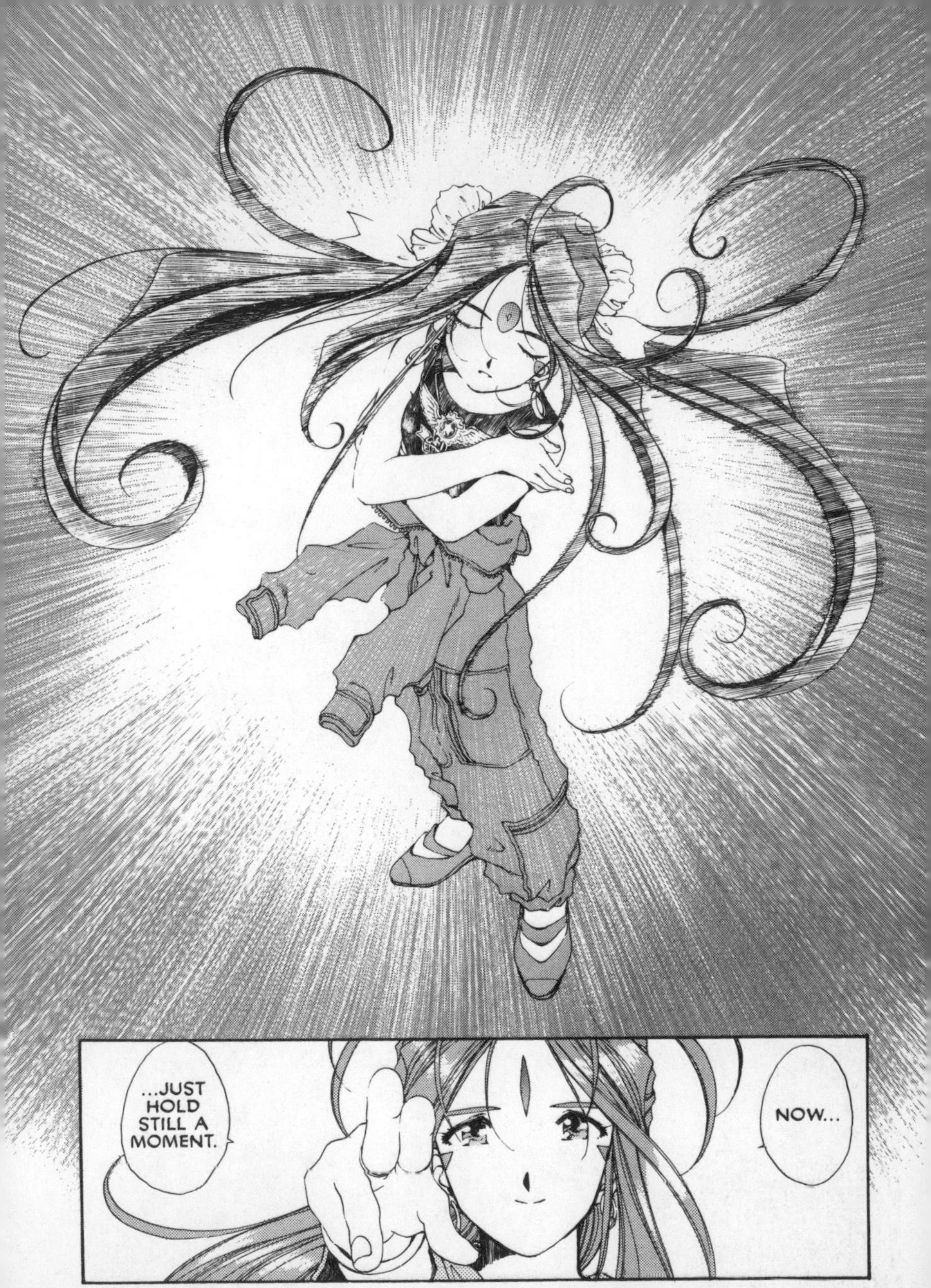
NOW...
...JUST HOLD STILL A MOMENT.

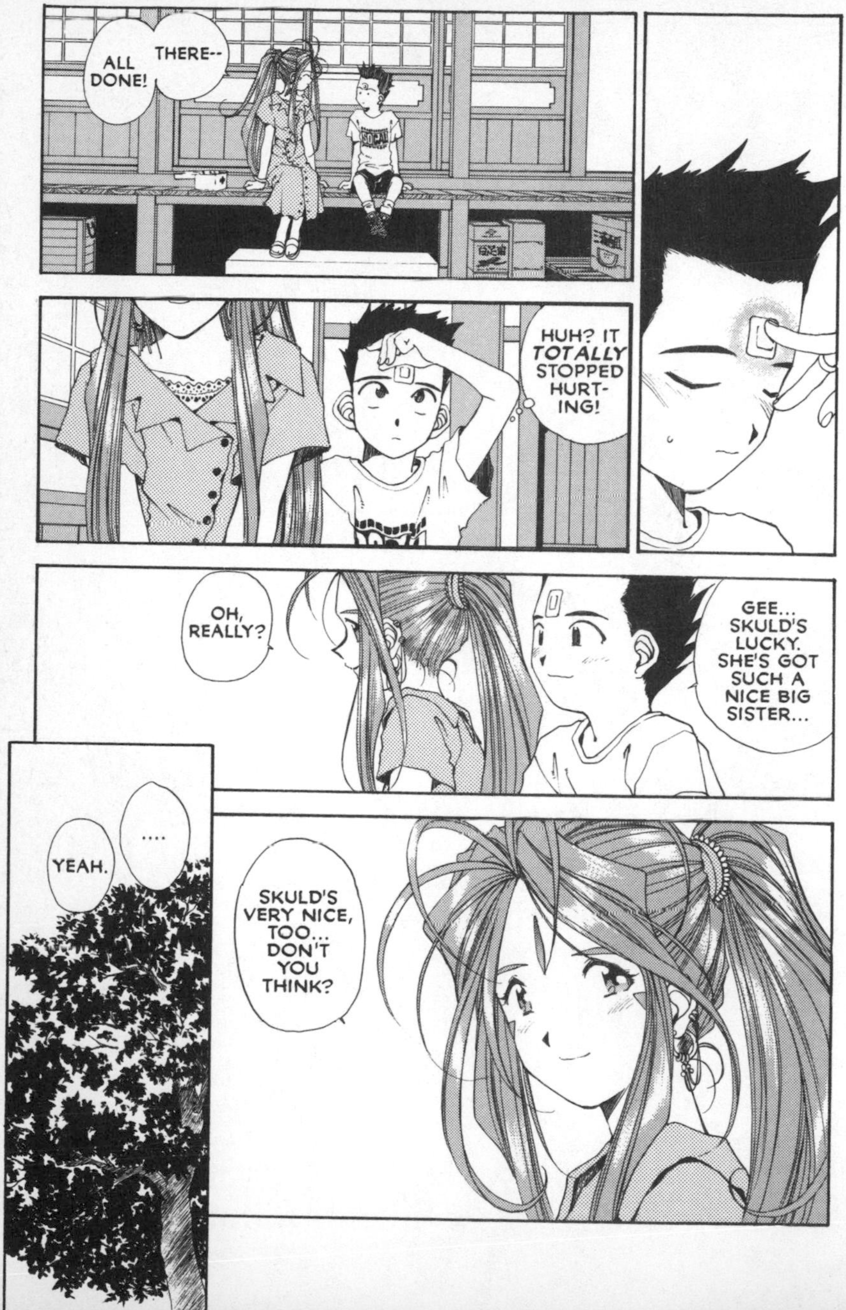
THERE-- ALL DONE!
HUH? IT *TOTALLY* STOPPED HURTING!
GEE... SKULD'S LUCKY. SHE'S GOT SUCH A NICE BIG SISTER...
OH, REALLY?
SKULD'S VERY NICE, TOO... DON'T YOU THINK?
....
YEAH.

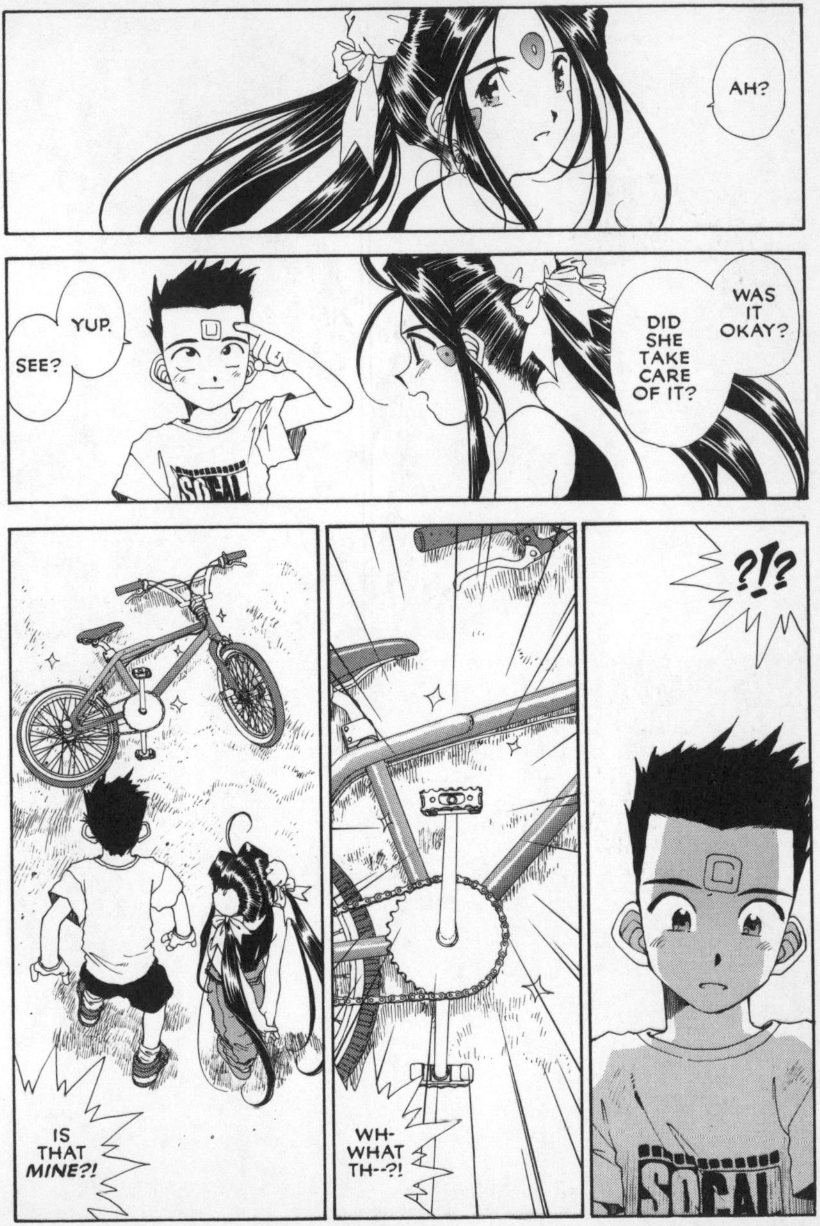
AH?
WAS IT OKAY?
DID SHE TAKE CARE OF IT?
YUP.
SEE?
SOCAL
?!?
SOCAL
WH- WHAT TH--?!
IS THAT *MINE?!*

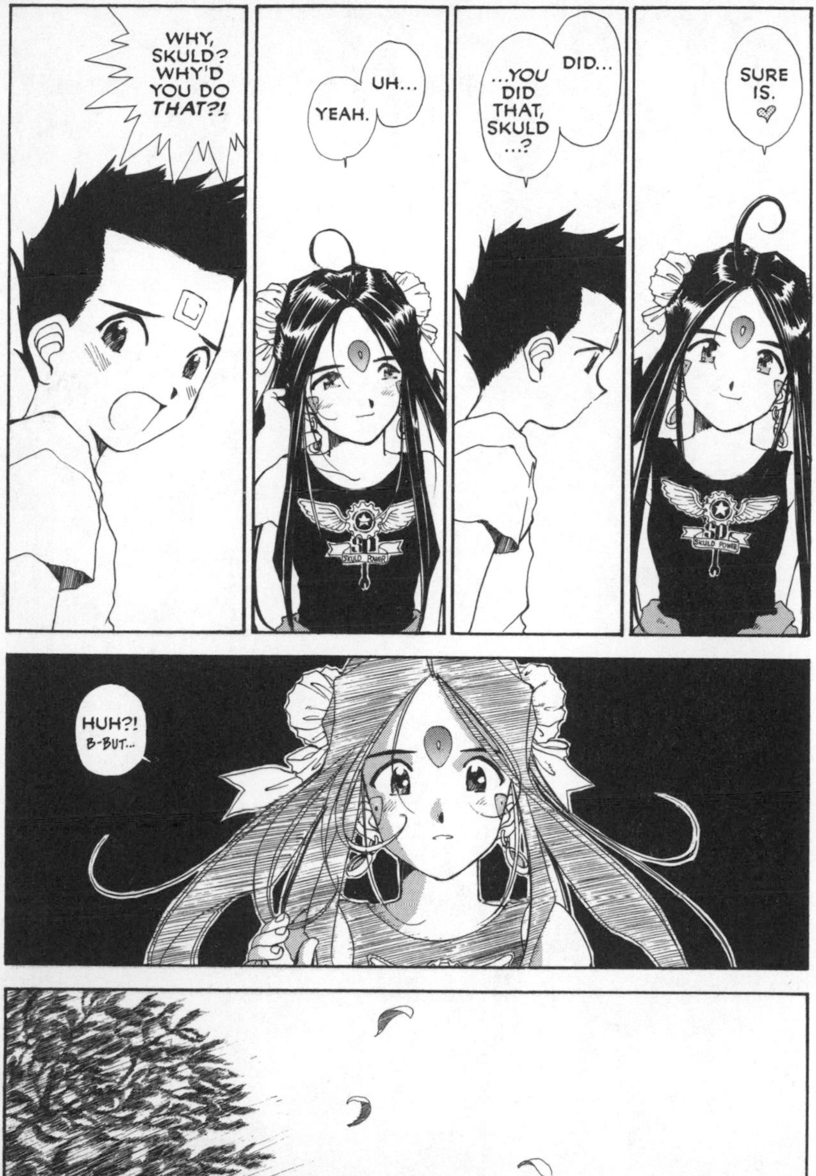
SURE IS. ♥
DID...
...YOU DID THAT, SKULD ...?
UH...
YEAH.
WHY, SKULD? WHY'D YOU DO *THAT?!*
HUH?! B-BUT...

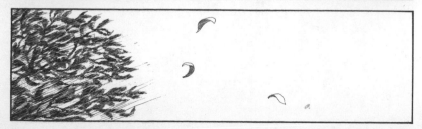

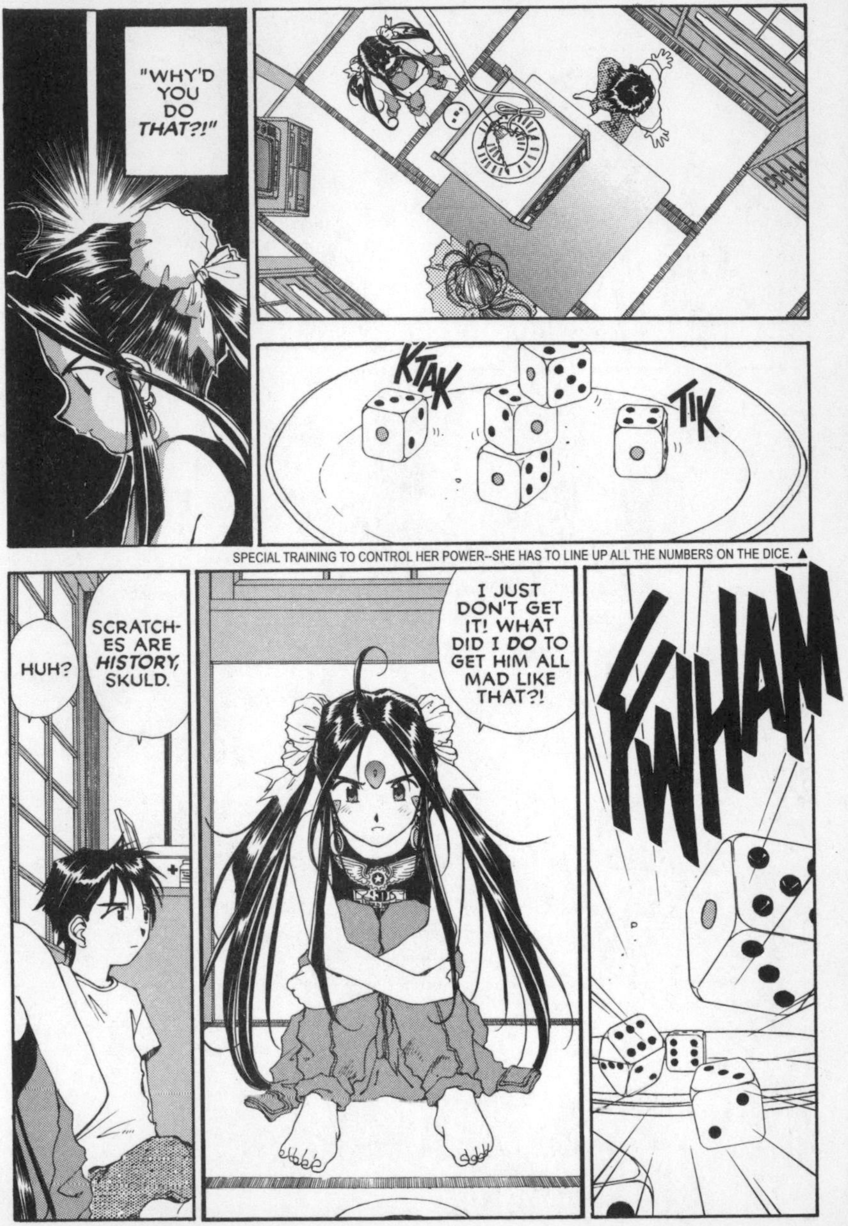
KTAK
TIK
"WHY'D YOU DO THAT?!"
FWHAM
I JUST DON'T GET IT! WHAT DID I DO TO GET HIM ALL MAD LIKE THAT?!
SCRATCH-ES ARE HISTORY, SKULD.
HUH?

SPECIAL TRAINING TO CONTROL HER POWER--SHE HAS TO LINE UP ALL THE NUMBERS ON THE DICE. ▲

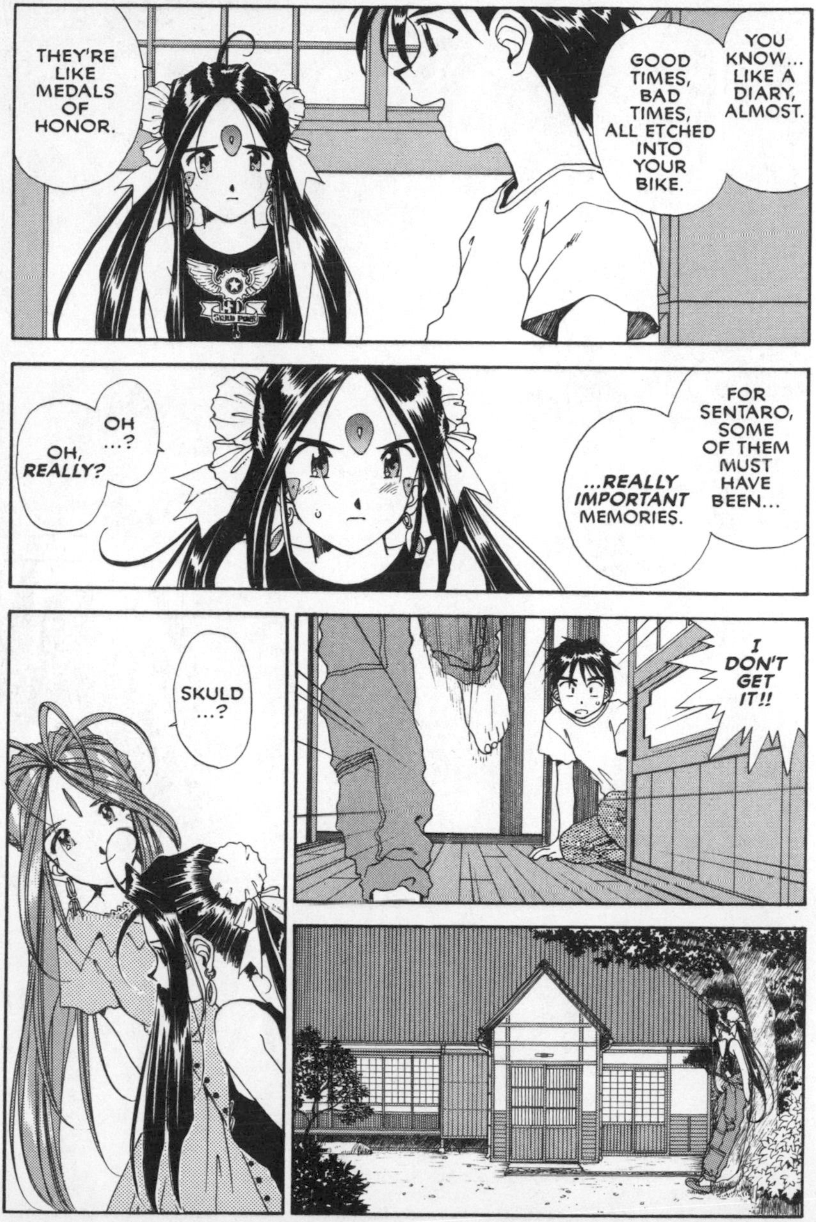
YOU KNOW... LIKE A DIARY, ALMOST.
GOOD TIMES, BAD TIMES, ALL ETCHED INTO YOUR BIKE.
THEY'RE LIKE MEDALS OF HONOR.
FOR SENTARO, SOME OF THEM MUST HAVE BEEN...
...REALLY IMPORTANT MEMORIES.
OH ...?
OH, REALLY?
I DON'T GET IT!!
SKULD ...?

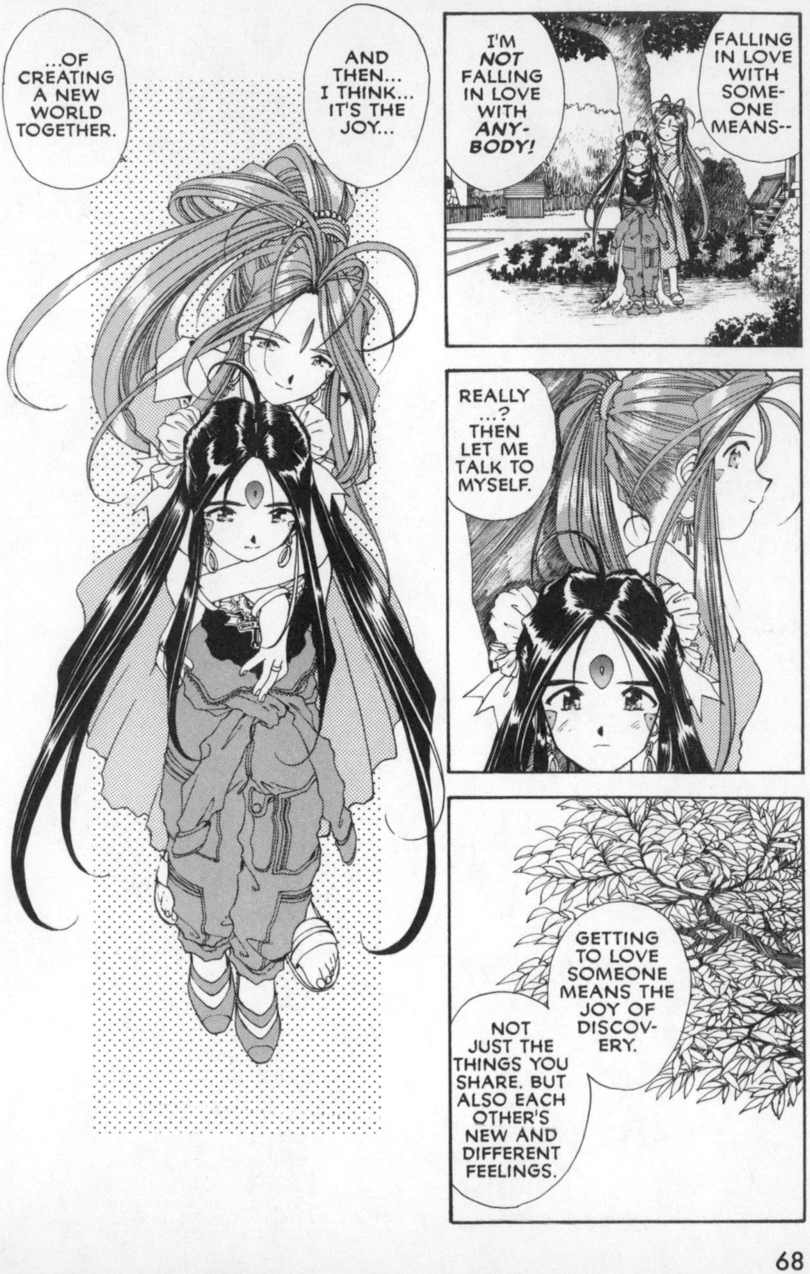
FALLING IN LOVE WITH SOME-ONE MEANS--
I'M NOT FALLING IN LOVE WITH ANY-BODY!
REALLY ...? THEN LET ME TALK TO MYSELF.
GETTING TO LOVE SOMEONE MEANS THE JOY OF DISCOV-ERY.
NOT JUST THE THINGS YOU SHARE. BUT ALSO EACH OTHER'S NEW AND DIFFERENT FEELINGS.
AND THEN... I THINK... IT'S THE JOY...
...OF CREATING A NEW WORLD TOGETHER.

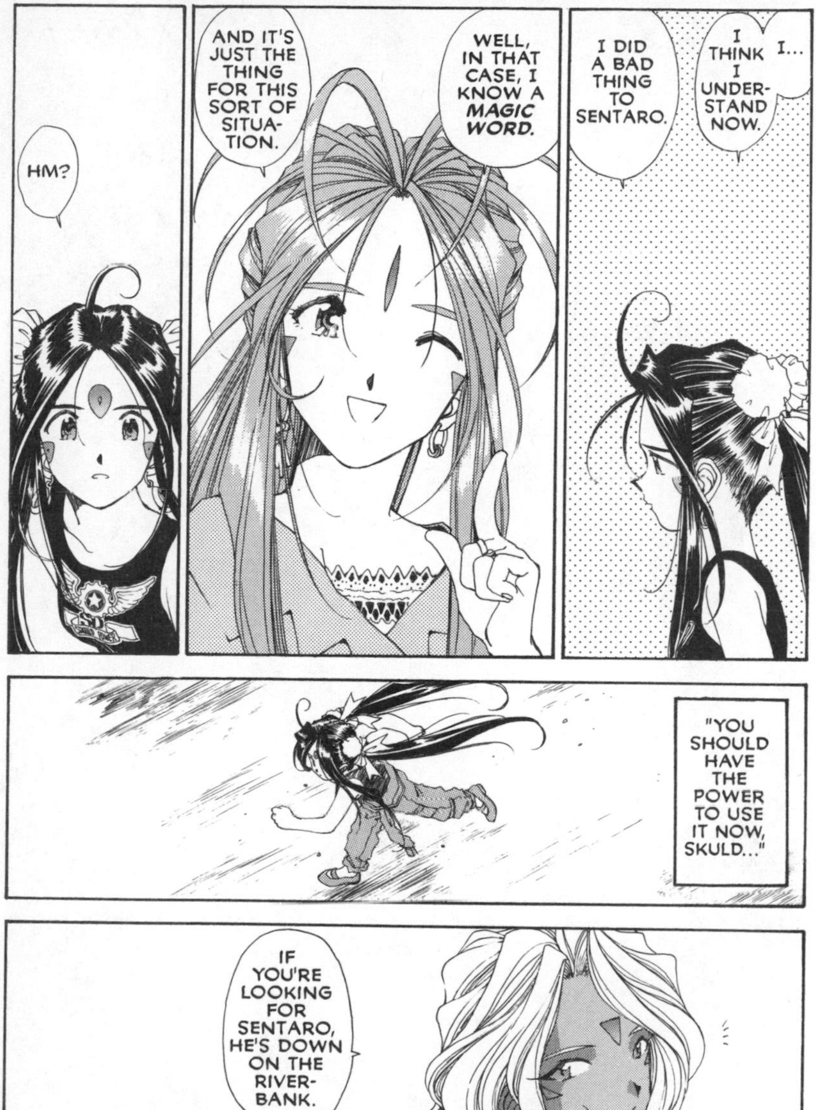
I...
I THINK I UNDERSTAND NOW.
I DID A BAD THING TO SENTARO.
WELL, IN THAT CASE, I KNOW A *MAGIC WORD.*
AND IT'S JUST THE THING FOR THIS SORT OF SITUATION.
HM?
"YOU SHOULD HAVE THE POWER TO USE IT NOW, SKULD..."
IF YOU'RE LOOKING FOR SENTARO, HE'S DOWN ON THE RIVERBANK.

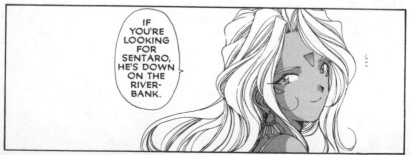

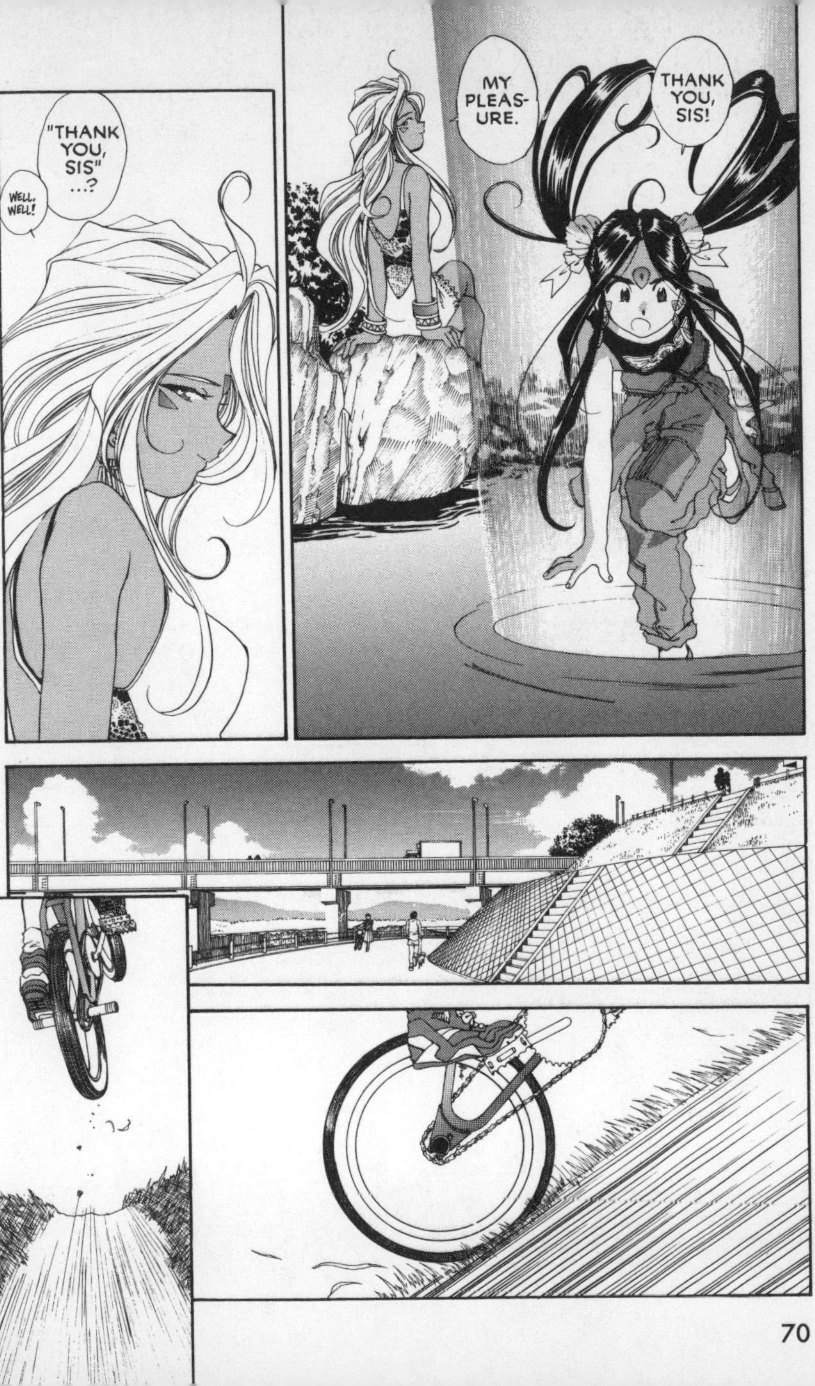
THANK YOU, SIS!
MY PLEASURE.
"THANK YOU, SIS" ...?
WELL, WELL!

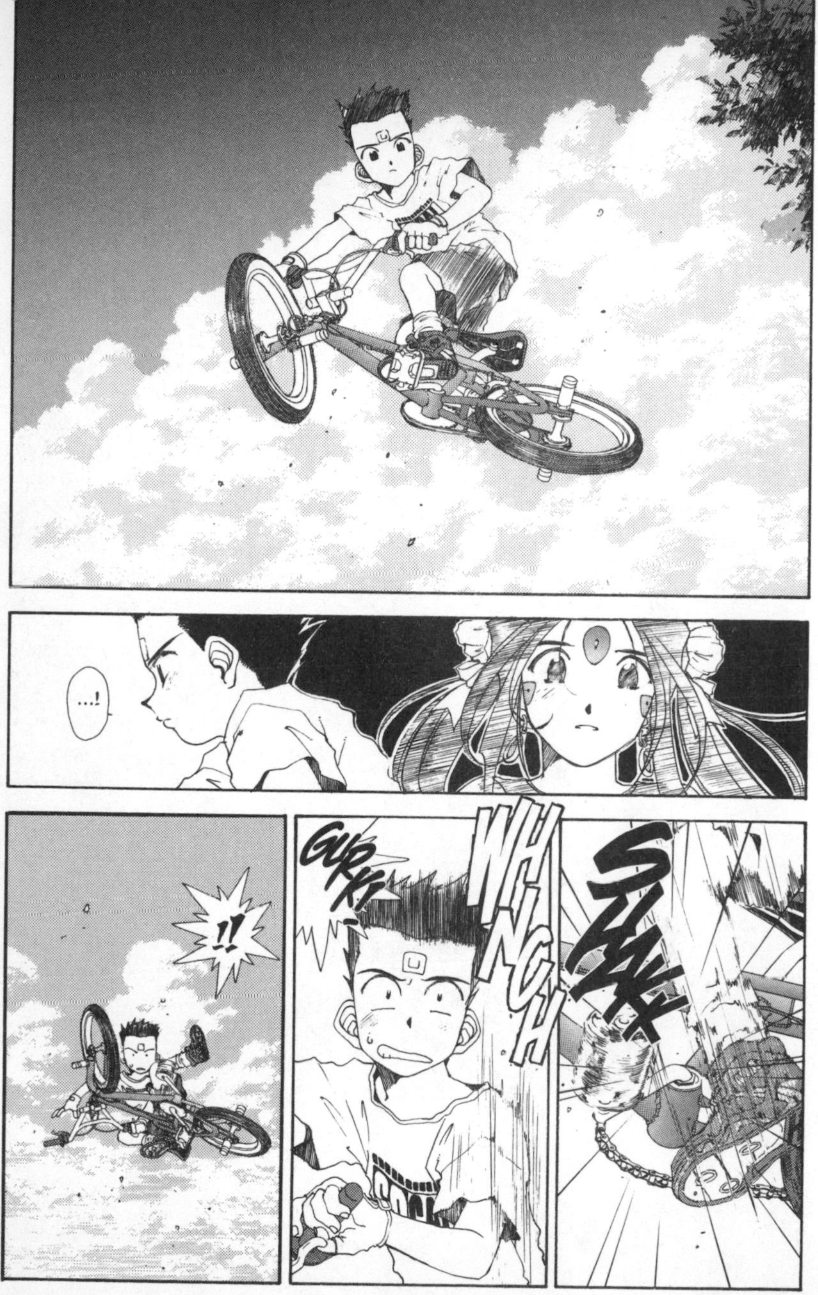
...!
GURK!
!!

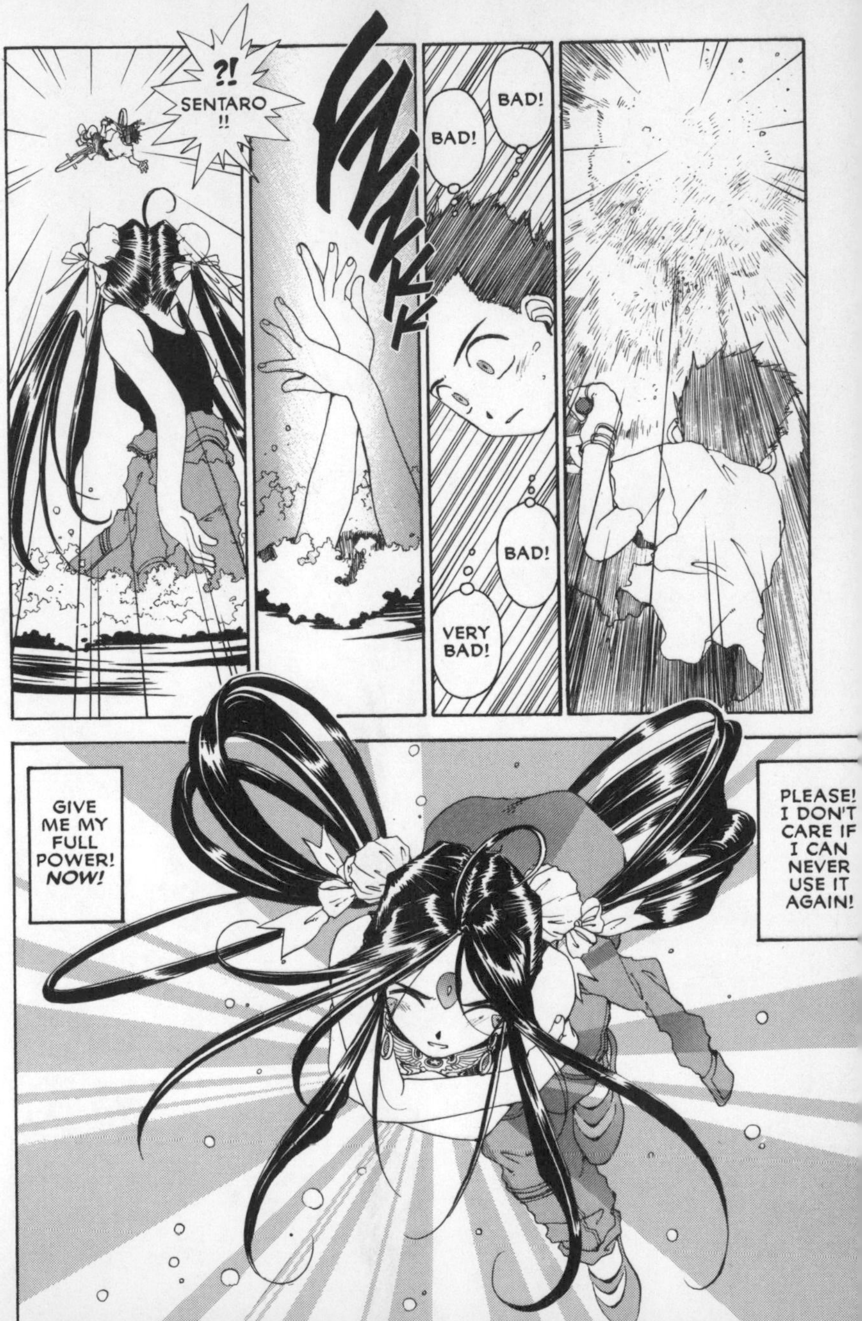
BAD!
BAD!
BAD!
VERY BAD!
?! SENTARO !!
PLEASE! I DON'T CARE IF I CAN NEVER USE IT AGAIN!
GIVE ME MY FULL POWER! NOW!

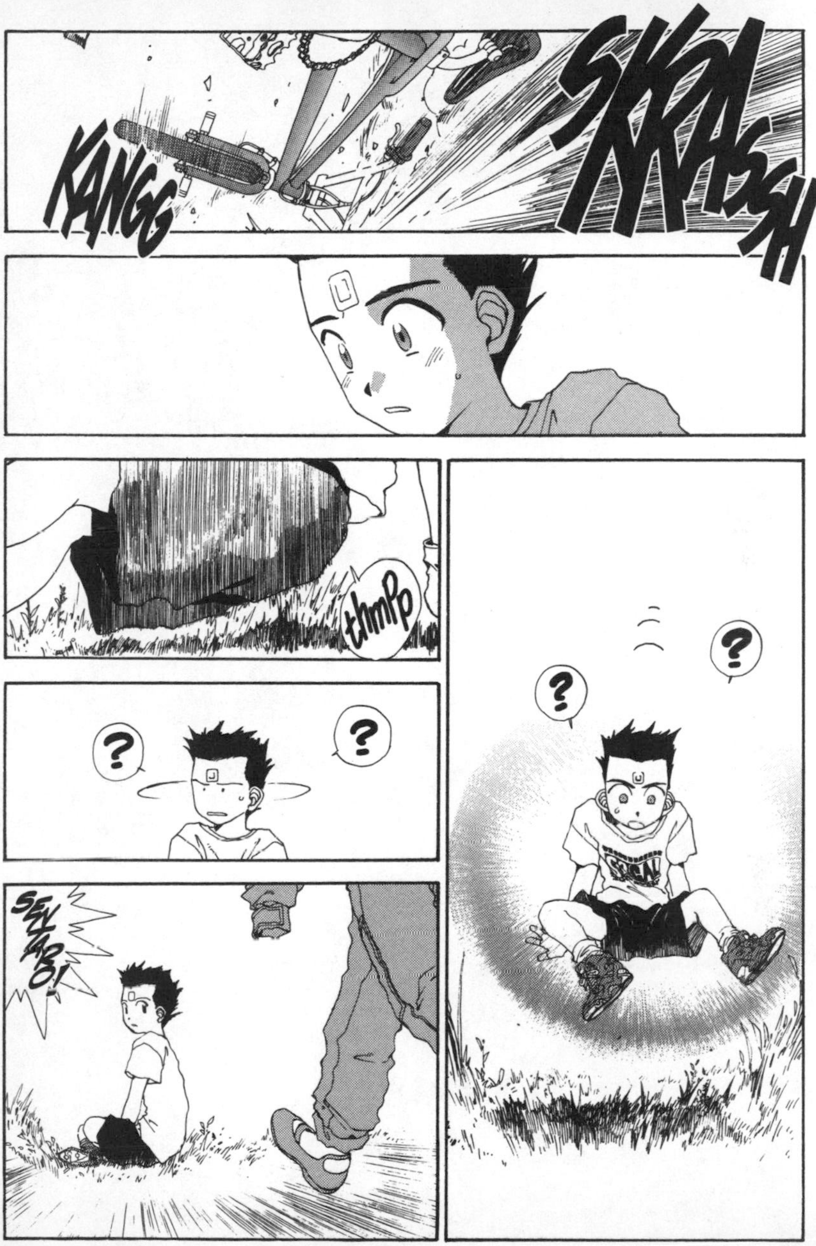
KANGG
thmpp
?
?
?
?

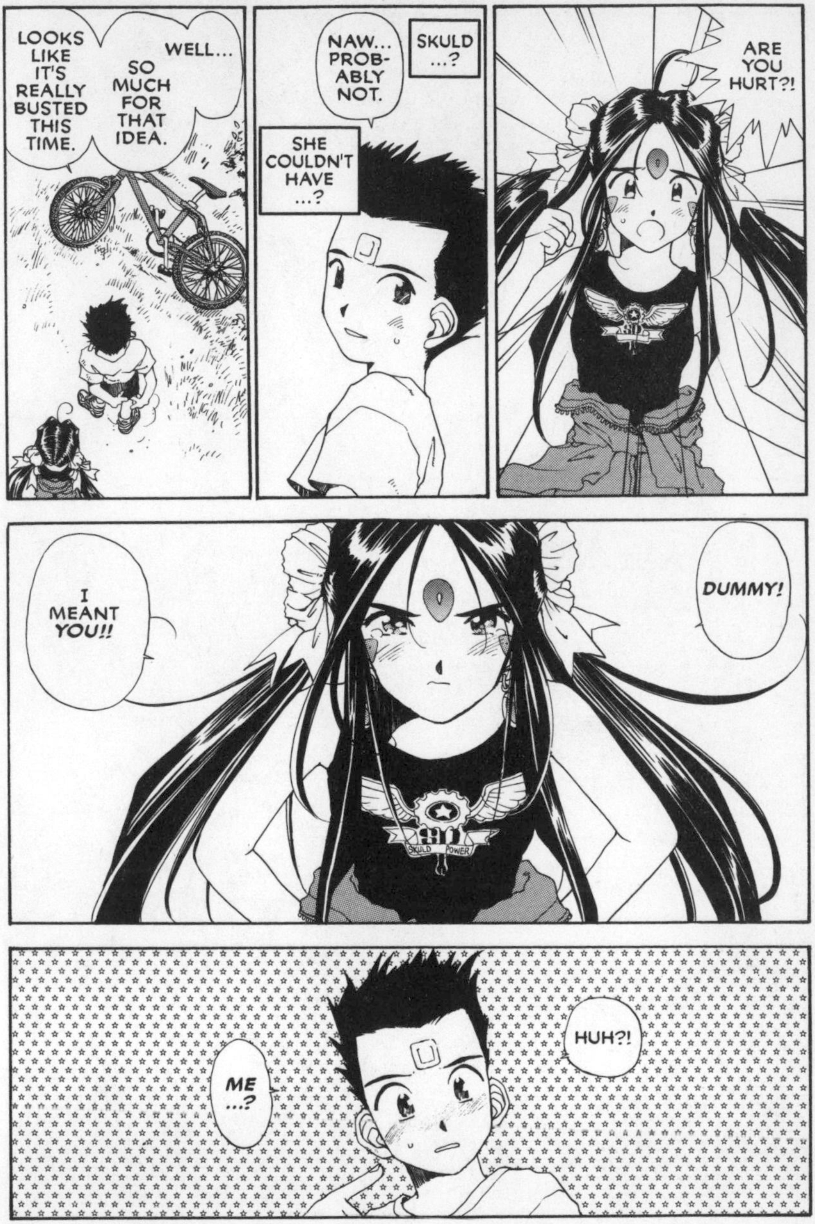
ARE YOU HURT?!
SKULD ...?
NAW... PROB-ABLY NOT.
SHE COULDN'T HAVE ...?
WELL...
SO MUCH FOR THAT IDEA.
LOOKS LIKE IT'S REALLY BUSTED THIS TIME.
DUMMY!
I MEANT *YOU!!*
HUH?!
ME ...?

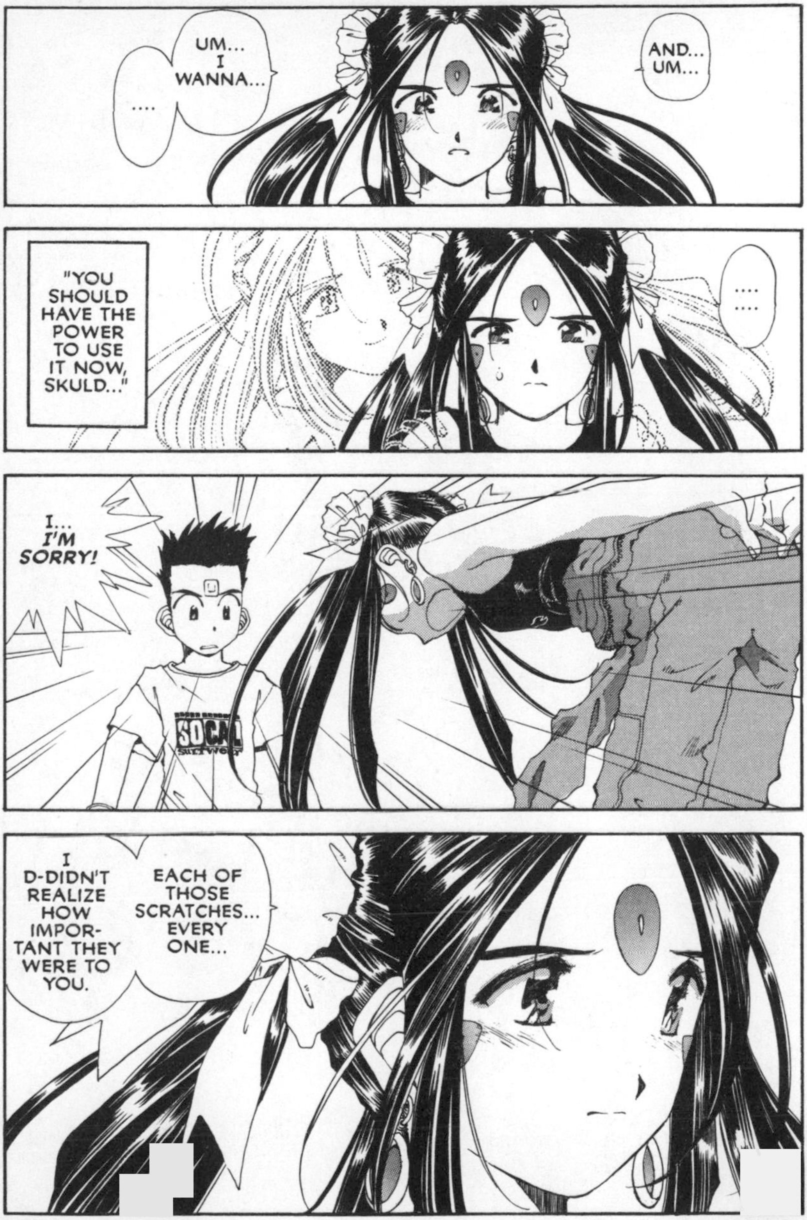
AND... UM...
UM... I WANNA...
....
....
"YOU SHOULD HAVE THE POWER TO USE IT NOW, SKULD..."
I... *I'M SORRY!*
EACH OF THOSE SCRATCHES... EVERY ONE...
I D-DIDN'T REALIZE HOW IMPOR-TANT THEY WERE TO YOU.

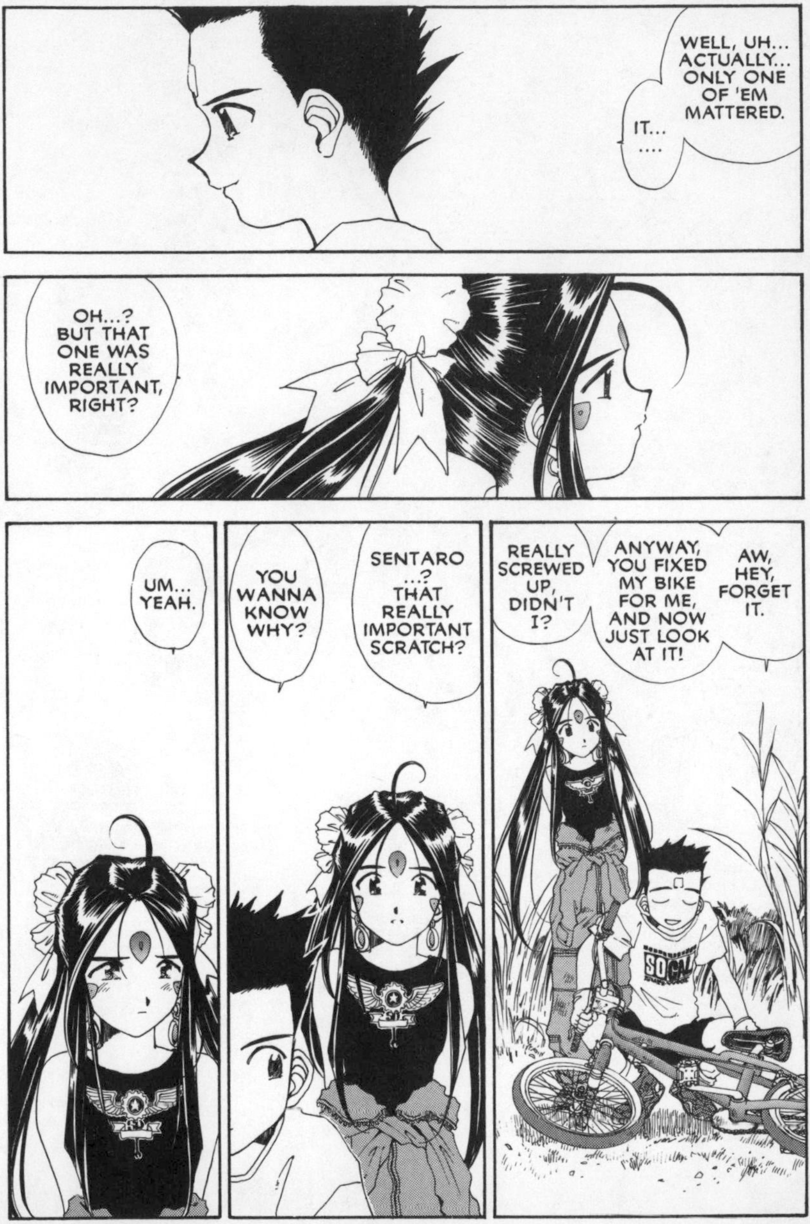
WELL, UH... ACTUALLY... ONLY ONE OF 'EM MATTERED.
IT... ....
OH...? BUT THAT ONE WAS REALLY IMPORTANT, RIGHT?
AW, HEY, FORGET IT.
ANYWAY, YOU FIXED MY BIKE FOR ME, AND NOW JUST LOOK AT IT!
REALLY SCREWED UP, DIDN'T I?
SENTARO ...? THAT REALLY IMPORTANT SCRATCH?
YOU WANNA KNOW WHY?
UM... YEAH.

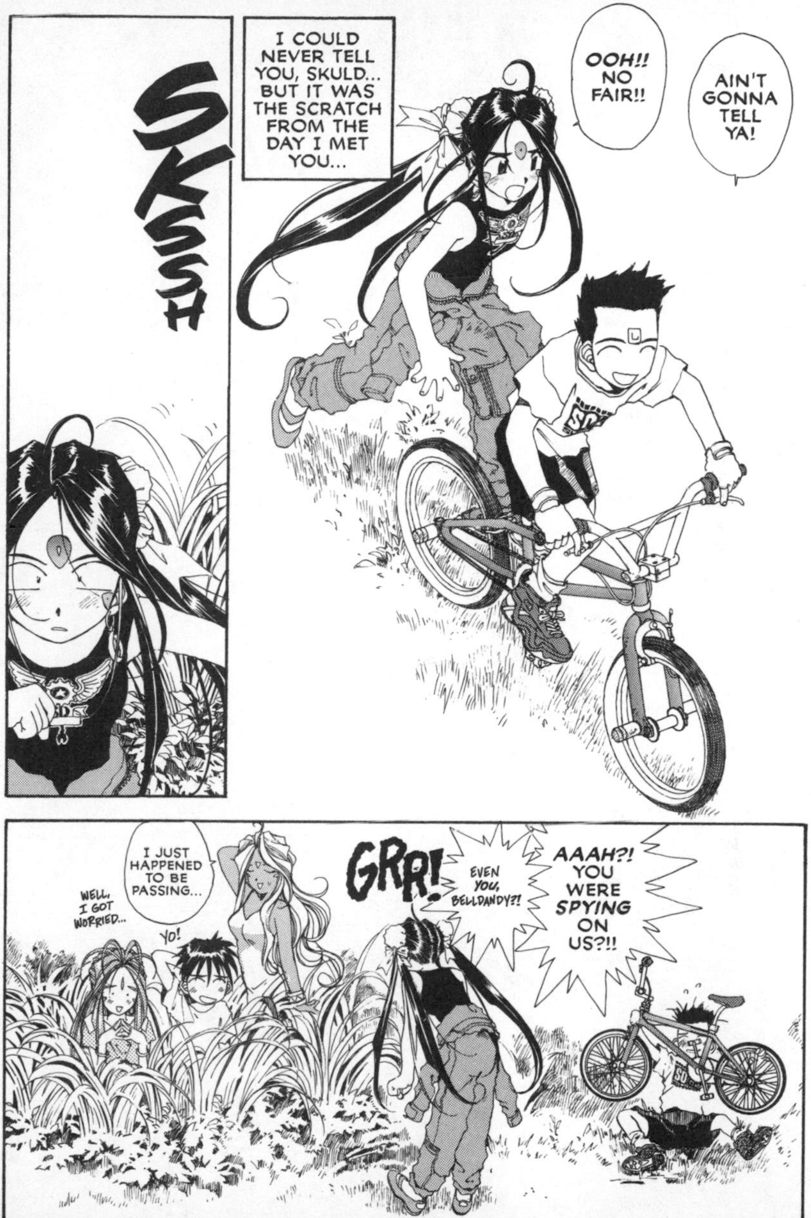
AIN'T GONNA TELL YA!
OOH!! NO FAIR!!
I COULD NEVER TELL YOU, SKULD... BUT IT WAS THE SCRATCH FROM THE DAY I MET YOU...
SKSSH
AAAH?! YOU WERE SPYING ON US?!!
EVEN YOU, BELLDANDY?!
GRR!
I JUST HAPPENED TO BE PASSING...
YO!
WELL, I GOT WORRIED...

CHAPTER 75

The Campus Queen Doesn't Trust Goddesses?!

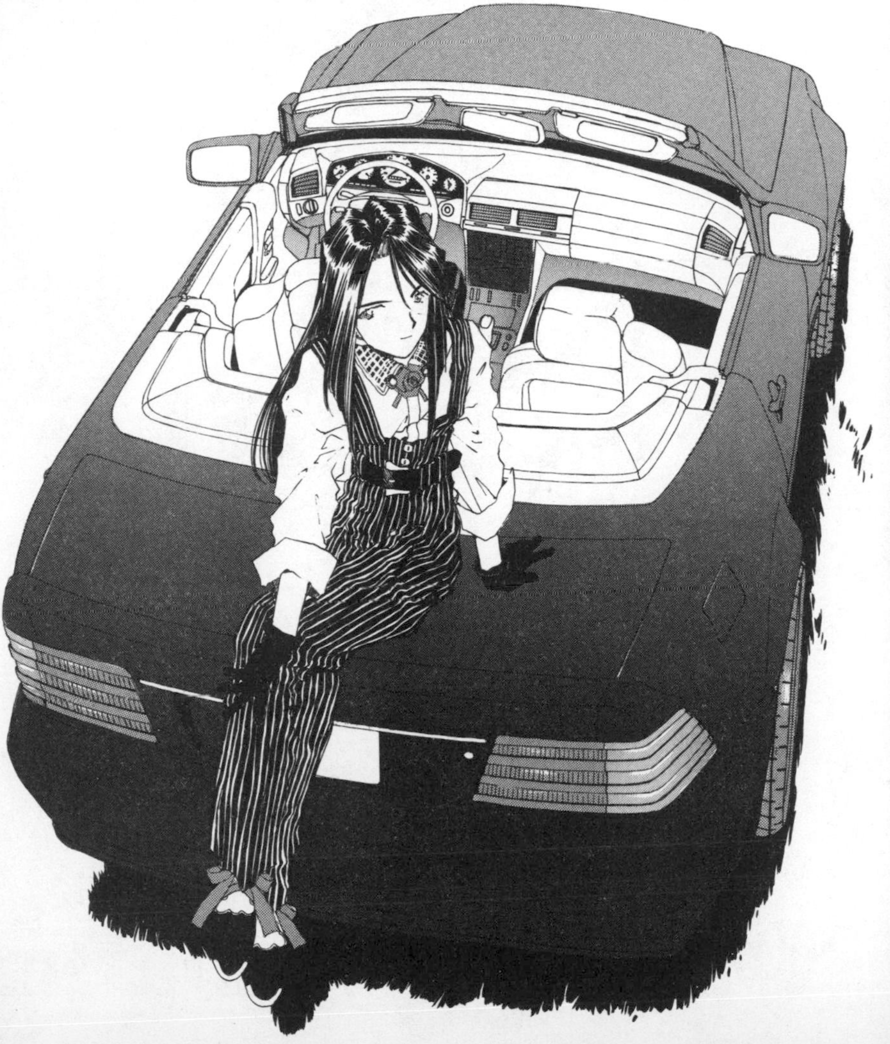

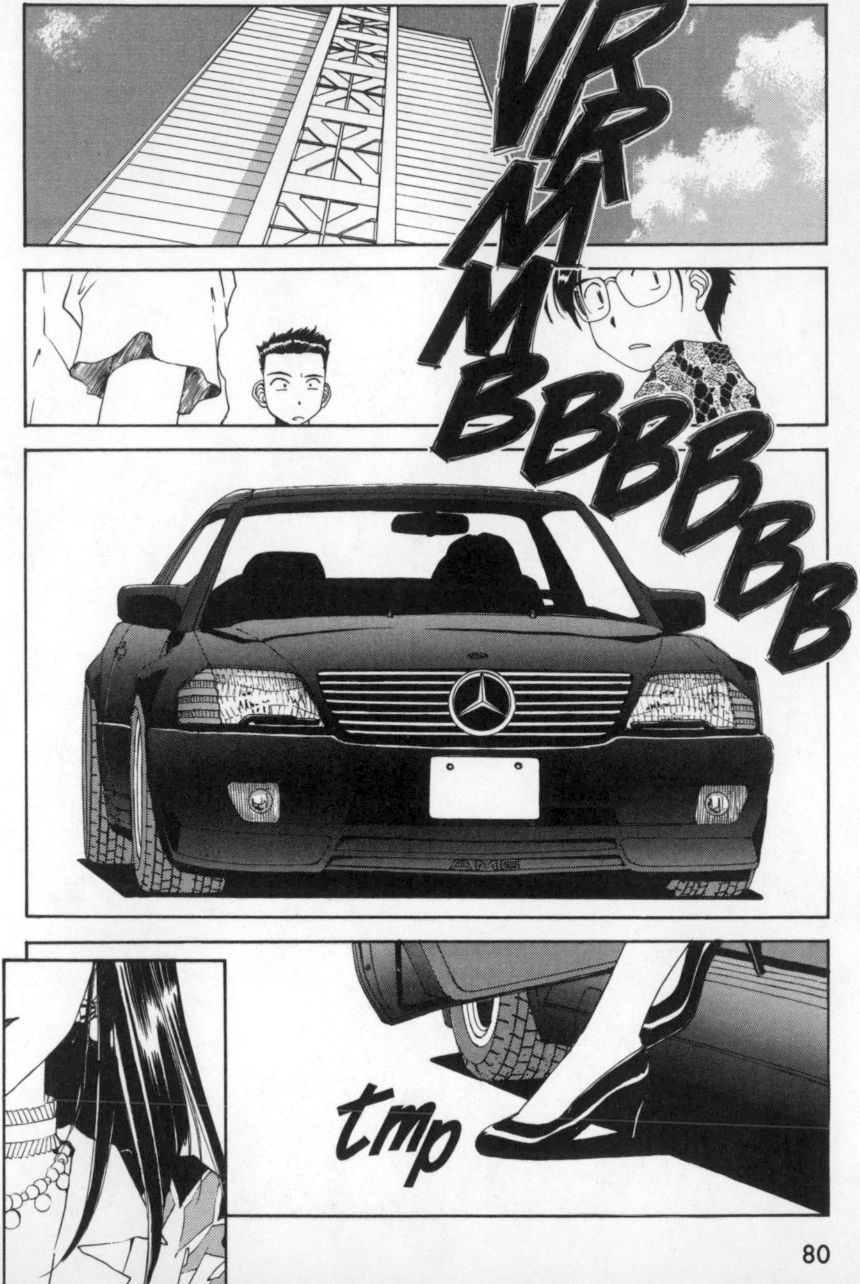
VRMMBBBBBBB
tmp

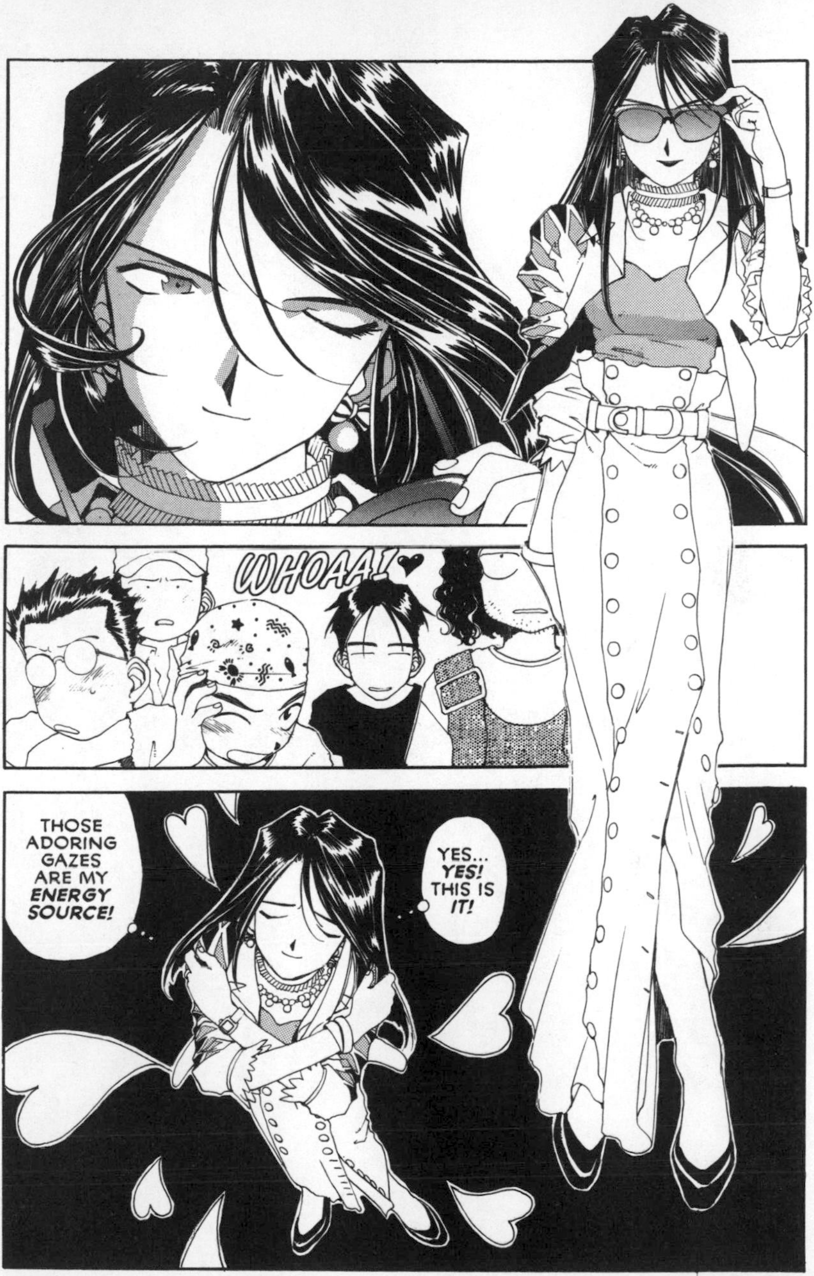
WHOAA!
YES... YES! THIS IS IT!
THOSE ADORING GAZES ARE MY ENERGY SOURCE!

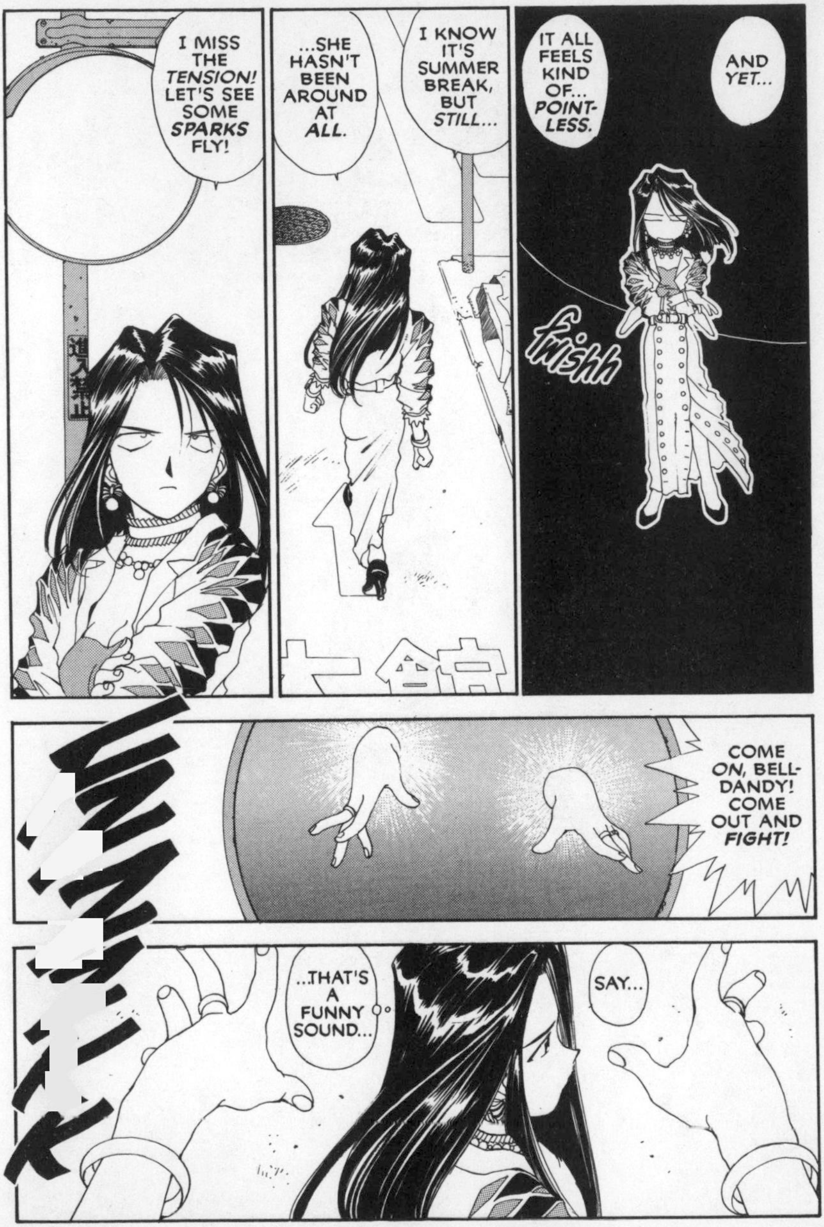
AND YET...
IT ALL FEELS KIND OF... POINTLESS.
frishh
I KNOW IT'S SUMMER BREAK, BUT STILL...
...SHE HASN'T BEEN AROUND AT ALL.
I MISS THE TENSION! LET'S SEE SOME SPARKS FLY!
COME ON, BELL-DANDY! COME OUT AND FIGHT!
SAY...
...THAT'S A FUNNY SOUND...

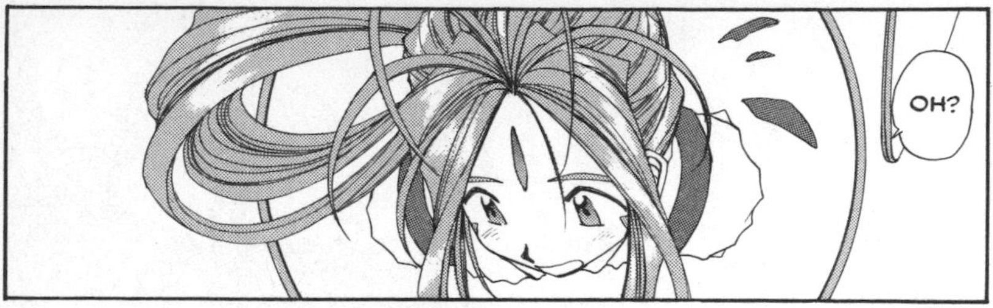
OH?
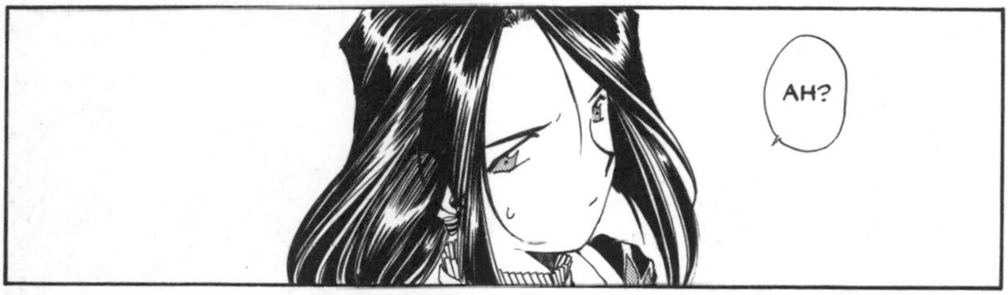
AH?
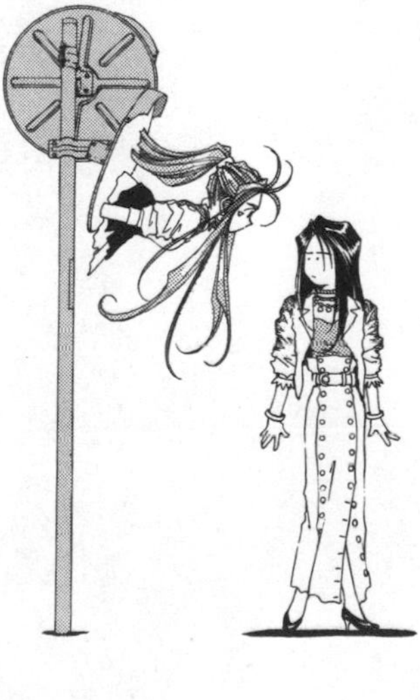

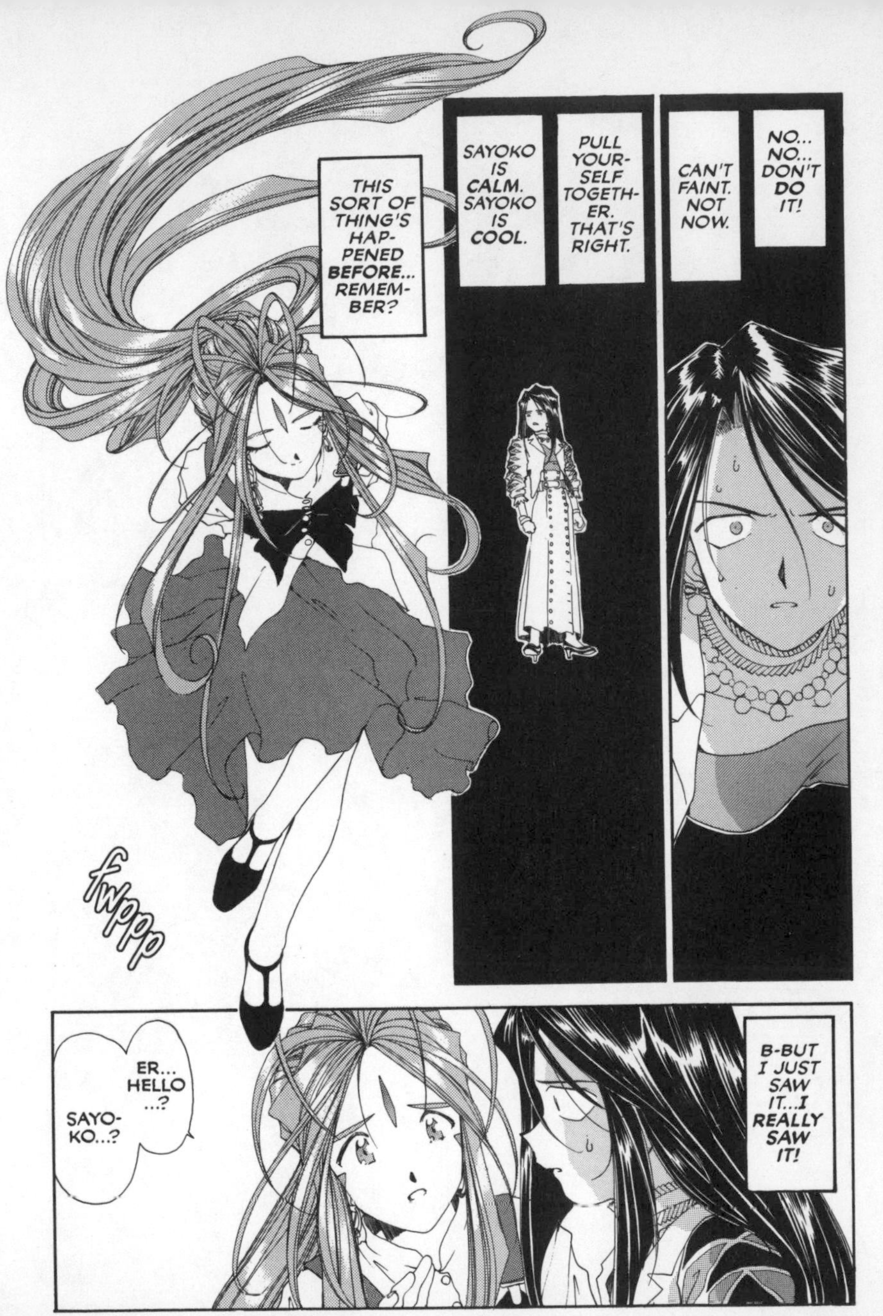
NO... NO... DON'T DO IT!
CAN'T FAINT. NOT NOW.
PULL YOURSELF TOGETHER. THAT'S RIGHT.
SAYOKO IS CALM. SAYOKO IS COOL.
THIS SORT OF THING'S HAPPENED BEFORE... REMEMBER?
fwppp
B-BUT I JUST SAW IT...I REALLY SAW IT!
ER... HELLO ...? SAYOKO...?

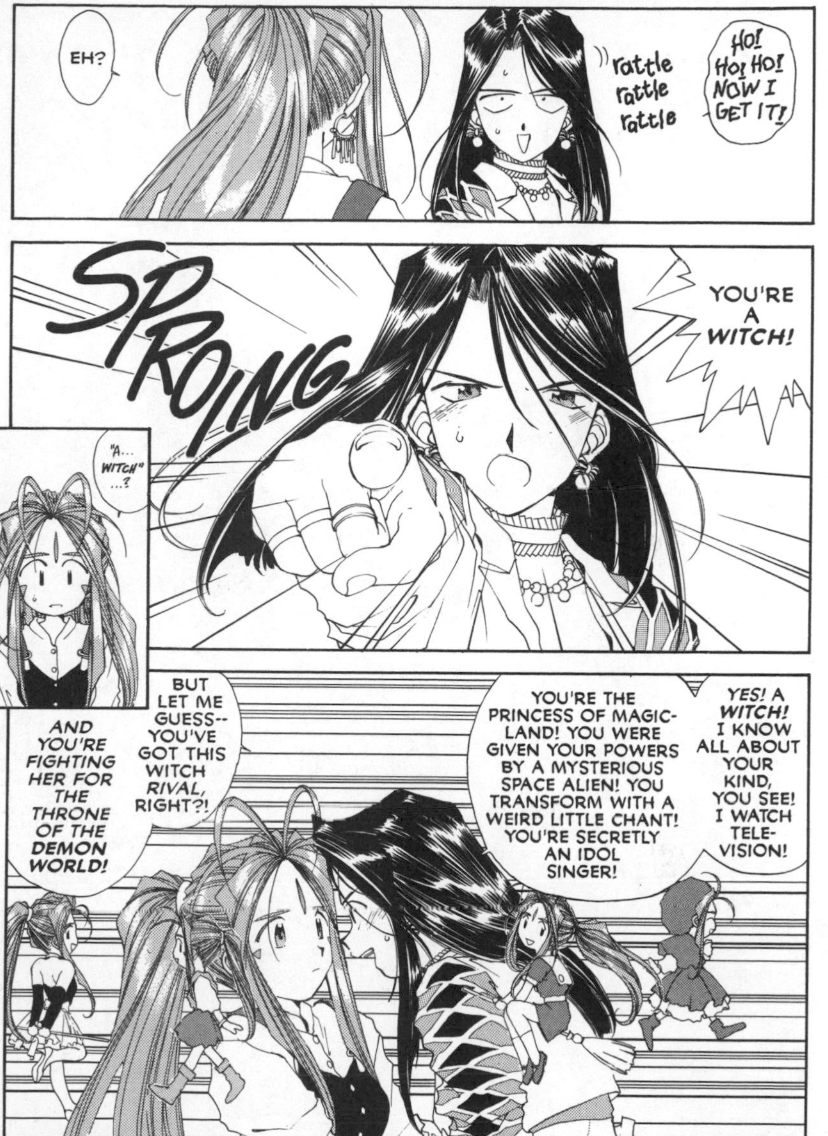
HO! HO! HO! NOW I GET IT!
rattle rattle rattle
EH?
YOU'RE A *WITCH!*
SPROING
"A... WITCH" ...?
YES! A *WITCH!* I KNOW ALL ABOUT YOUR KIND, YOU SEE! I WATCH TELE-VISION!
YOU'RE THE PRINCESS OF MAGIC-LAND! YOU WERE GIVEN YOUR POWERS BY A MYSTERIOUS SPACE ALIEN! YOU TRANSFORM WITH A WEIRD LITTLE CHANT! YOU'RE SECRETLY AN IDOL SINGER!
BUT LET ME GUESS-- YOU'VE GOT THIS WITCH *RIVAL,* RIGHT?!
AND YOU'RE FIGHTING HER FOR THE THRONE OF THE DEMON WORLD!

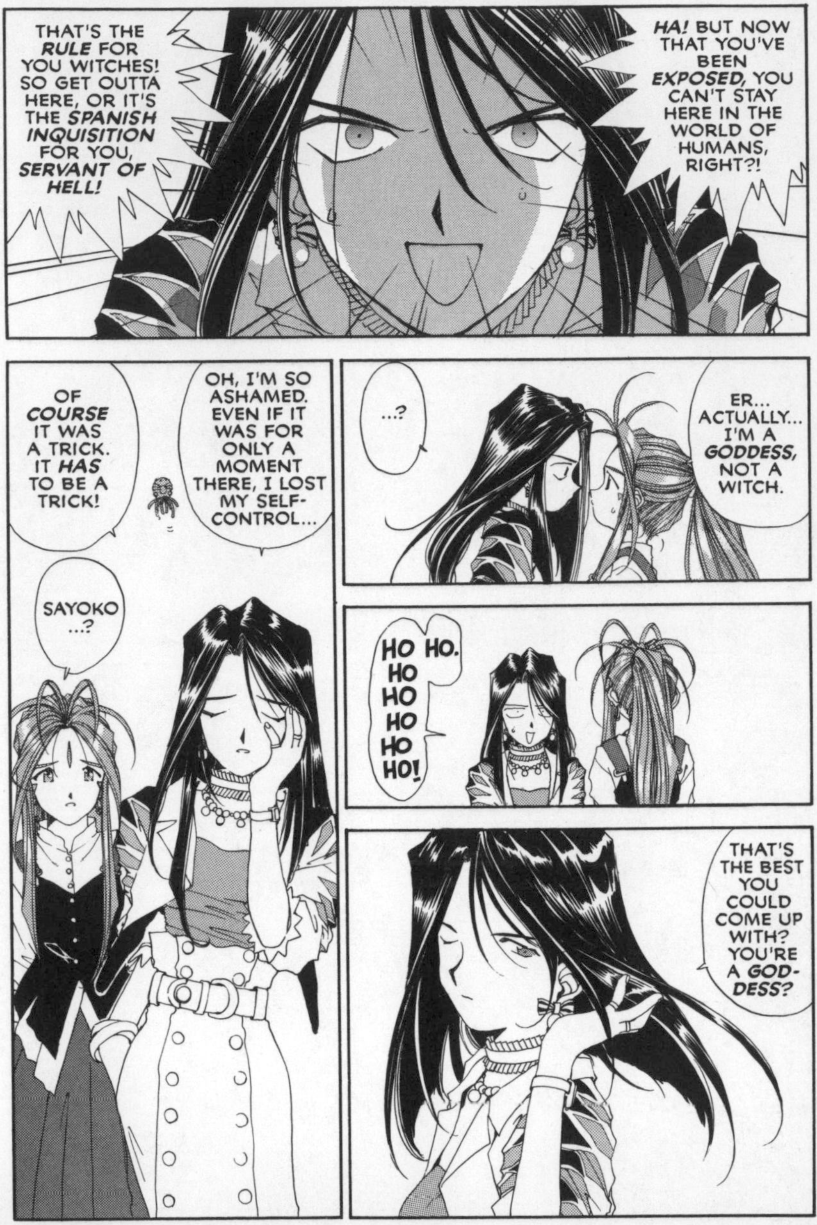
HA! BUT NOW THAT YOU'VE BEEN EXPOSED, YOU CAN'T STAY HERE IN THE WORLD OF HUMANS, RIGHT?!
THAT'S THE RULE FOR YOU WITCHES! SO GET OUTTA HERE, OR IT'S THE SPANISH INQUISITION FOR YOU, SERVANT OF HELL!
ER... ACTUALLY... I'M A GODDESS, NOT A WITCH.
...?
HO HO. HO HO HO HO HO!
THAT'S THE BEST YOU COULD COME UP WITH? YOU'RE A GOD-DESS?
OH, I'M SO ASHAMED. EVEN IF IT WAS FOR ONLY A MOMENT THERE, I LOST MY SELF-CONTROL...
OF COURSE IT WAS A TRICK. IT HAS TO BE A TRICK!
SAYOKO ...?

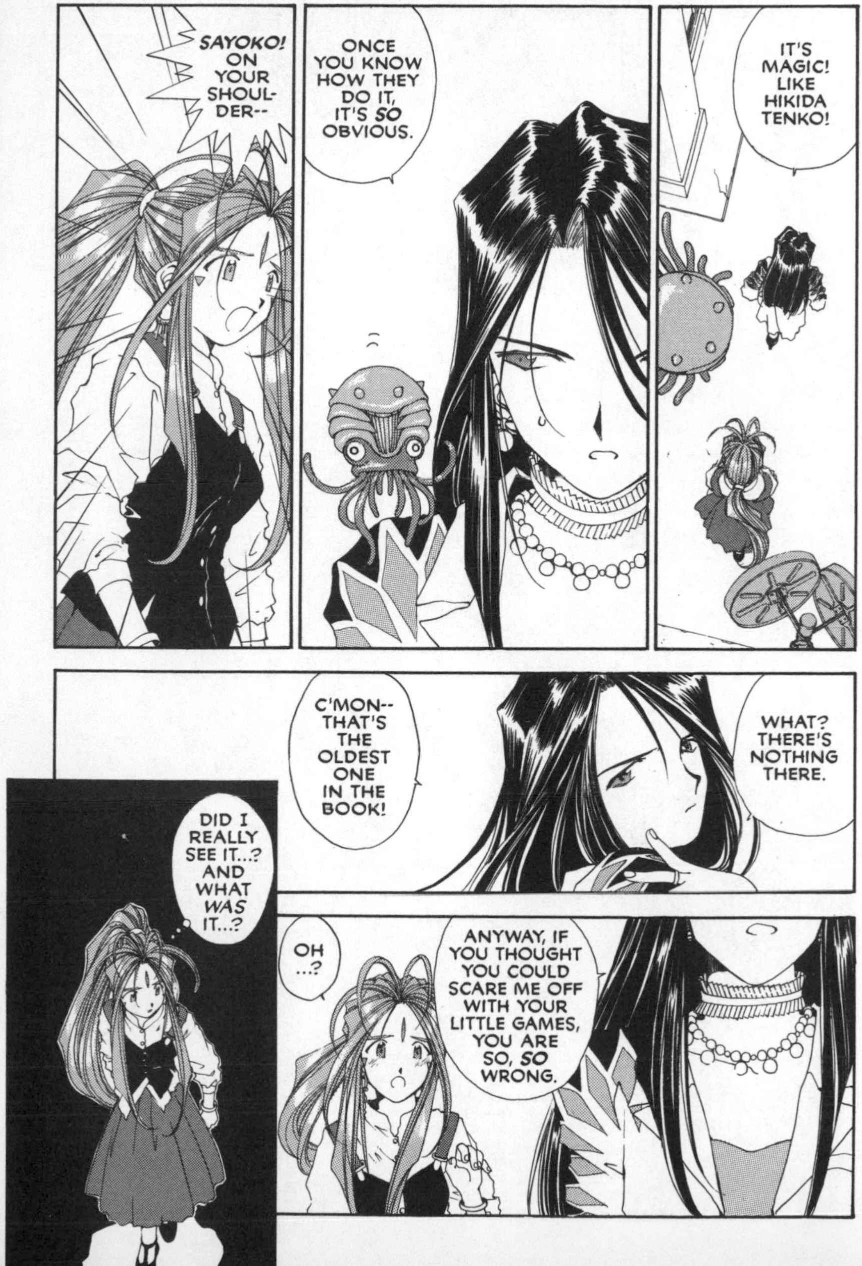
IT'S MAGIC! LIKE HIKIDA TENKO!
ONCE YOU KNOW HOW THEY DO IT, IT'S *SO* OBVIOUS.
SAYOKO! ON YOUR SHOULDER--
WHAT? THERE'S NOTHING THERE.
C'MON-- THAT'S THE OLDEST ONE IN THE BOOK!
ANYWAY, IF YOU THOUGHT YOU COULD SCARE ME OFF WITH YOUR LITTLE GAMES, YOU ARE SO, *SO* WRONG.
OH ...?
DID I REALLY SEE IT...? AND WHAT *WAS* IT...?

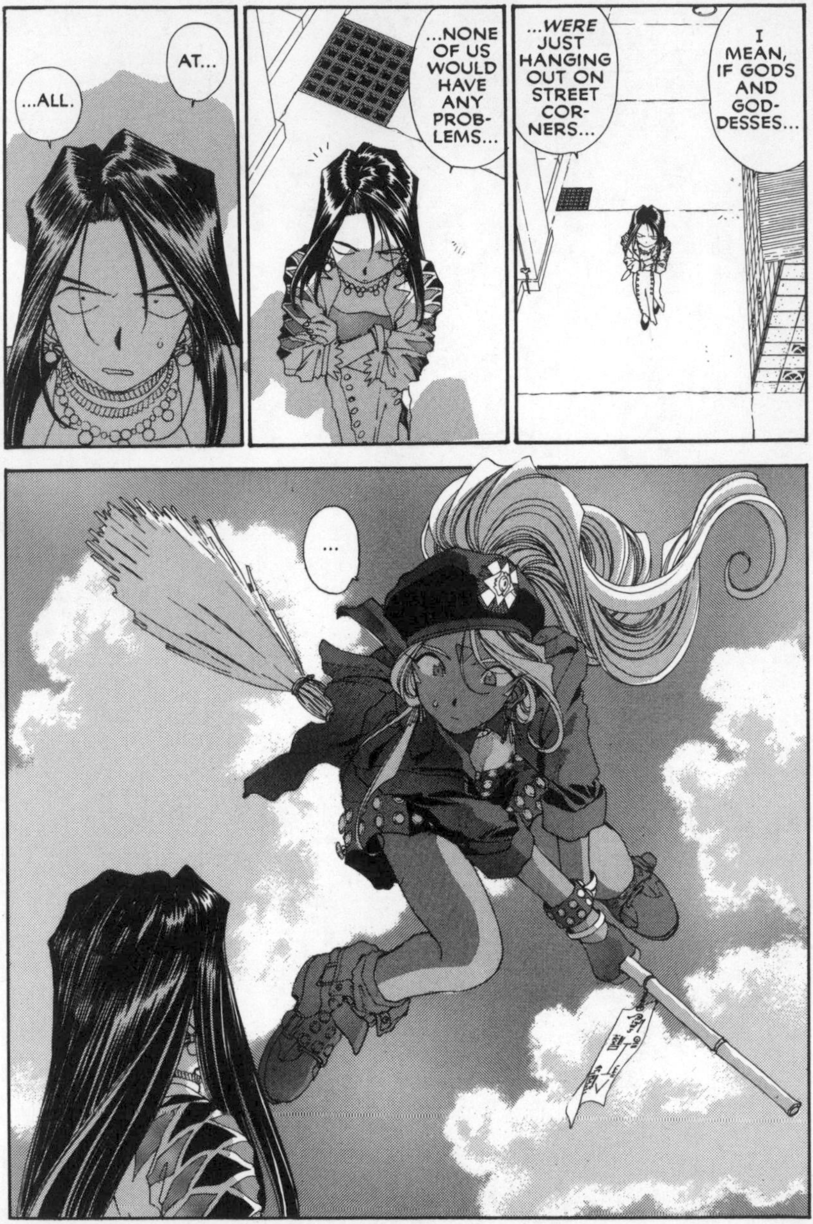
I MEAN, IF GODS AND GOD-DESSES...
...WERE JUST HANGING OUT ON STREET COR-NERS...
...NONE OF US WOULD HAVE ANY PROB-LEMS...
AT...
...ALL.
...

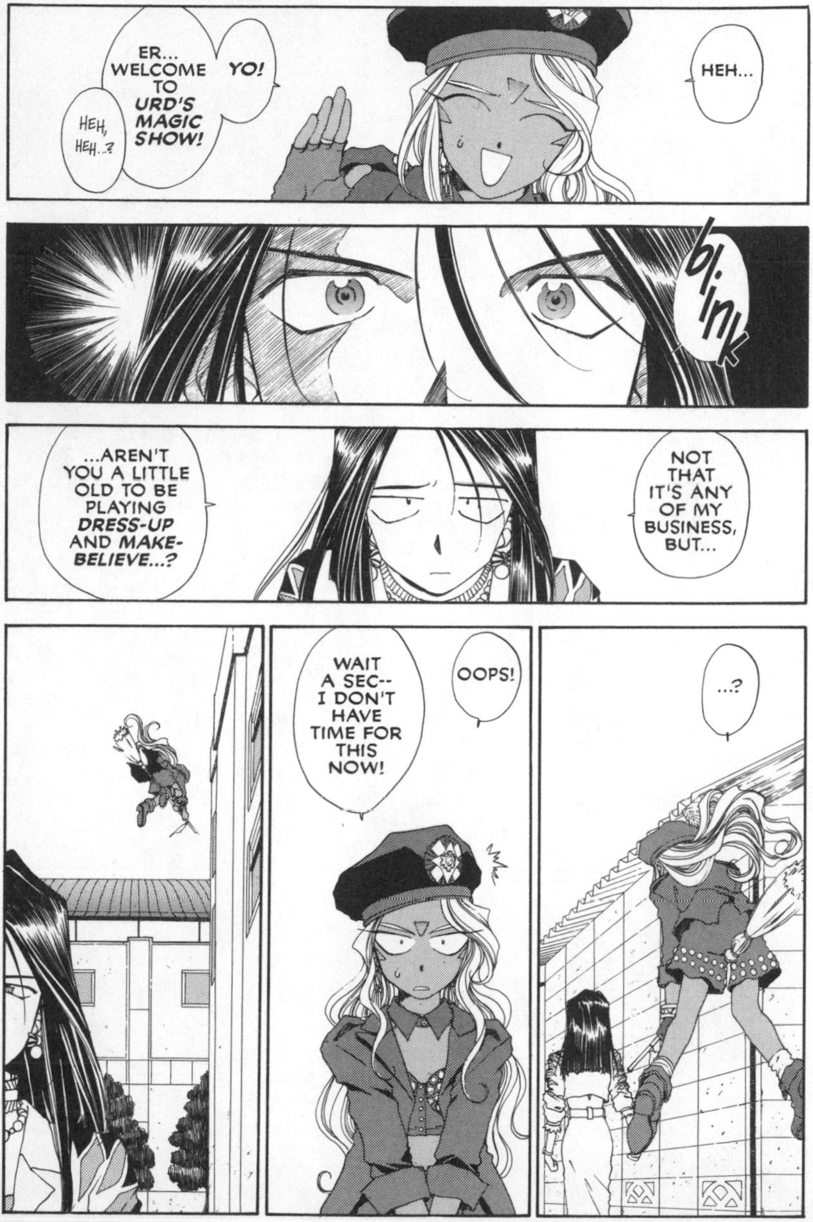
HEH...
YO!
ER... WELCOME TO URD'S MAGIC SHOW!
HEH, HEH..?
blink
NOT THAT IT'S ANY OF MY BUSINESS, BUT...
...AREN'T YOU A LITTLE OLD TO BE PLAYING DRESS-UP AND MAKE-BELIEVE...?
...?
OOPS!
WAIT A SEC-- I DON'T HAVE TIME FOR THIS NOW!

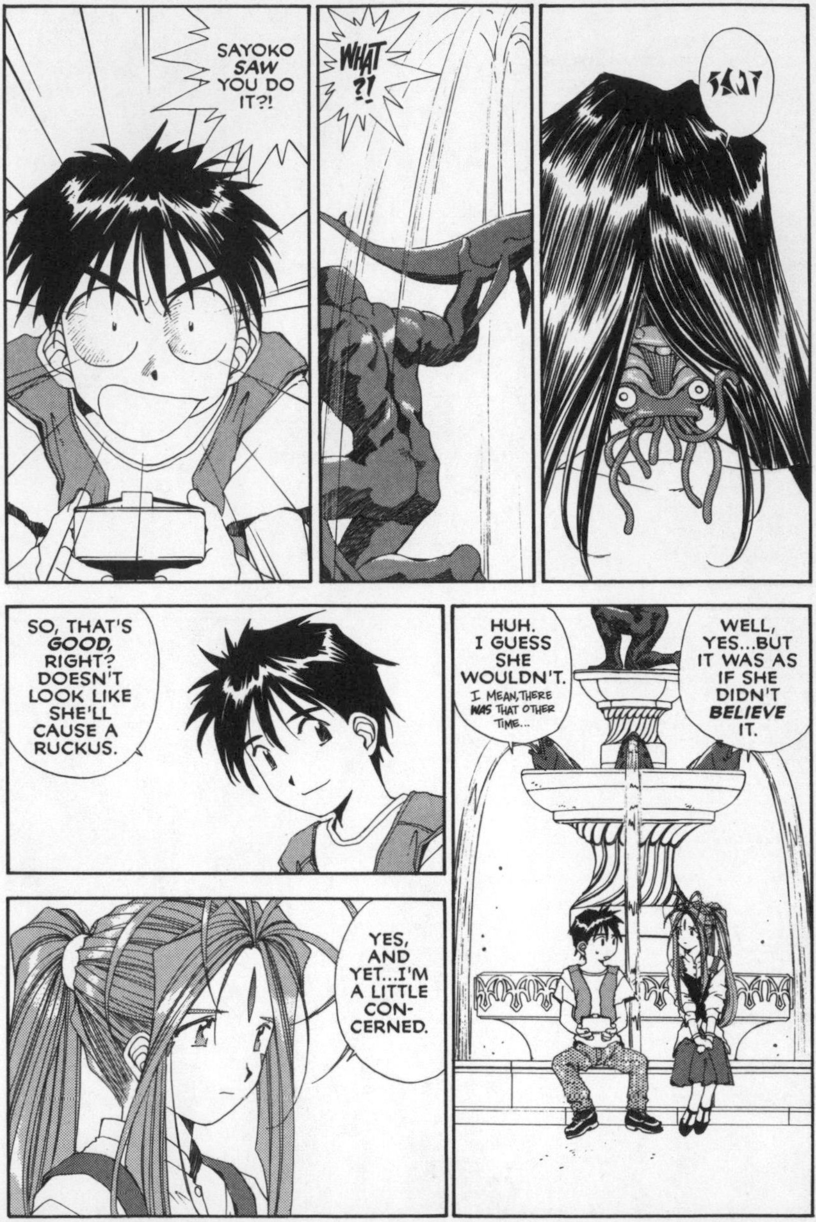
WHAT ?!
SAYOKO SAW YOU DO IT?!
WELL, YES...BUT IT WAS AS IF SHE DIDN'T BELIEVE IT.
HUH. I GUESS SHE WOULDN'T.
I MEAN, THERE WAS THAT OTHER TIME...
SO, THAT'S GOOD, RIGHT? DOESN'T LOOK LIKE SHE'LL CAUSE A RUCKUS.
YES, AND YET...I'M A LITTLE CON-CERNED.

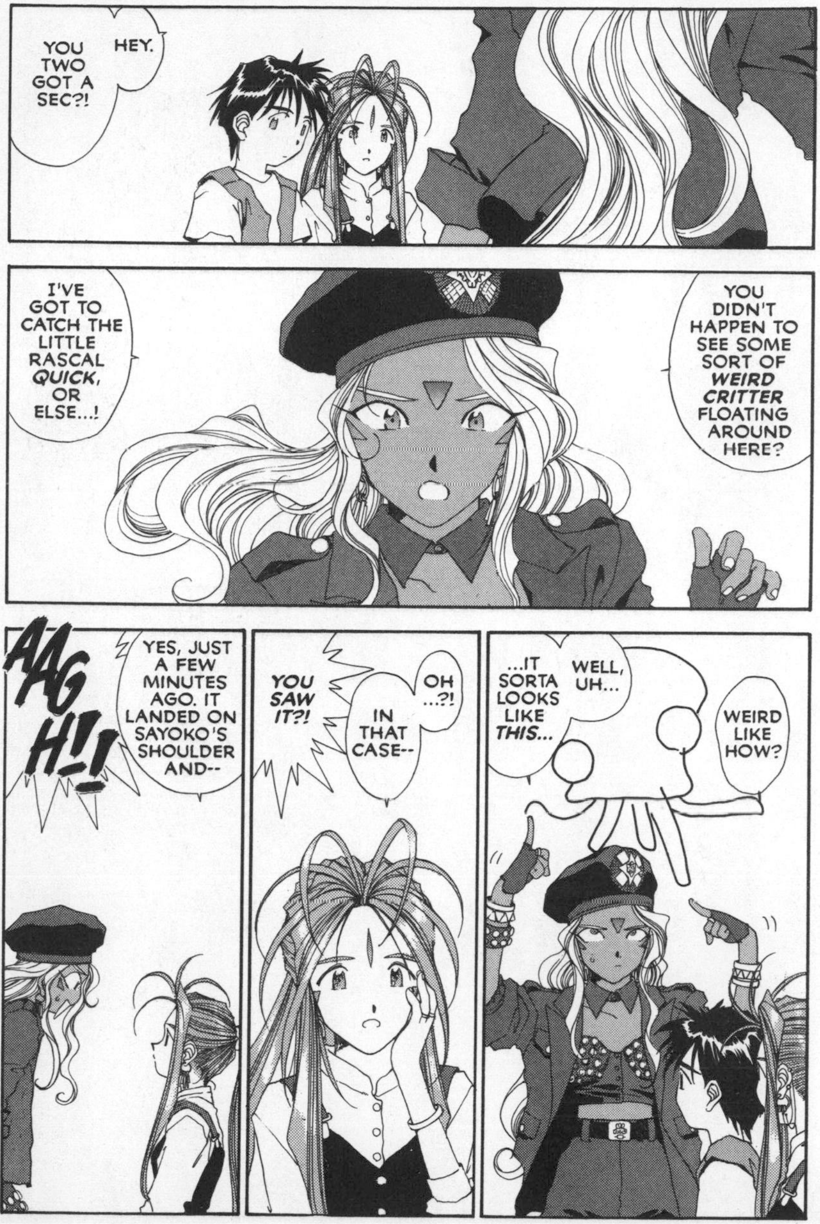
HEY.
YOU TWO GOT A SEC?!
YOU DIDN'T HAPPEN TO SEE SOME SORT OF WEIRD CRITTER FLOATING AROUND HERE?
I'VE GOT TO CATCH THE LITTLE RASCAL QUICK, OR ELSE...!
WEIRD LIKE HOW?
WELL, UH...
...IT SORTA LOOKS LIKE THIS...
OH ...?!
IN THAT CASE--
YOU SAW IT?!
YES, JUST A FEW MINUTES AGO. IT LANDED ON SAYOKO'S SHOULDER AND--
AAGH!!!

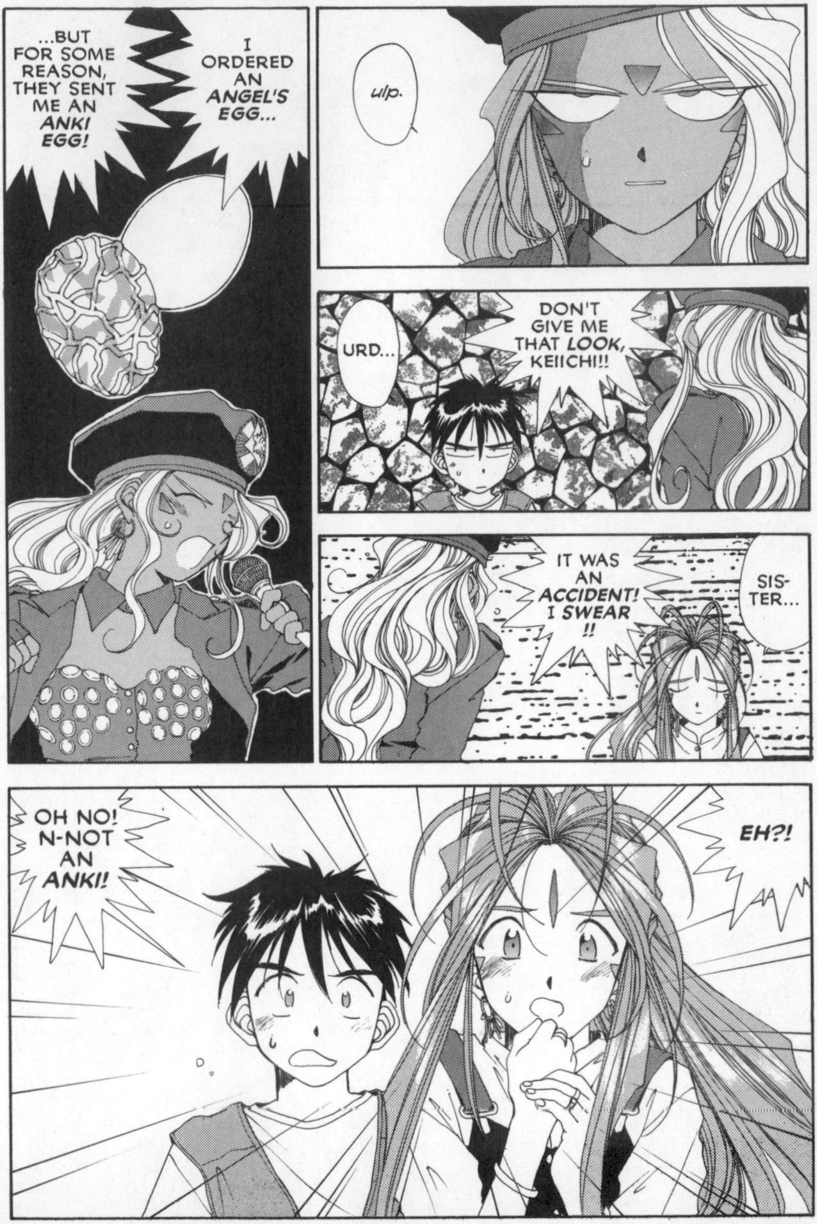
ulp.
DON'T GIVE ME THAT LOOK, KEIICHI!!
URD...
SIS- TER...
IT WAS AN ACCIDENT! I SWEAR !!
I ORDERED AN ANGEL'S EGG...
...BUT FOR SOME REASON, THEY SENT ME AN ANKI EGG!
EH?!
OH NO! N-NOT AN ANKI!

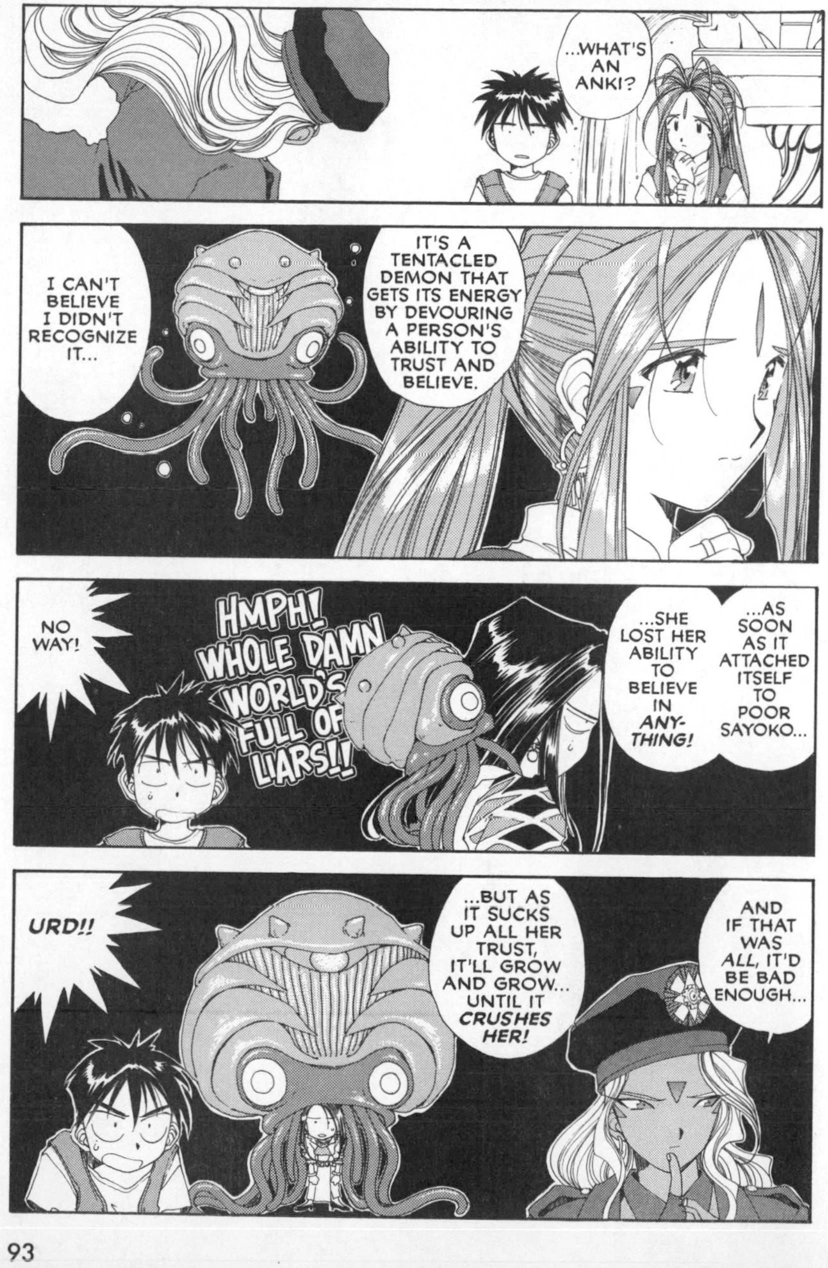
...WHAT'S AN ANKI?
IT'S A TENTACLED DEMON THAT GETS ITS ENERGY BY DEVOURING A PERSON'S ABILITY TO TRUST AND BELIEVE.
I CAN'T BELIEVE I DIDN'T RECOGNIZE IT...
...AS SOON AS IT ATTACHED ITSELF TO POOR SAYOKO...
...SHE LOST HER ABILITY TO BELIEVE IN ANY-THING!
HMPH! WHOLE DAMN WORLD'S FULL OF LIARS!!
NO WAY!
AND IF THAT WAS ALL, IT'D BE BAD ENOUGH...
...BUT AS IT SUCKS UP ALL HER TRUST, IT'LL GROW AND GROW... UNTIL IT CRUSHES HER!
URD!!

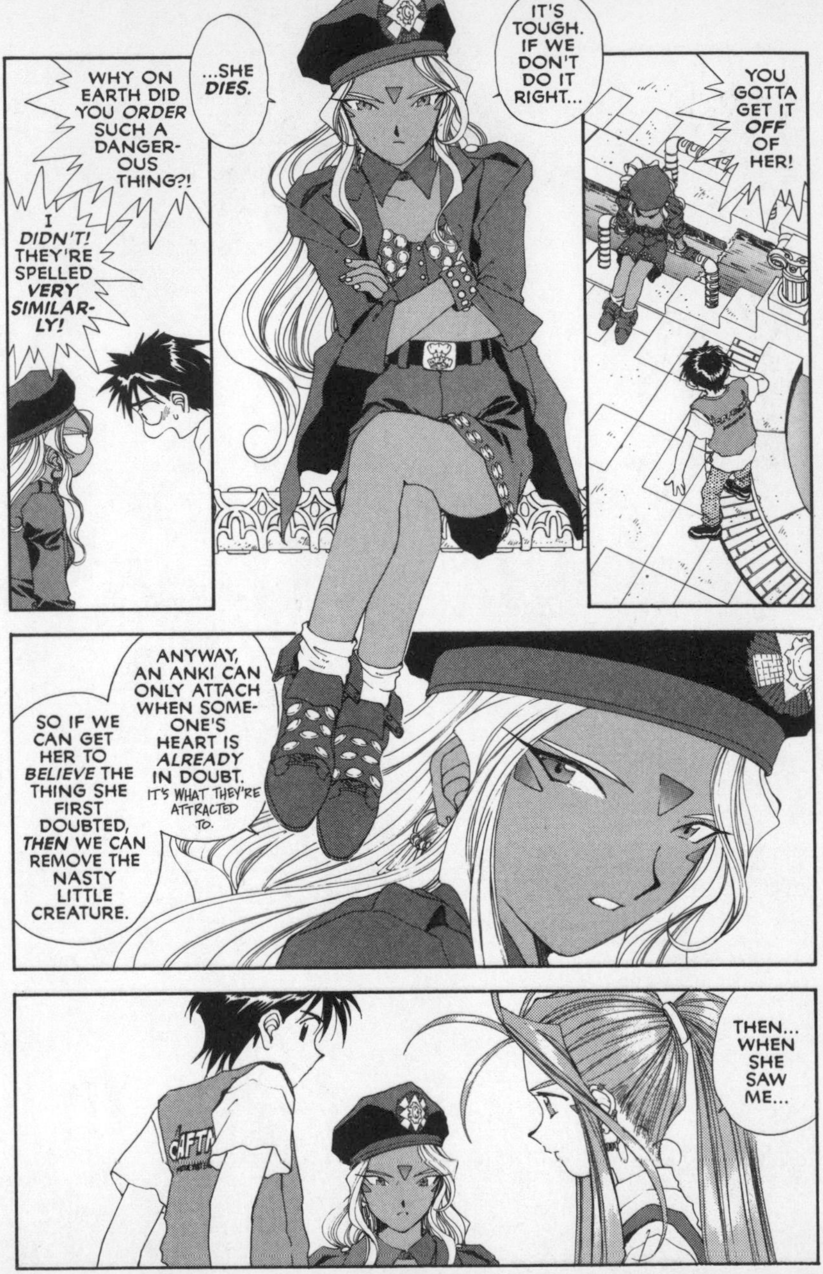
YOU GOTTA GET IT OFF OF HER!
IT'S TOUGH. IF WE DON'T DO IT RIGHT...
...SHE DIES.
WHY ON EARTH DID YOU ORDER SUCH A DANGER-OUS THING?!
I DIDN'T! THEY'RE SPELLED VERY SIMILAR-LY!
ANYWAY, AN ANKI CAN ONLY ATTACH WHEN SOME-ONE'S HEART IS ALREADY IN DOUBT. IT'S WHAT THEY'RE ATTRACTED TO.
SO IF WE CAN GET HER TO BELIEVE THE THING SHE FIRST DOUBTED, THEN WE CAN REMOVE THE NASTY LITTLE CREATURE.
THEN... WHEN SHE SAW ME...

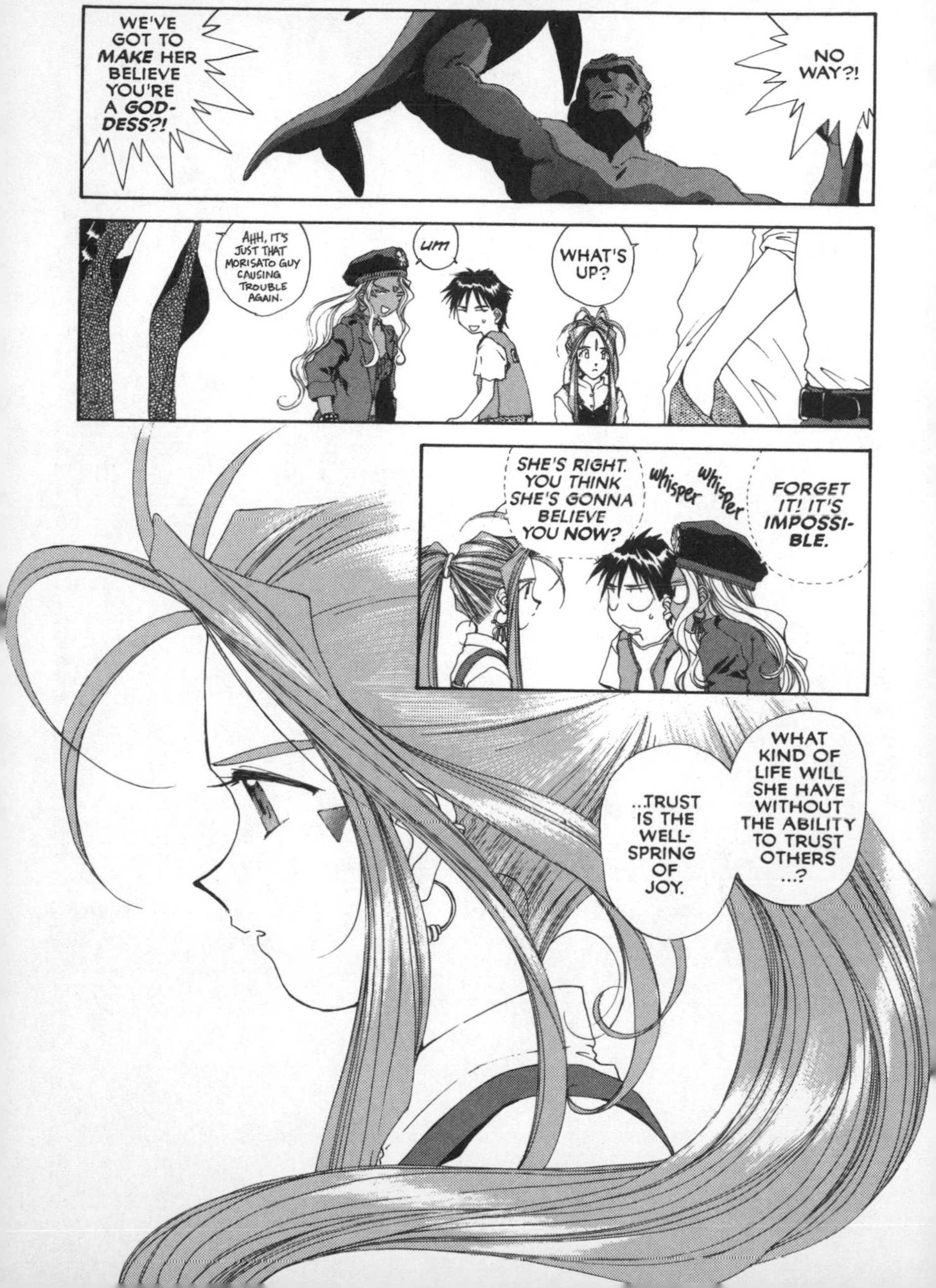
NO WAY?!
WE'VE GOT TO MAKE HER BELIEVE YOU'RE A GOD-DESS?!
WHAT'S UP?
um
AHH, IT'S JUST THAT MORISATO GUY CAUSING TROUBLE AGAIN.
FORGET IT! IT'S IMPOSSI-BLE.
whisper
whisper
SHE'S RIGHT. YOU THINK SHE'S GONNA BELIEVE YOU NOW?
WHAT KIND OF LIFE WILL SHE HAVE WITHOUT THE ABILITY TO TRUST OTHERS ...?
...TRUST IS THE WELL-SPRING OF JOY.

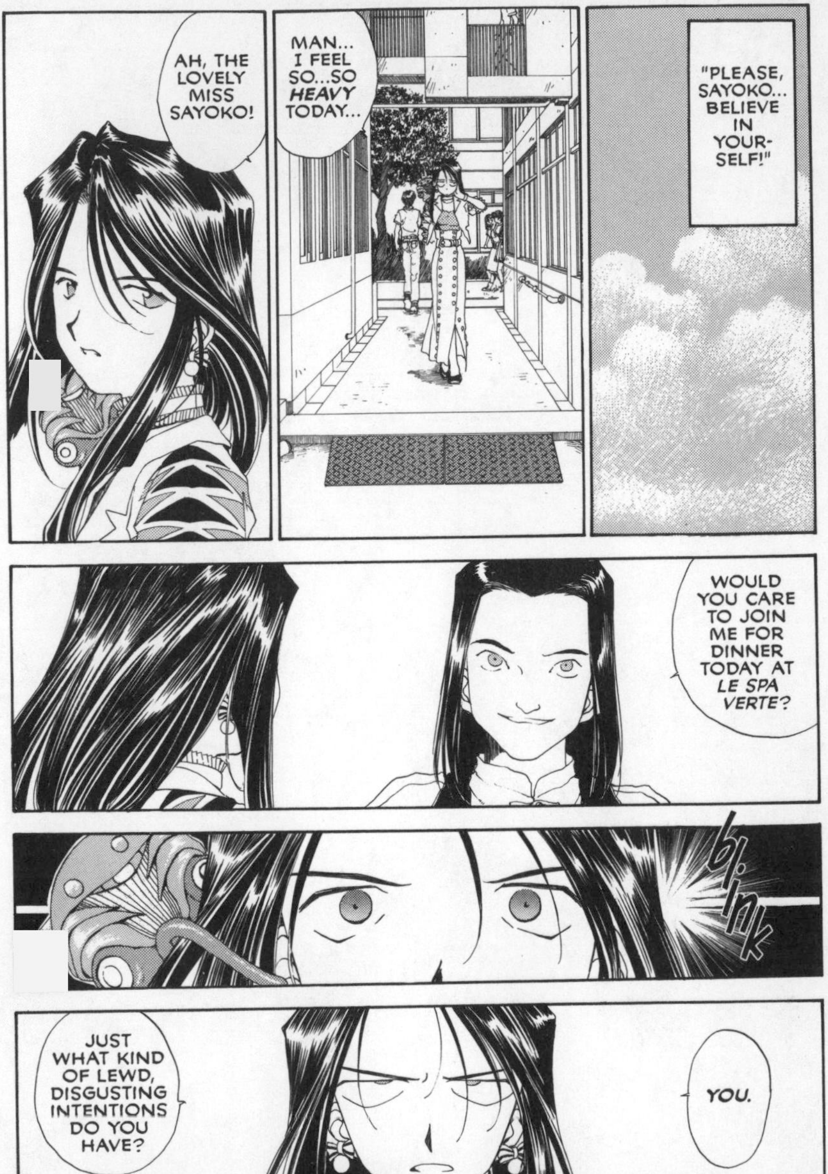
"PLEASE, SAYOKO... BELIEVE IN YOURSELF!"
MAN... I FEEL SO...SO *HEAVY* TODAY...
AH, THE LOVELY MISS SAYOKO!
WOULD YOU CARE TO JOIN ME FOR DINNER TODAY AT *LE SPA VERTE*?
blink
YOU.
JUST WHAT KIND OF LEWD, DISGUSTING INTENTIONS DO YOU HAVE?

HUH?
IT'S TRUE! I KNOW IT!! YOU MEN ARE ALL ALIKE! YOU ONLY TREAT US NICE BECAUSE YOU WANT OUR BODIES!
AGHH! YOU'RE SO DISGUSTING! LOATH-SOME! FILTHY!
Whooosh
SAYOKO!
SATOKO?
Whooosh
ER... WOULD YOU MIND COMING WITH US A MINUTE?
YOU'RE PLANNING TO KIDNAP ME, AREN'T YOU? YEP.
...?
NO, NO, NO.

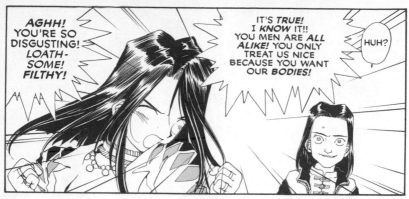

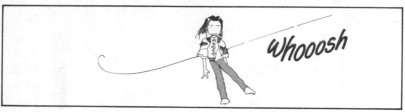

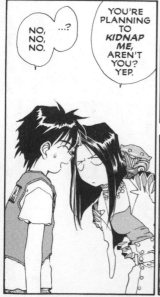

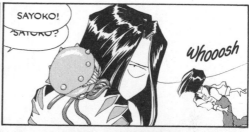

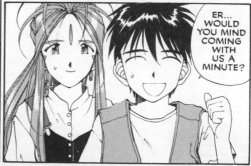

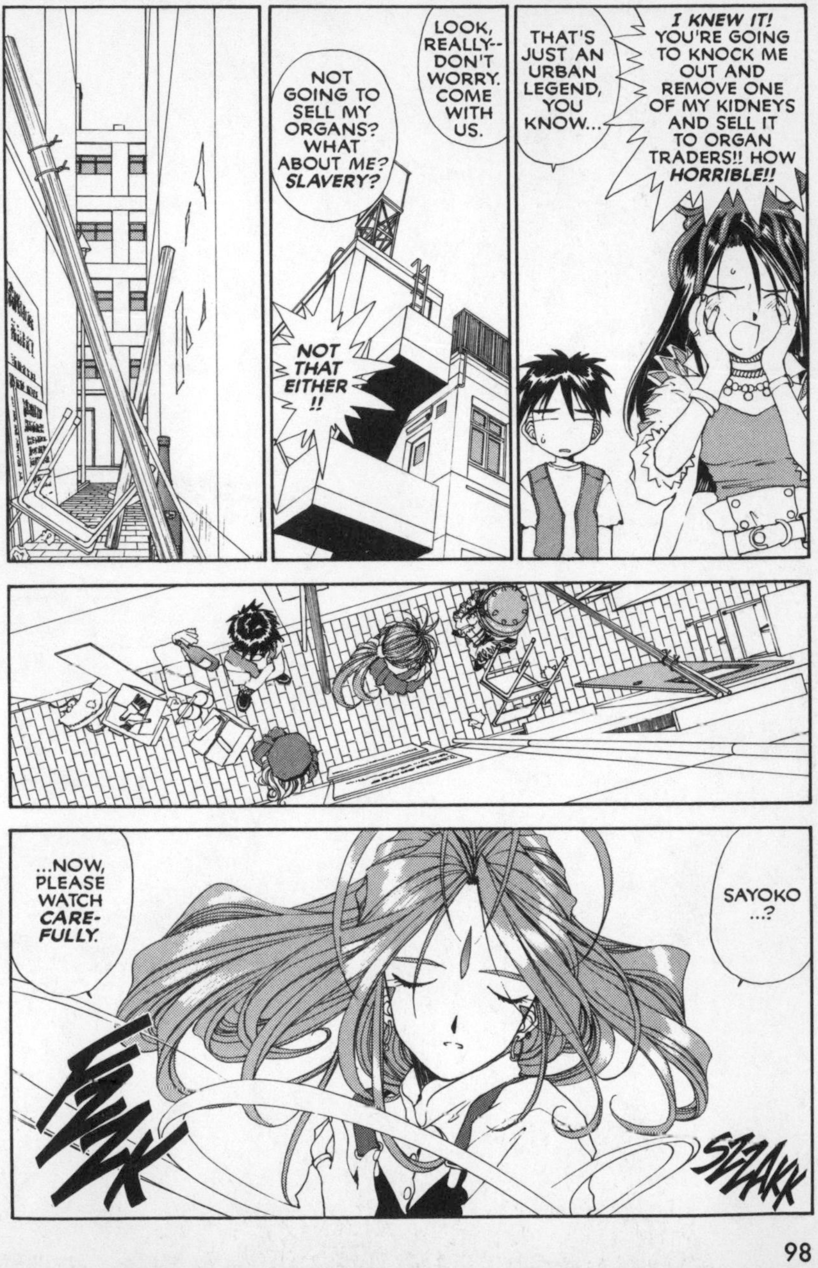
I KNEW IT! YOU'RE GOING TO KNOCK ME OUT AND REMOVE ONE OF MY KIDNEYS AND SELL IT TO ORGAN TRADERS!! HOW HORRIBLE!!
THAT'S JUST AN URBAN LEGEND, YOU KNOW...
LOOK, REALLY-- DON'T WORRY. COME WITH US.
NOT GOING TO SELL MY ORGANS? WHAT ABOUT ME? SLAVERY?
NOT THAT EITHER!!
SAYOKO ...?
...NOW, PLEASE WATCH CARE-FULLY.
SZZAKK

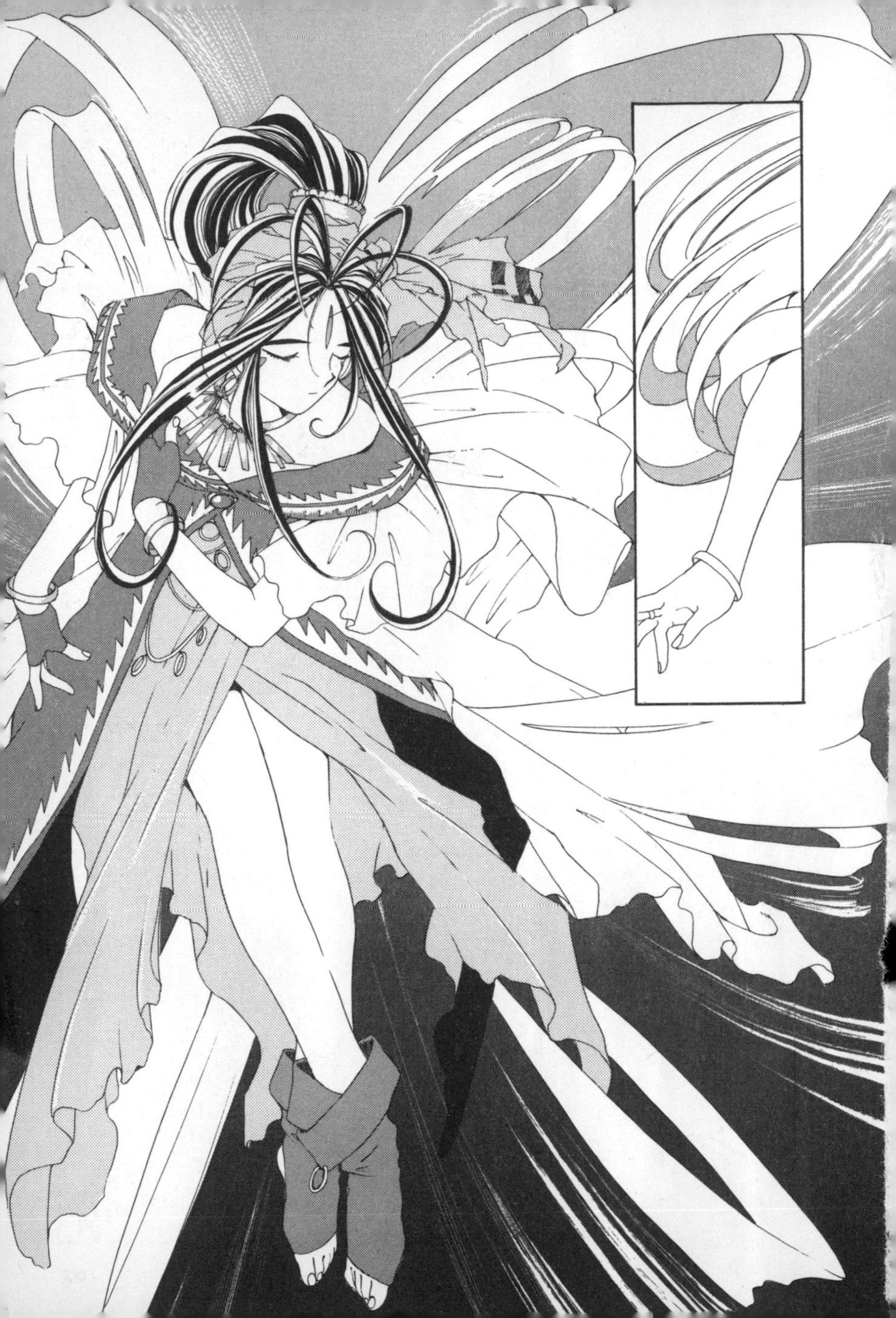

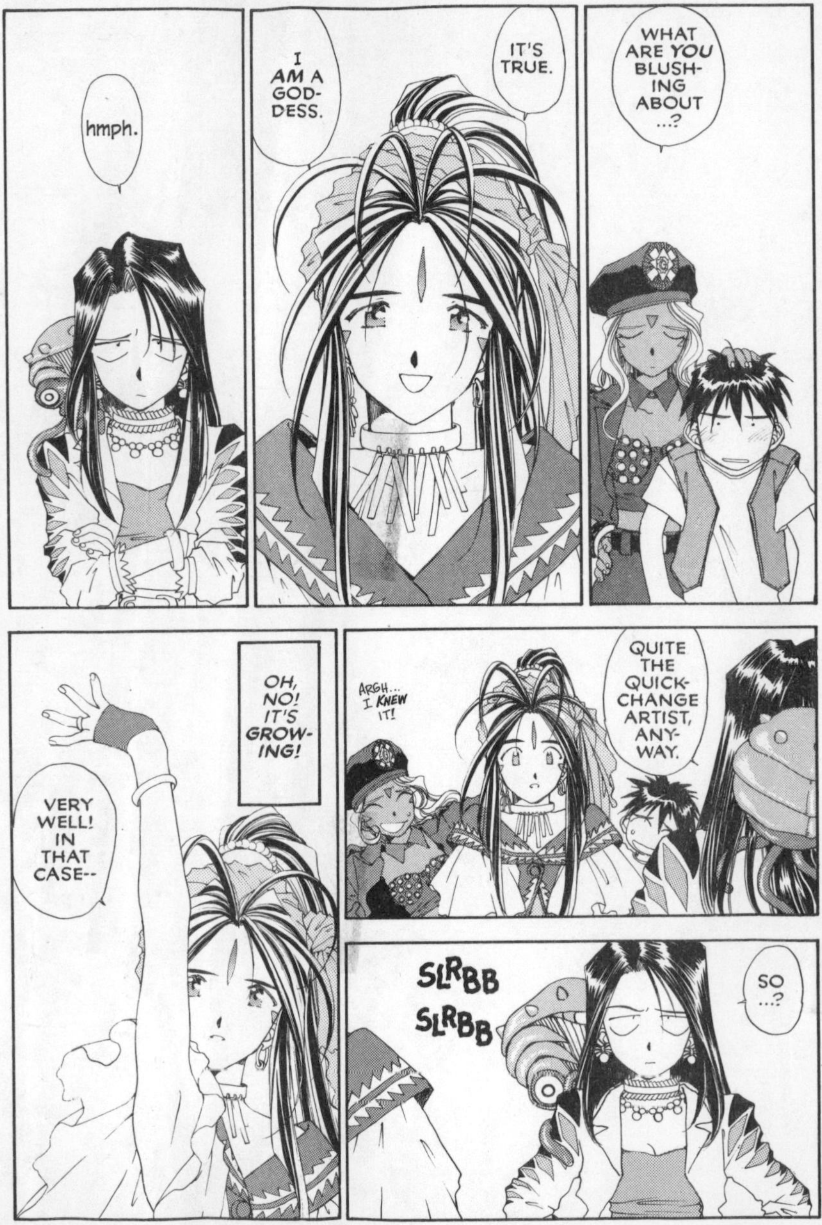
WHAT ARE YOU BLUSHING ABOUT ...?
IT'S TRUE.
I AM A GODDESS.
hmph.
QUITE THE QUICK-CHANGE ARTIST, ANYWAY.
ARGH... I KNEW IT!
SO ...?
SLRBB
SLRBB
OH, NO! IT'S GROWING!
VERY WELL! IN THAT CASE--

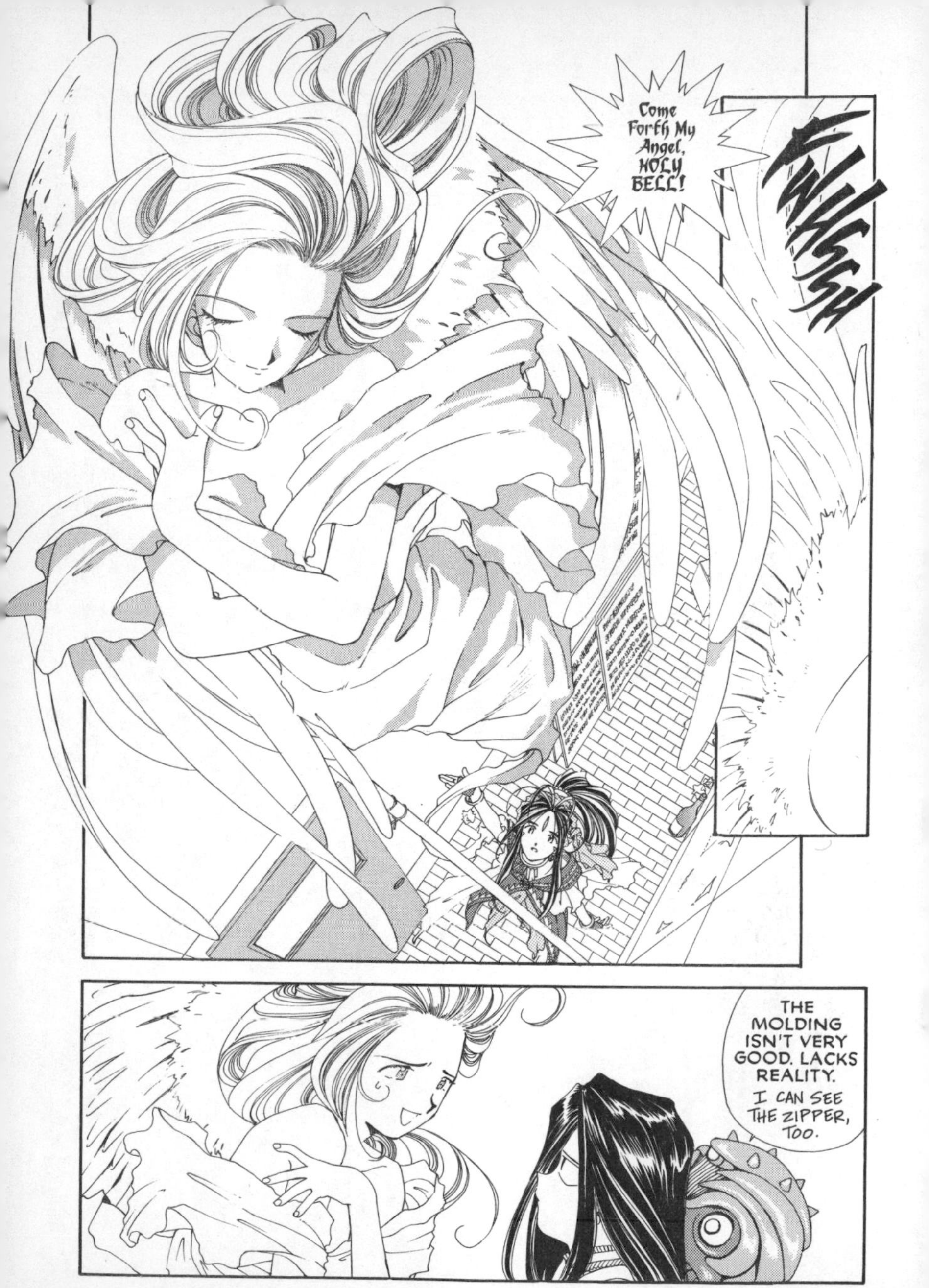
Come Forth My Angel, HOLY BELL!
FWHSSH
THE MOLDING ISN'T VERY GOOD. LACKS REALITY.
I CAN SEE THE ZIPPER, TOO.

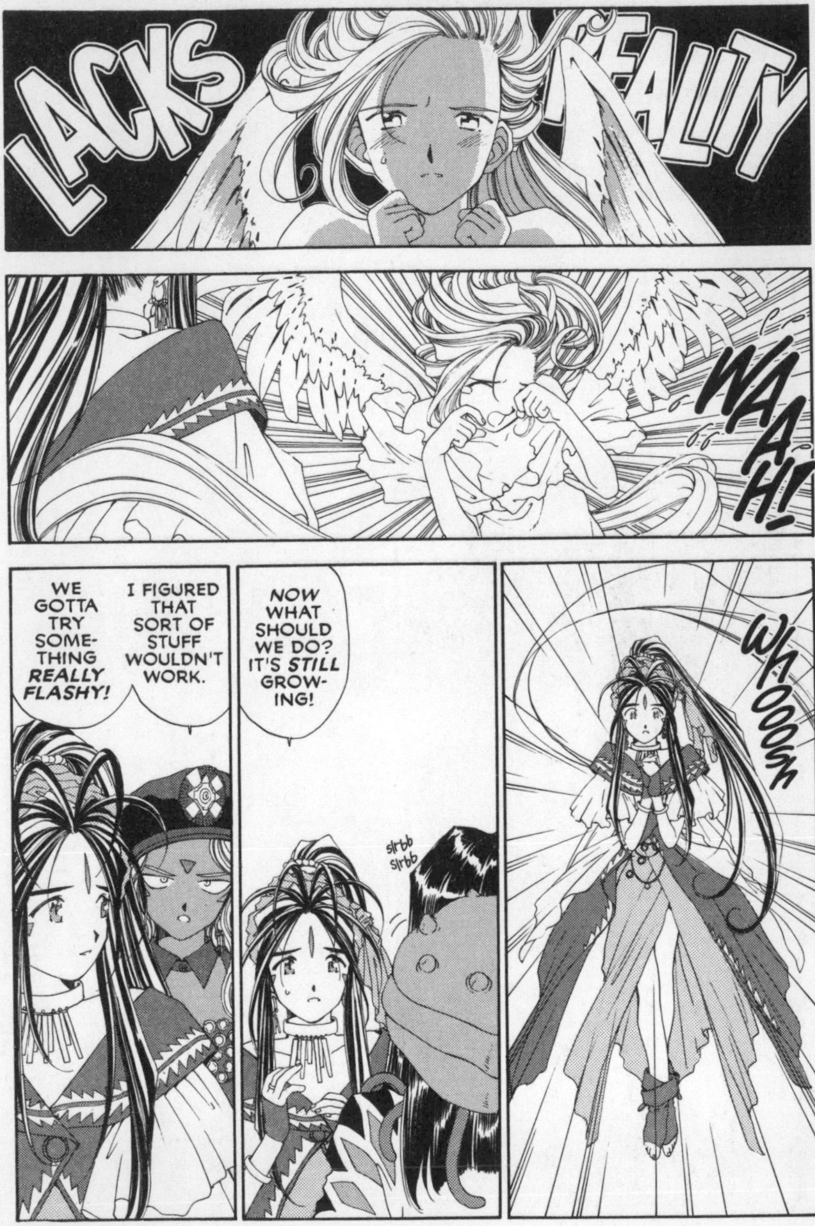
LACKS REALITY
WAAH!
WHOOOOM
NOW WHAT SHOULD WE DO? IT'S STILL GROWING!
slrbb slrbb
I FIGURED THAT SORT OF STUFF WOULDN'T WORK.
WE GOTTA TRY SOMETHING REALLY FLASHY!

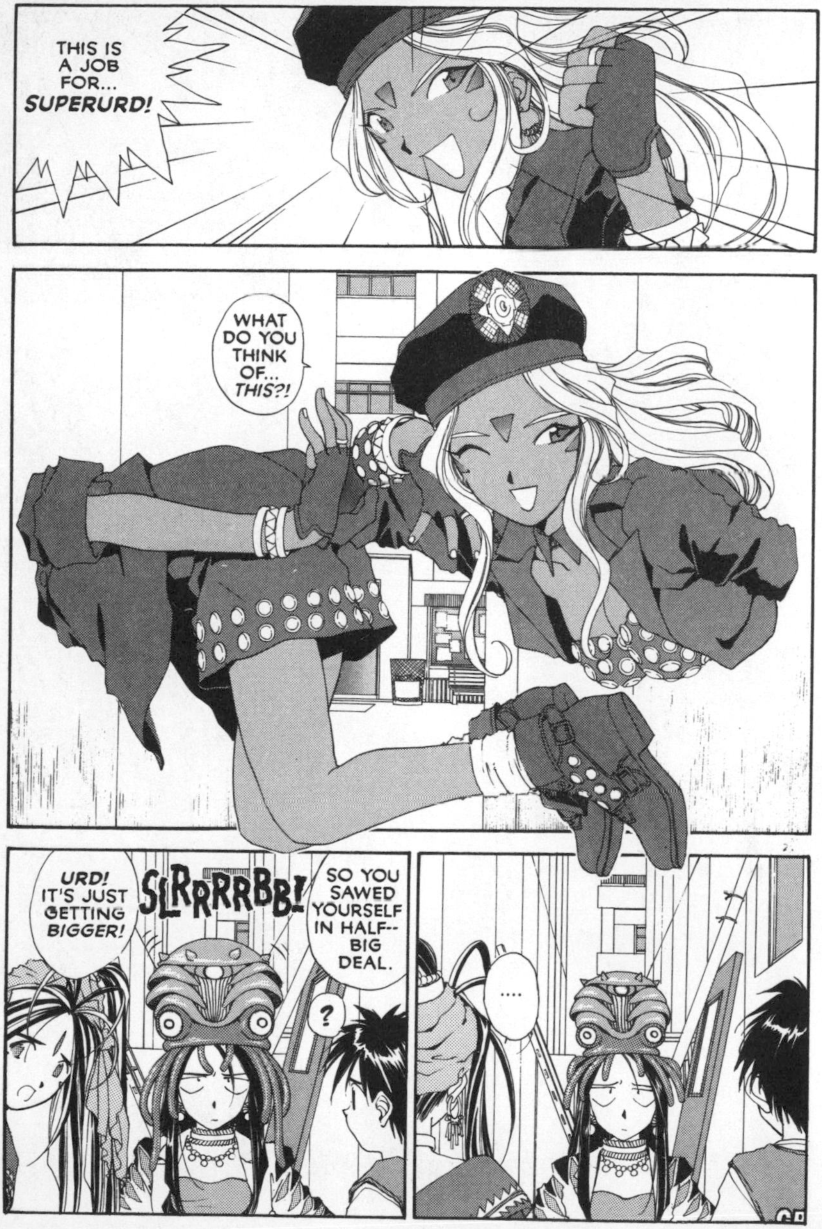
THIS IS A JOB FOR... SUPERURD!
WHAT DO YOU THINK OF... THIS?!
....
SO YOU SAWED YOURSELF IN HALF-- BIG DEAL.
SLRRRRBB!
URD! IT'S JUST GETTING BIGGER!
?

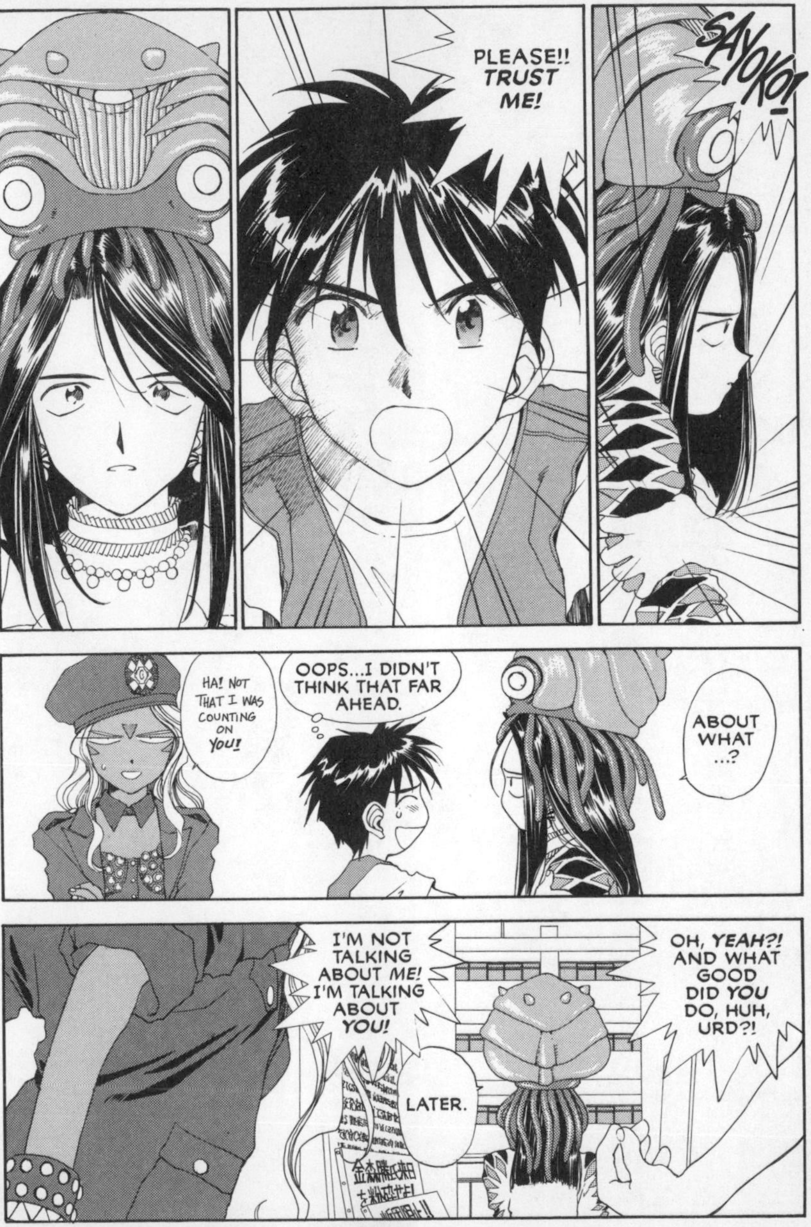
SAYOKO!
PLEASE!! TRUST ME!
ABOUT WHAT ...?
OOPS...I DIDN'T THINK THAT FAR AHEAD.
HA! NOT THAT I WAS COUNTING ON YOU!
OH, YEAH?! AND WHAT GOOD DID YOU DO, HUH, URD?!
I'M NOT TALKING ABOUT ME! I'M TALKING ABOUT YOU!
LATER.

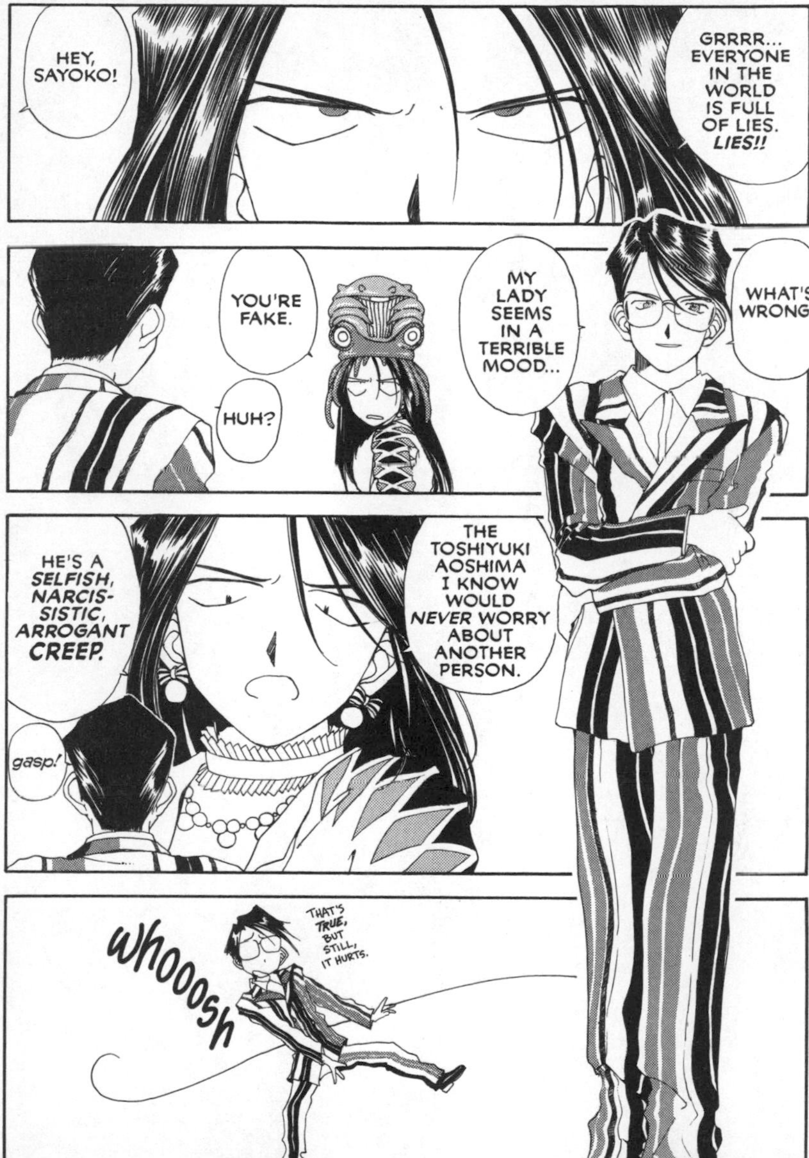
GRRRR... EVERYONE IN THE WORLD IS FULL OF LIES. *LIES!!*
HEY, SAYOKO!
WHAT'S WRONG?
MY LADY SEEMS IN A TERRIBLE MOOD...
YOU'RE FAKE.
HUH?
THE TOSHIYUKI AOSHIMA I KNOW WOULD *NEVER* WORRY ABOUT ANOTHER PERSON.
HE'S A *SELFISH, NARCISSISTIC, ARROGANT* **CREEP.**
gasp!
THAT'S *TRUE,* BUT STILL, IT HURTS.
whoooosh

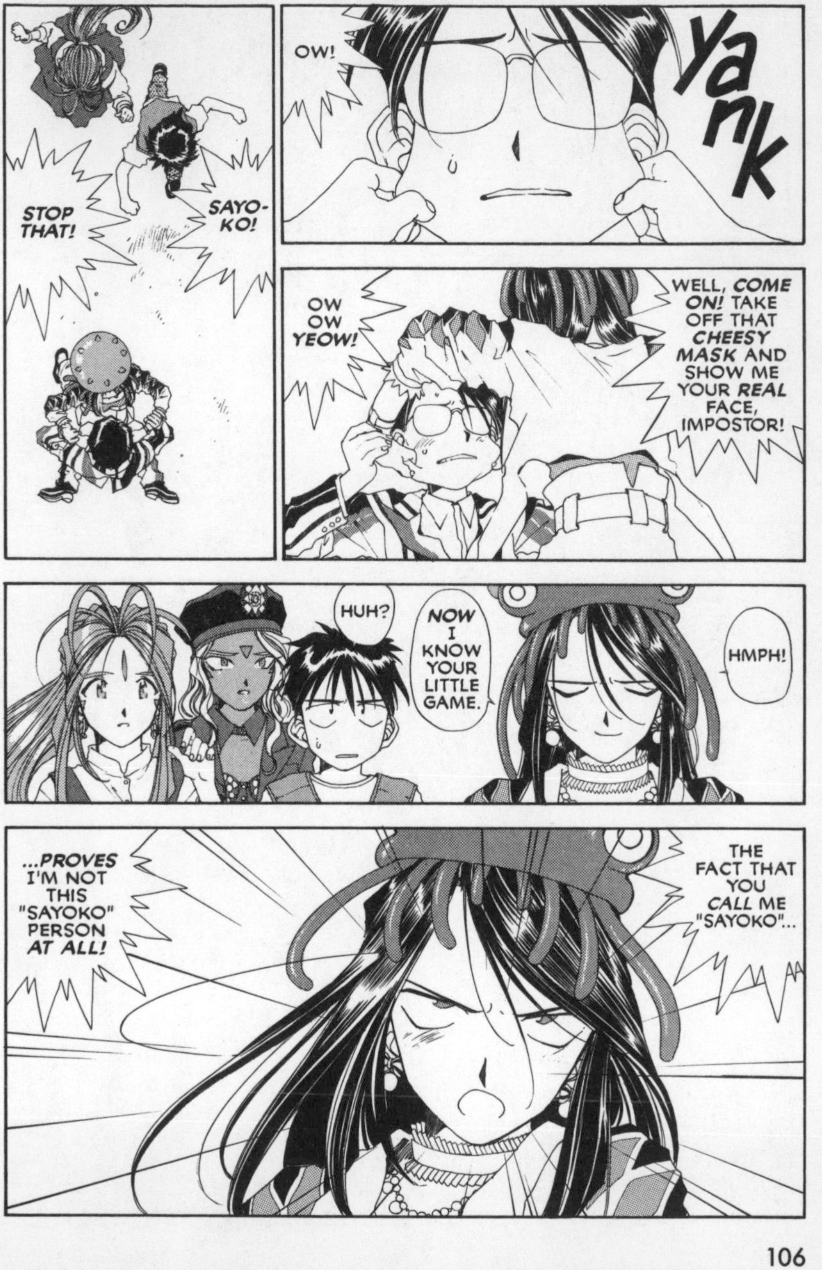
yank
OW!
WELL, COME ON! TAKE OFF THAT CHEESY MASK AND SHOW ME YOUR REAL FACE, IMPOSTOR!
OW OW YEOW!
SAYO-KO!
STOP THAT!
HMPH!
NOW I KNOW YOUR LITTLE GAME.
HUH?
THE FACT THAT YOU CALL ME "SAYOKO"...
...PROVES I'M NOT THIS "SAYOKO" PERSON AT ALL!

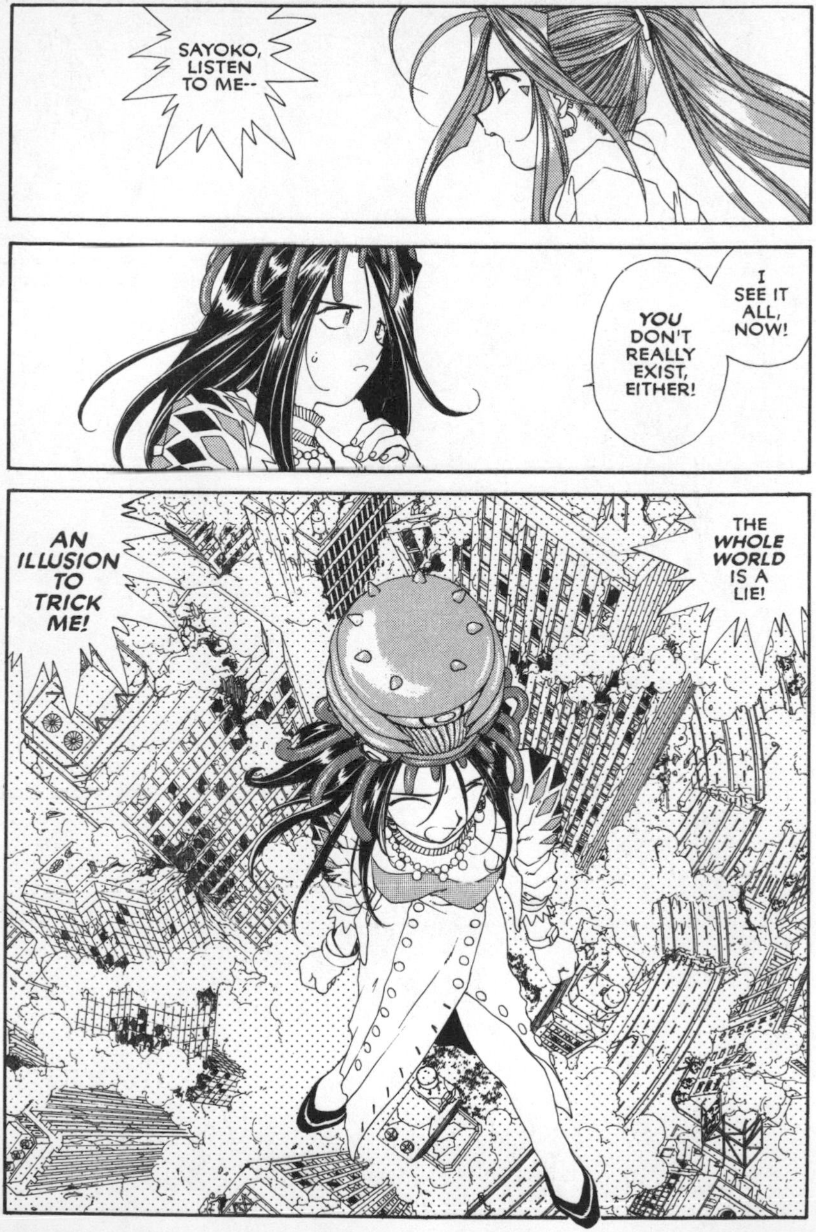
SAYOKO, LISTEN TO ME--
I SEE IT ALL, NOW!
YOU DON'T REALLY EXIST, EITHER!
THE WHOLE WORLD IS A LIE!
AN ILLUSION TO TRICK ME!

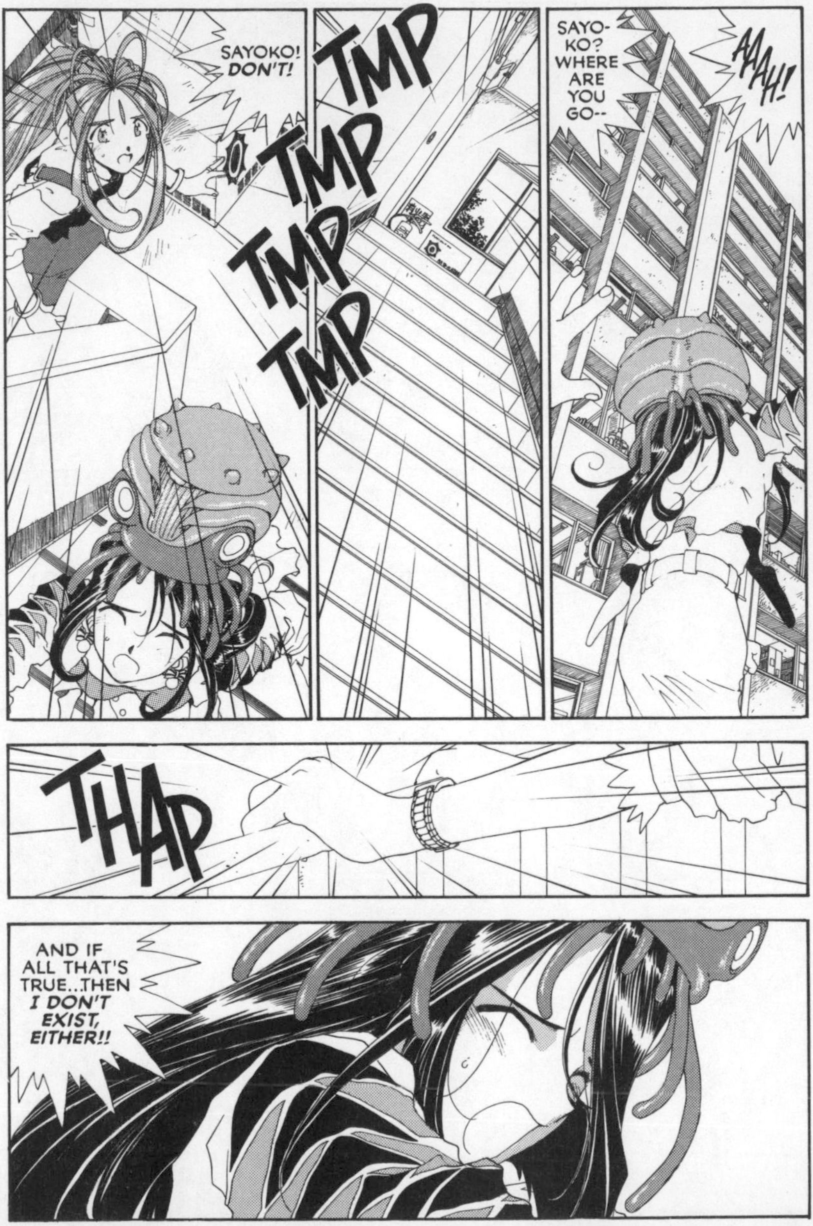

SAYO-KO? WHERE ARE YOU GO--
AAAAH!
TMP TMP TMP TMP
SAYOKO! DON'T!
THAP
AND IF ALL THAT'S TRUE...THEN I DON'T EXIST, EITHER!!

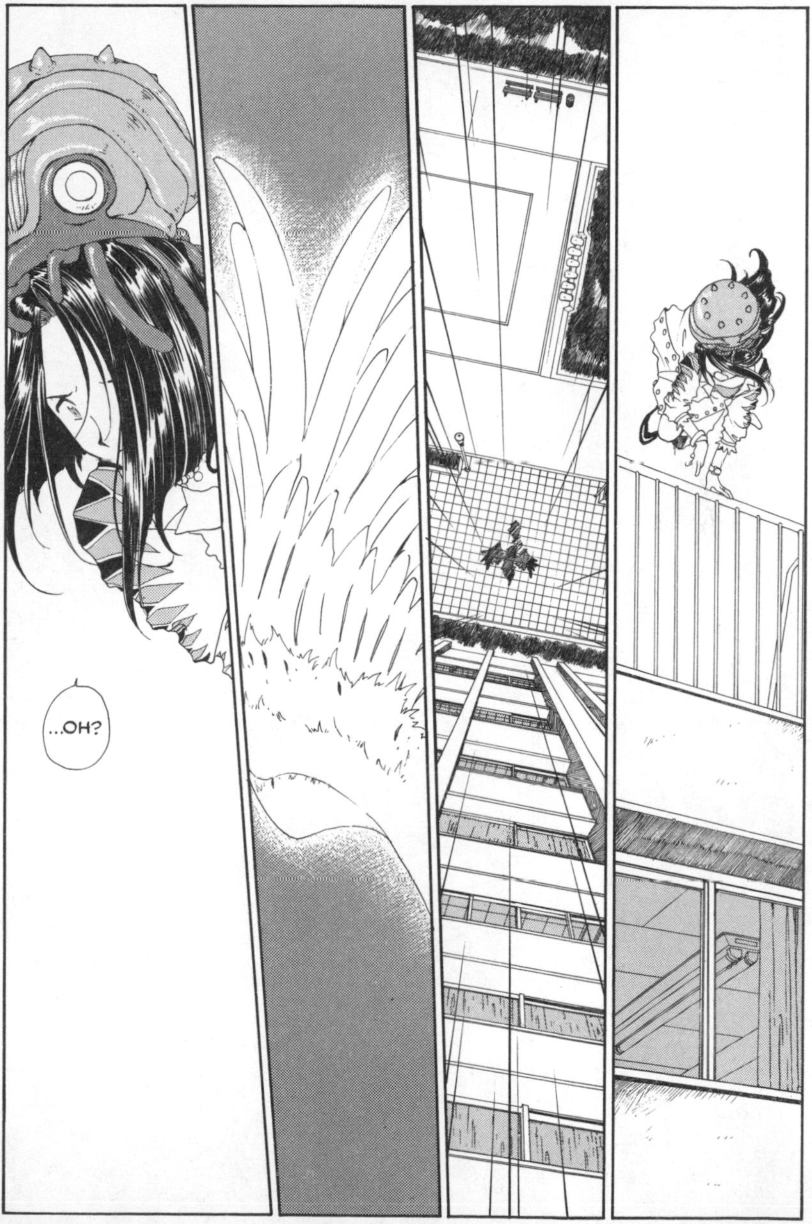
...OH?

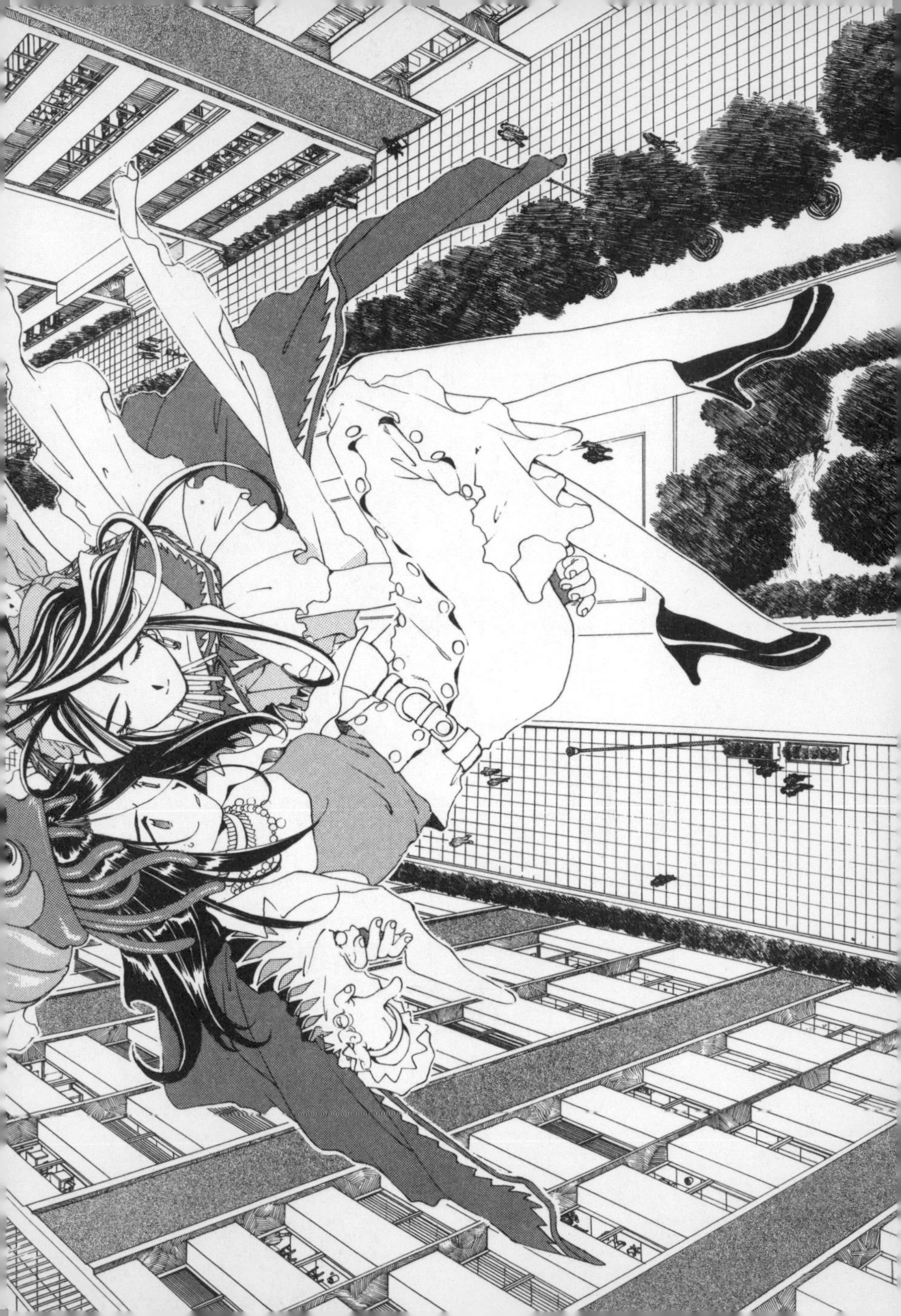

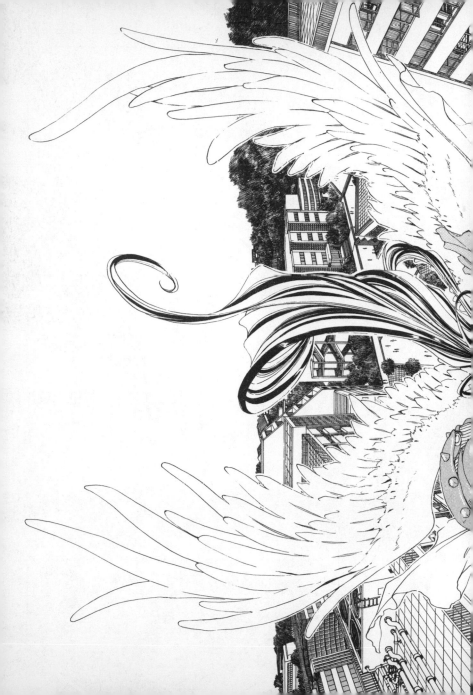

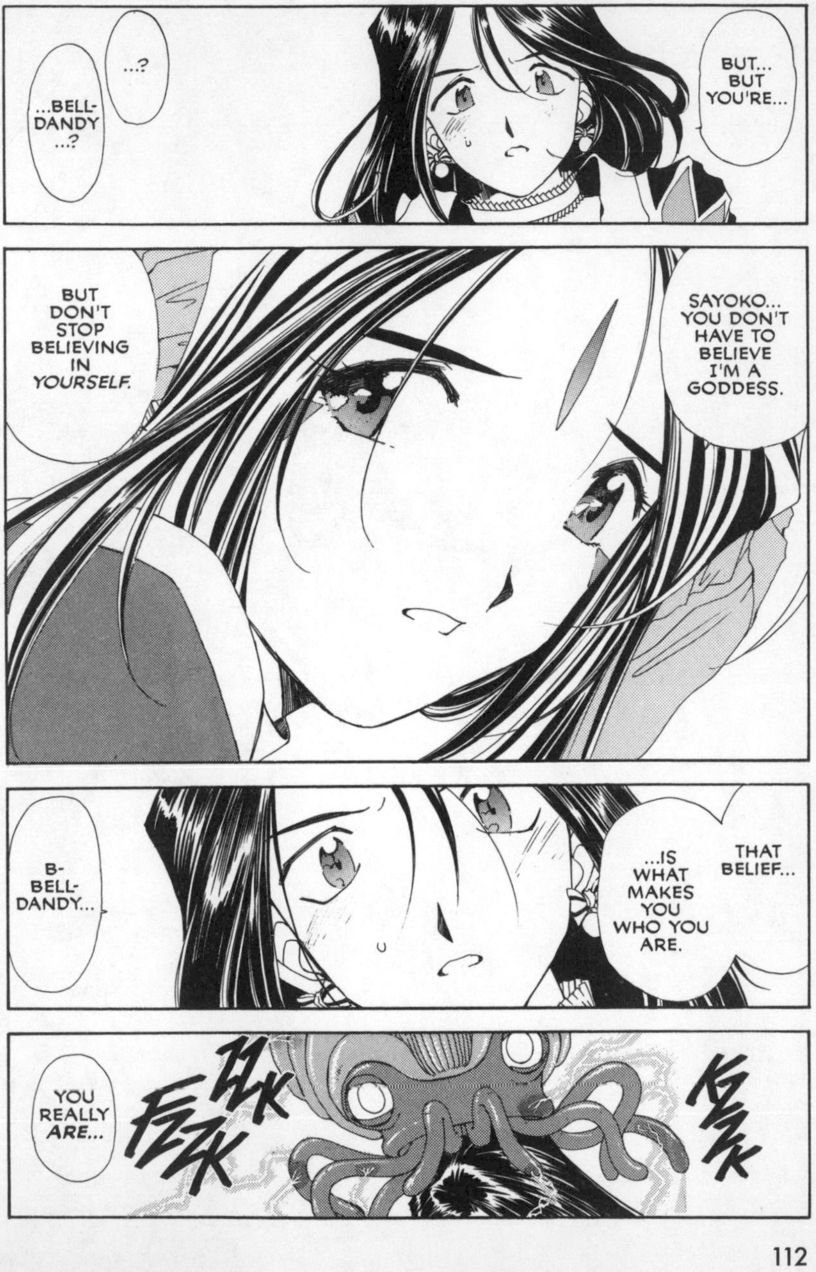
BUT... BUT YOU'RE...
...?
...BELL-DANDY ...?
SAYOKO... YOU DON'T HAVE TO BELIEVE I'M A GODDESS.
BUT DON'T STOP BELIEVING IN *YOURSELF*.
THAT BELIEF...
...IS WHAT MAKES YOU WHO YOU ARE.
B-BELL-DANDY...
KZZK
ZZK
FZZK
YOU REALLY *ARE*...

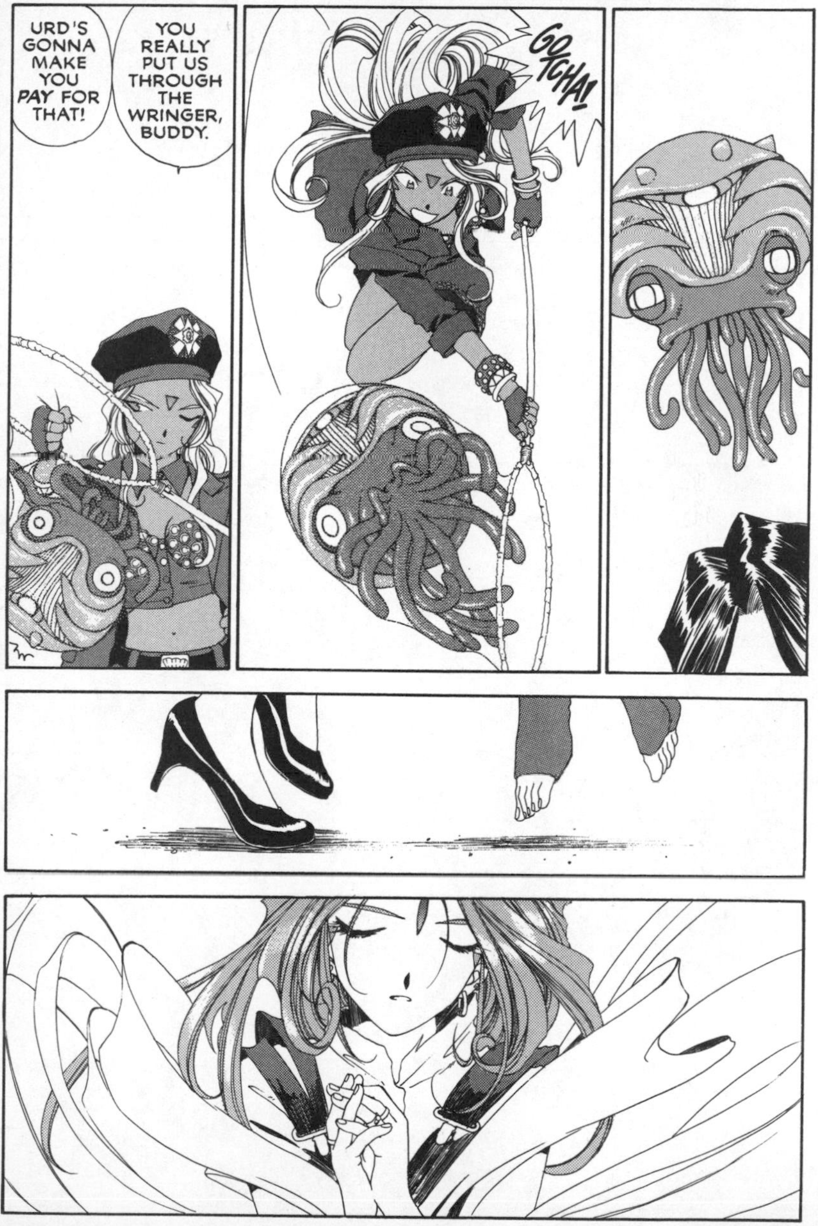
GOTCHA!
YOU REALLY PUT US THROUGH THE WRINGER, BUDDY.
URD'S GONNA MAKE YOU *PAY* FOR THAT!

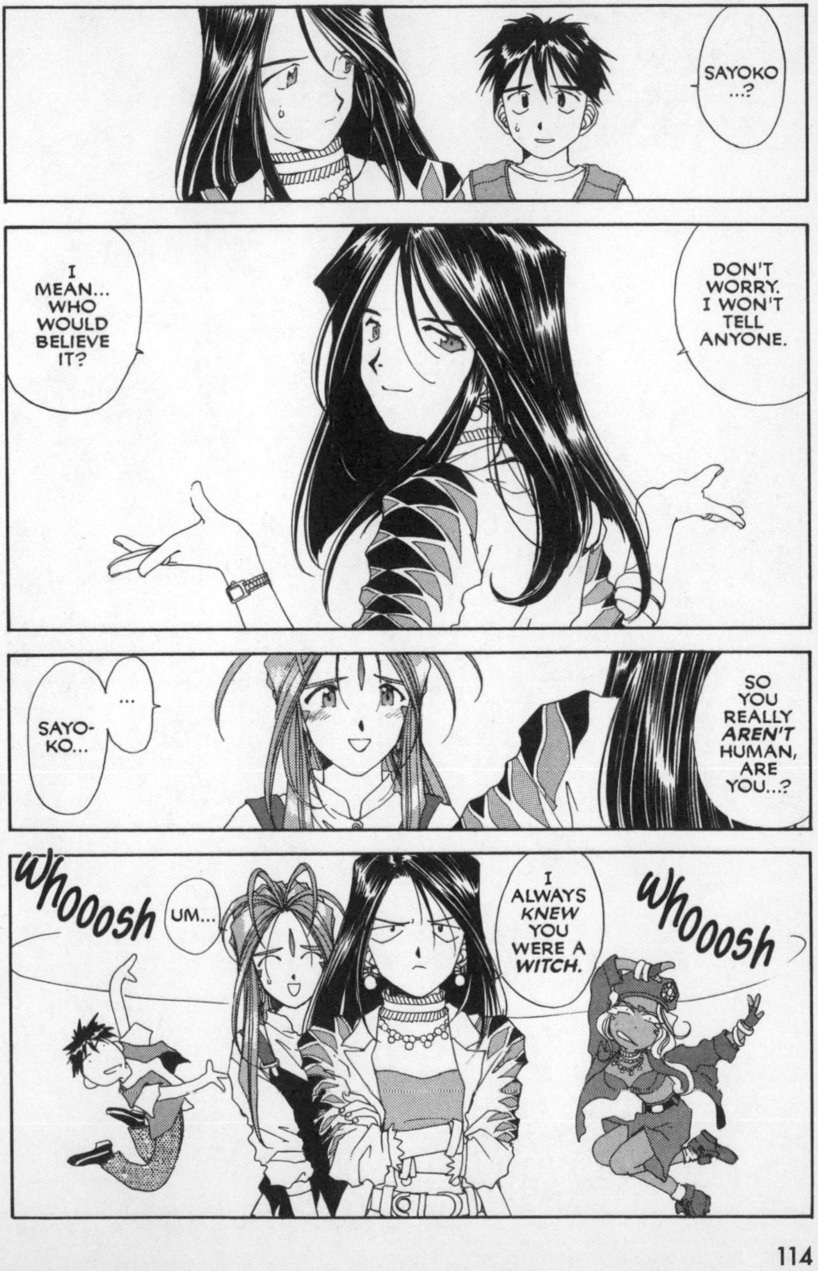
SAYOKO ...?
DON'T WORRY. I WON'T TELL ANYONE.
I MEAN... WHO WOULD BELIEVE IT?
SO YOU REALLY AREN'T HUMAN, ARE YOU...?
... SAYOKO...
whooosh
I ALWAYS KNEW YOU WERE A WITCH.
UM...
whooosh

CHAPTER 76

First Director of the Motor Club

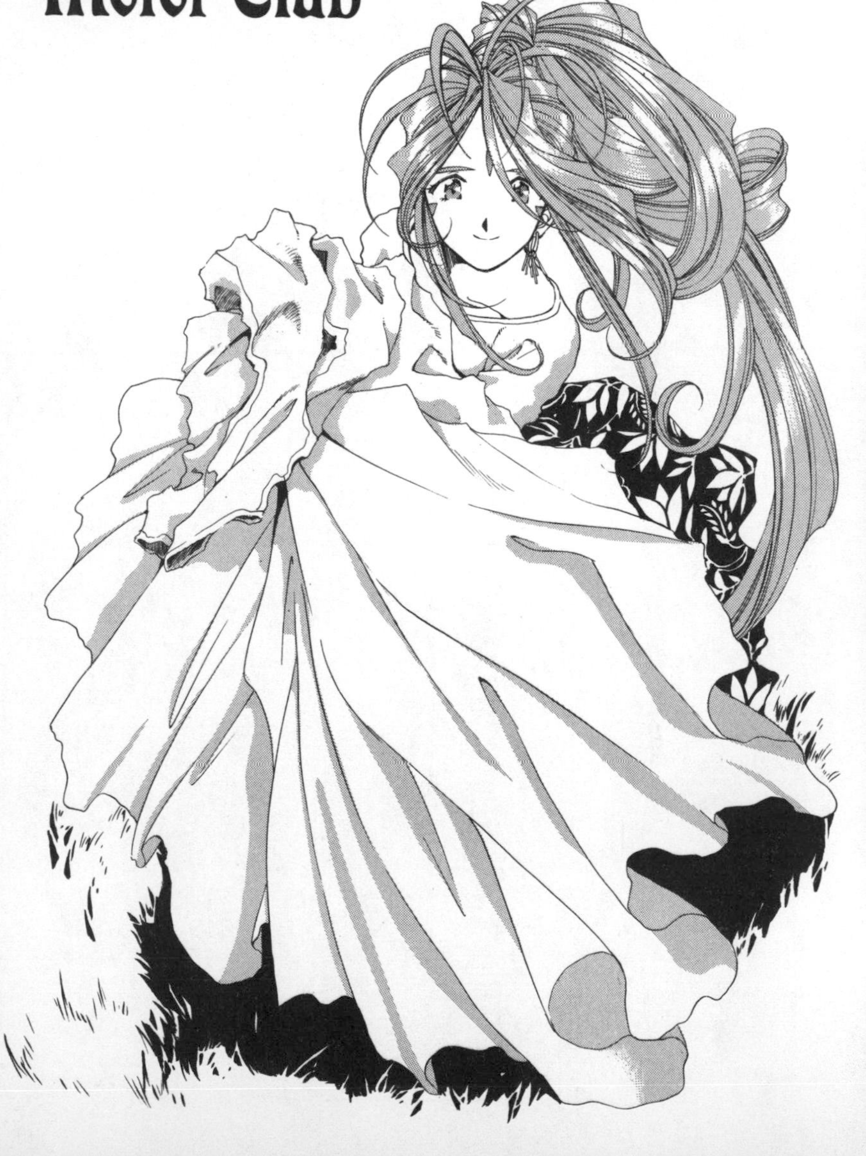

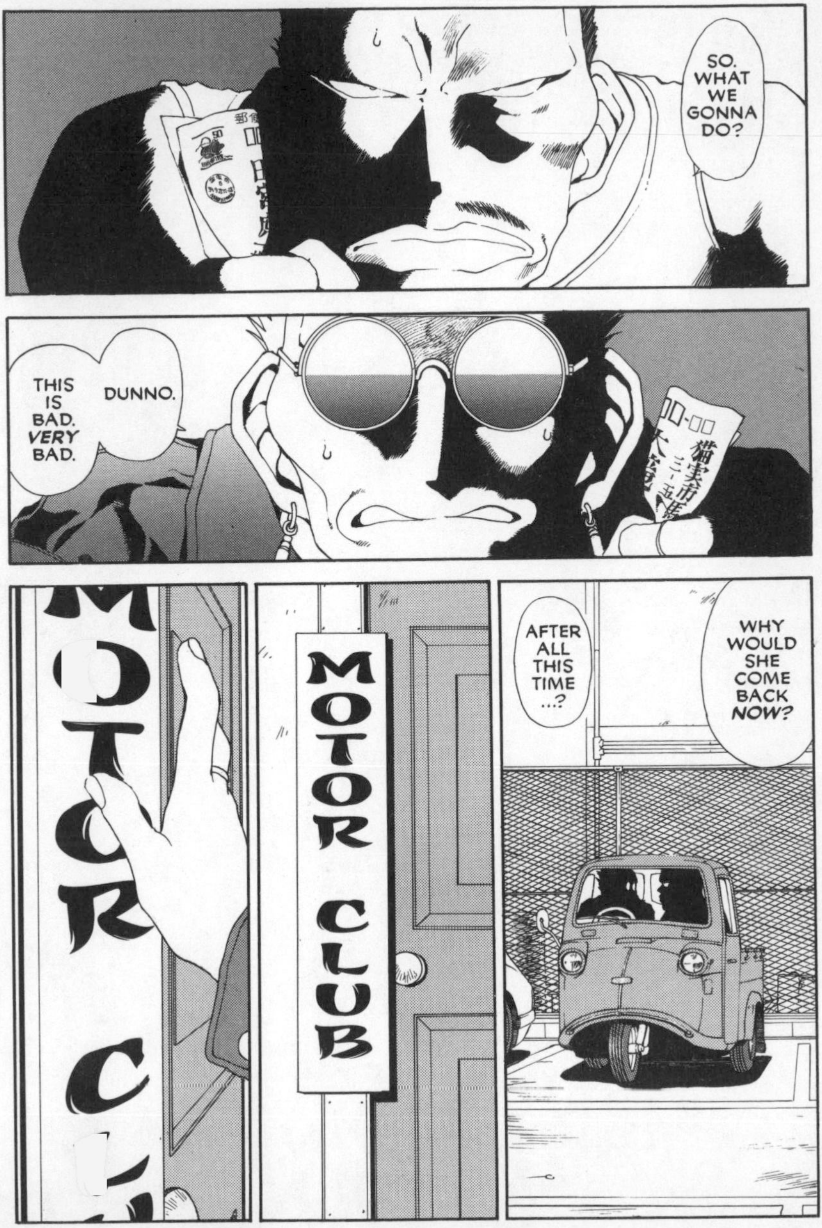
SO. WHAT WE GONNA DO?
DUNNO.
THIS IS BAD. *VERY* BAD.
WHY WOULD SHE COME BACK *NOW?*
AFTER ALL THIS TIME ...?
MOTOR CLUB

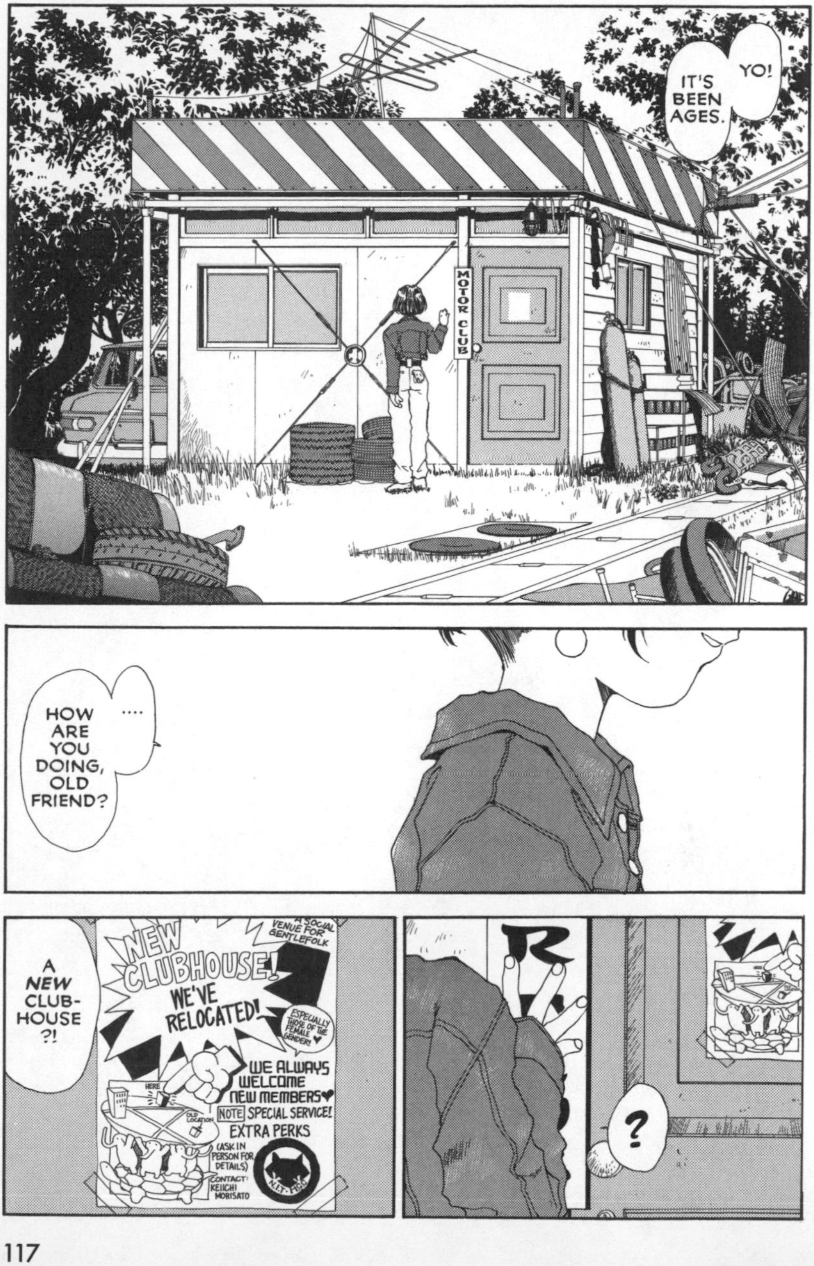
YO!
IT'S BEEN AGES.
....
HOW ARE YOU DOING, OLD FRIEND?
?
A SOCIAL VENUE FOR GENTLEFOLK
NEW CLUBHOUSE!
WE'VE RELOCATED!
ESPECIALLY THOSE OF THE FEMALE GENDER! ♥
WE ALWAYS WELCOME NEW MEMBERS ♥
HERE
OLD LOCATION
NOTE SPECIAL SERVICE!
EXTRA PERKS
(ASK IN PERSON FOR DETAILS)
CONTACT: KEIICHI MORISATO
N.I.T. M.C.
A *NEW* CLUBHOUSE?!

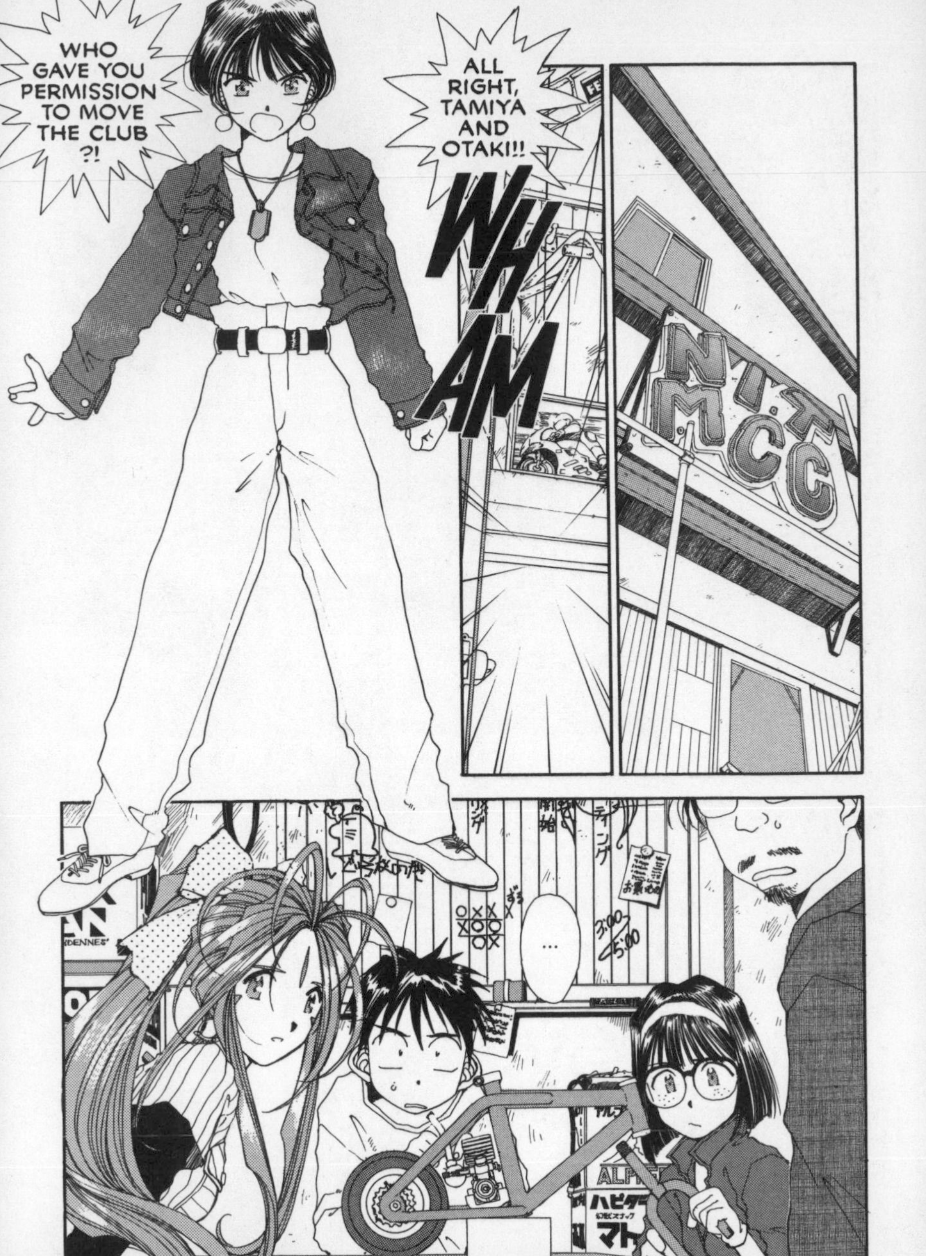
ALL RIGHT, TAMIYA AND OTAKI!!
WHAM
NIT MCC
WHO GAVE YOU PERMISSION TO MOVE THE CLUB ?!
...

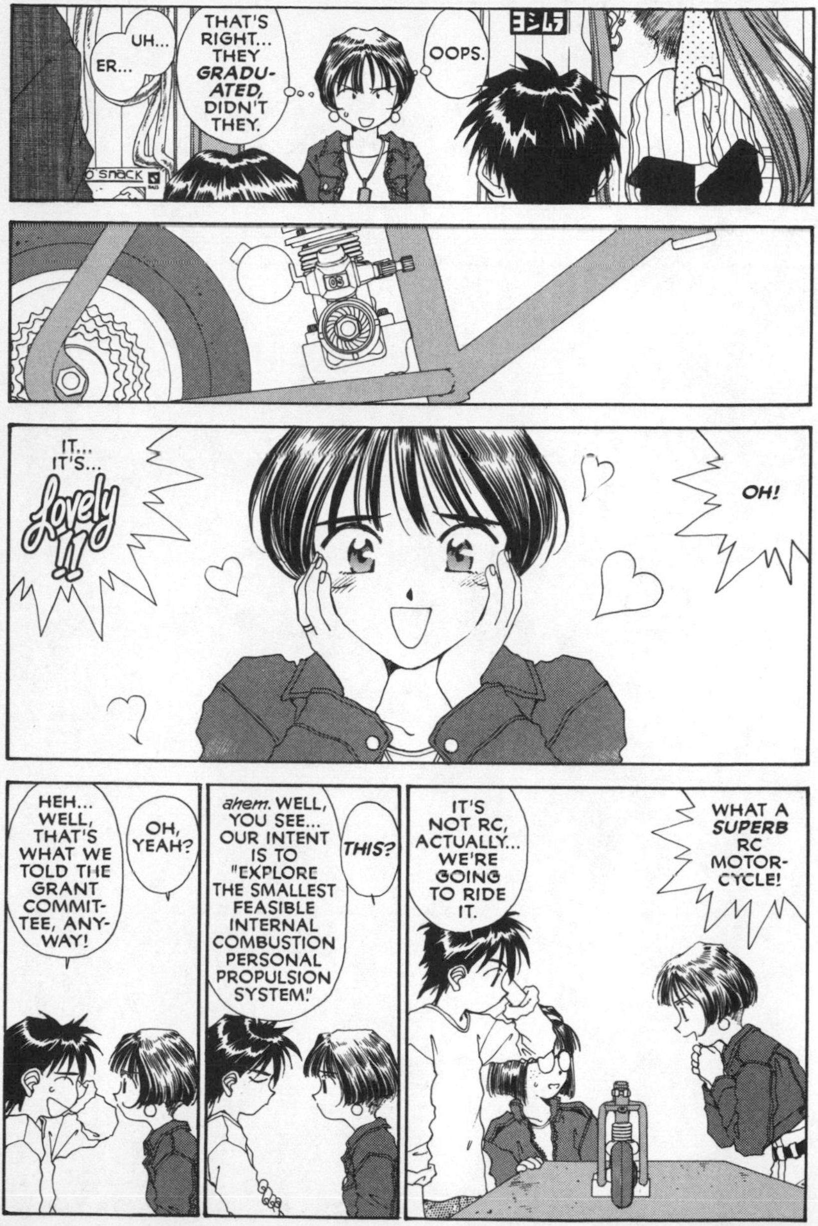
ヨシムラ
OOPS.
THAT'S RIGHT... THEY *GRADUATED,* DIDN'T THEY.
UH... ER...
O'snack
OH!
IT... IT'S... Lovely!!
WHAT A *SUPERB* RC MOTORCYCLE!
IT'S NOT RC, ACTUALLY... WE'RE GOING TO RIDE IT.
THIS?
ahem. WELL, YOU SEE... OUR INTENT IS TO "EXPLORE THE SMALLEST FEASIBLE INTERNAL COMBUSTION PERSONAL PROPULSION SYSTEM."
OH, YEAH?
HEH... WELL, THAT'S WHAT WE TOLD THE GRANT COMMITTEE, ANYWAY!

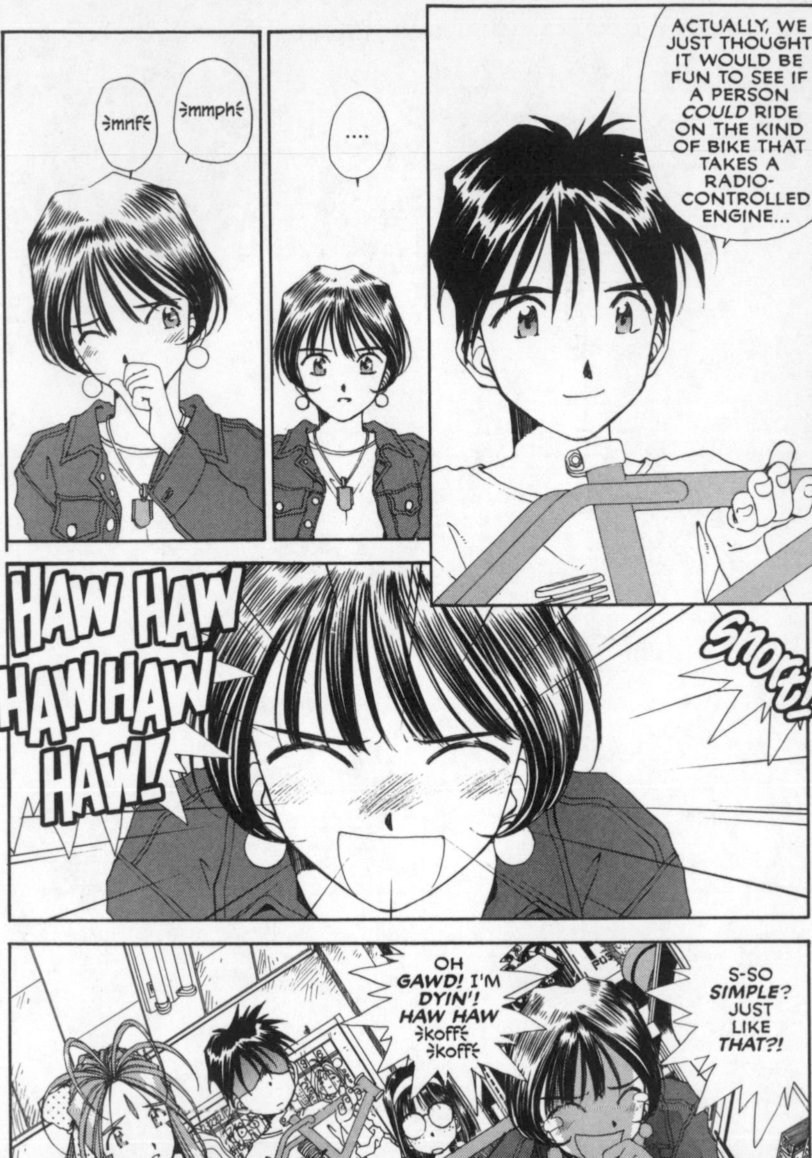
ACTUALLY, WE JUST THOUGHT IT WOULD BE FUN TO SEE IF A PERSON *COULD* RIDE ON THE KIND OF BIKE THAT TAKES A RADIO-CONTROLLED ENGINE...
....
mmph
mnf
Snort!
HAW HAW HAW HAW HAW!
S-SO *SIMPLE*? JUST LIKE *THAT*?!
OH *GAWD!* I'M *DYIN'!* HAW HAW koff koff

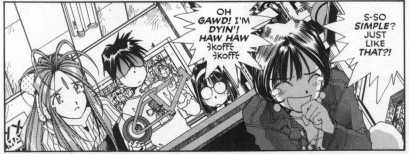

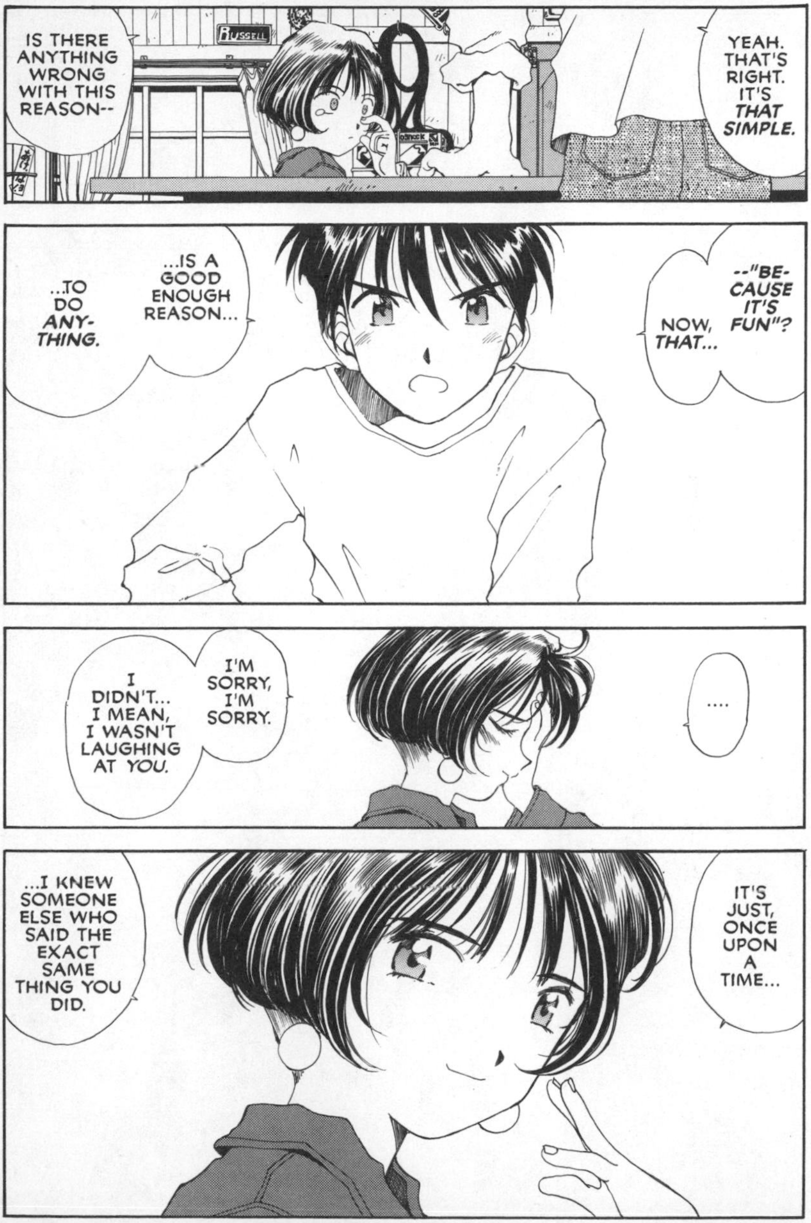
YEAH. THAT'S RIGHT. IT'S *THAT SIMPLE.*
IS THERE ANYTHING WRONG WITH THIS REASON--
--"BE-CAUSE IT'S FUN"?
NOW, THAT...
...IS A GOOD ENOUGH REASON...
...TO DO *ANY-THING.*
....
I'M SORRY, I'M SORRY.
I DIDN'T... I MEAN, I WASN'T LAUGHING AT *YOU.*
IT'S JUST, ONCE UPON A TIME...
...I KNEW SOMEONE ELSE WHO SAID THE EXACT SAME THING YOU DID.

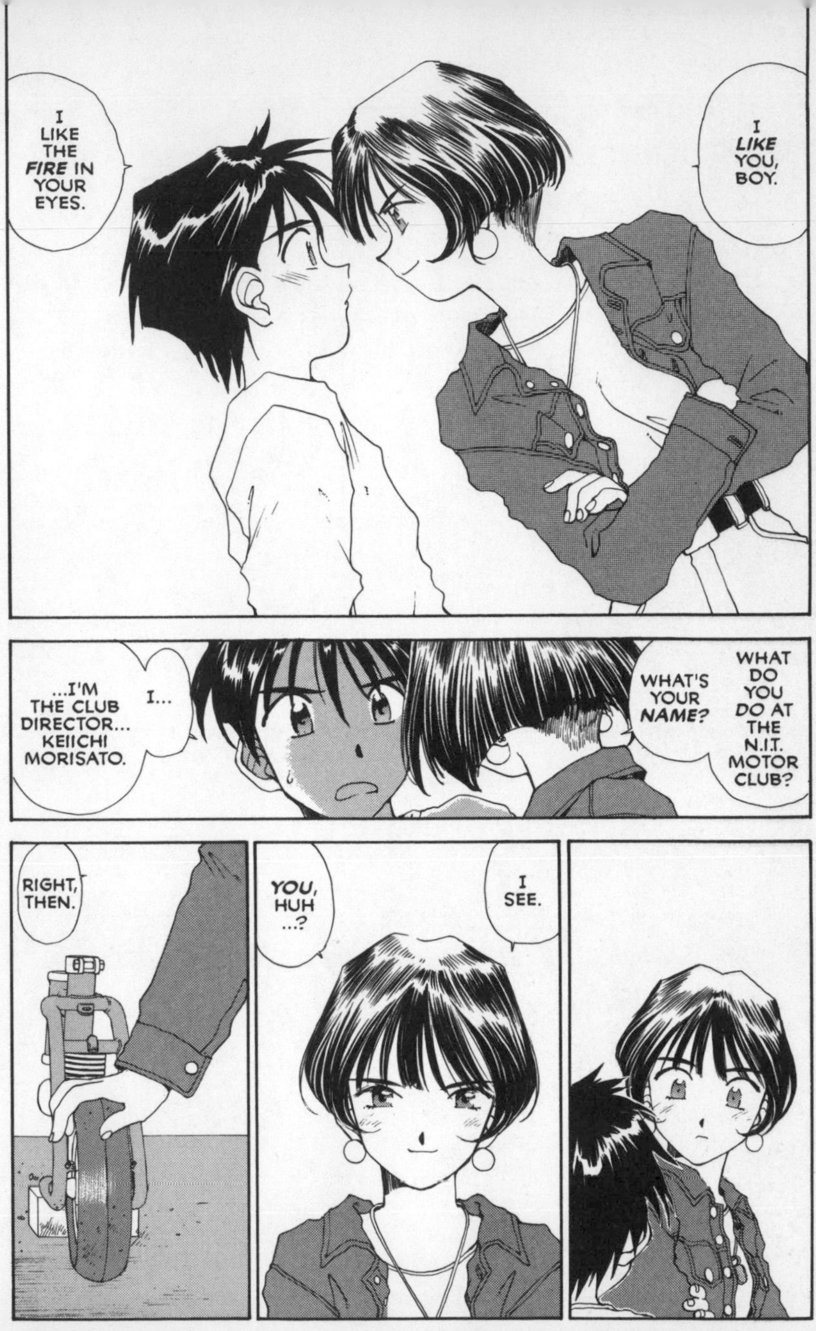
I LIKE YOU, BOY.
I LIKE THE FIRE IN YOUR EYES.
WHAT DO YOU DO AT THE N.I.T. MOTOR CLUB?
WHAT'S YOUR NAME?
I...
...I'M THE CLUB DIRECTOR... KEIICHI MORISATO.
I SEE.
YOU, HUH ...?
RIGHT, THEN.

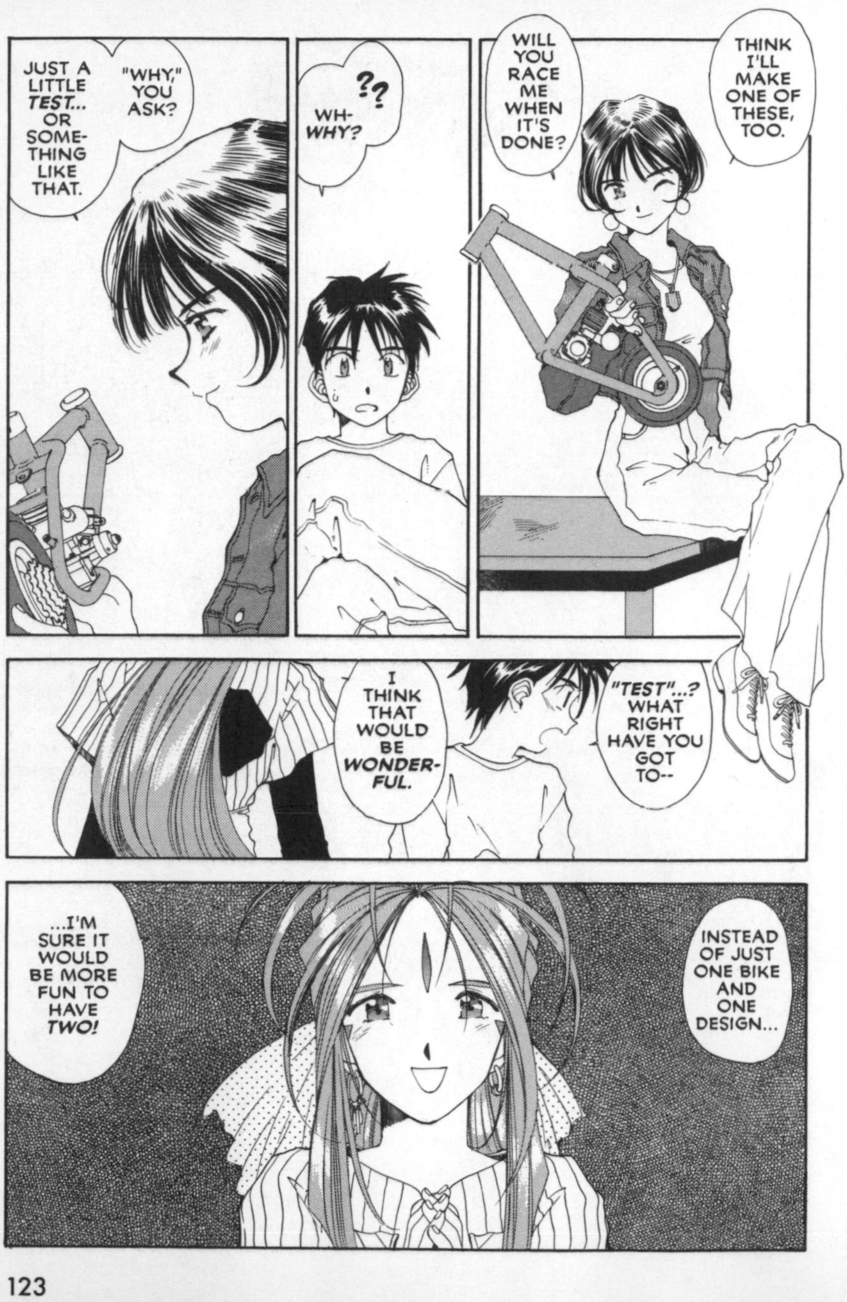
THINK I'LL MAKE ONE OF THESE, TOO.
WILL YOU RACE ME WHEN IT'S DONE?
??
WH- *WHY?*
"WHY," YOU ASK?
JUST A LITTLE *TEST...* OR SOMETHING LIKE THAT.
"TEST"...? WHAT RIGHT HAVE YOU GOT TO--
I THINK THAT WOULD BE *WONDERFUL.*
INSTEAD OF JUST ONE BIKE AND ONE DESIGN...
...I'M SURE IT WOULD BE MORE FUN TO HAVE *TWO!*

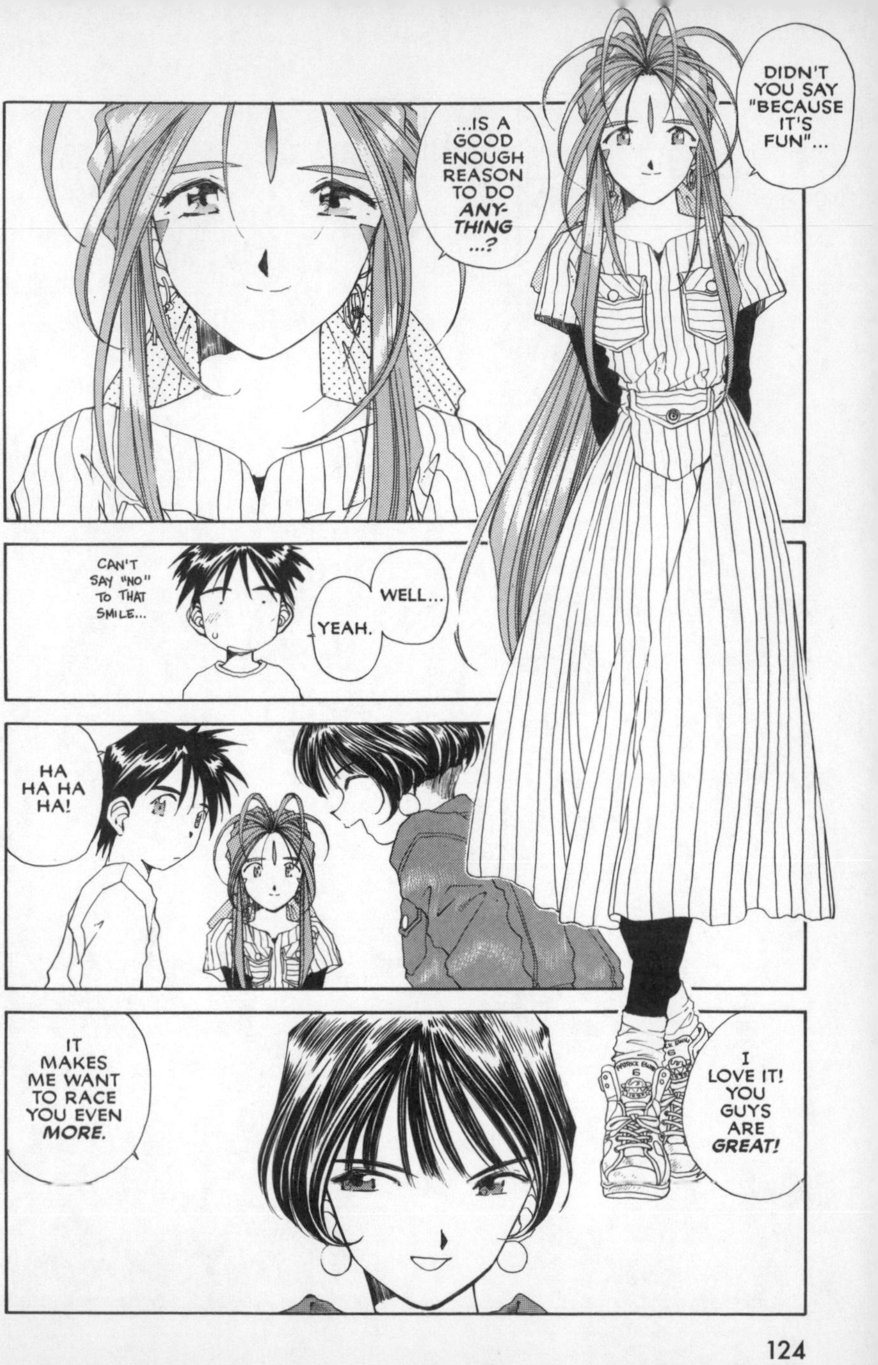
DIDN'T YOU SAY "BECAUSE IT'S FUN"...
...IS A GOOD ENOUGH REASON TO DO ANYTHING ...?
WELL... YEAH.
CAN'T SAY "NO" TO THAT SMILE...
HA HA HA HA!
I LOVE IT! YOU GUYS ARE GREAT!
IT MAKES ME WANT TO RACE YOU EVEN MORE.

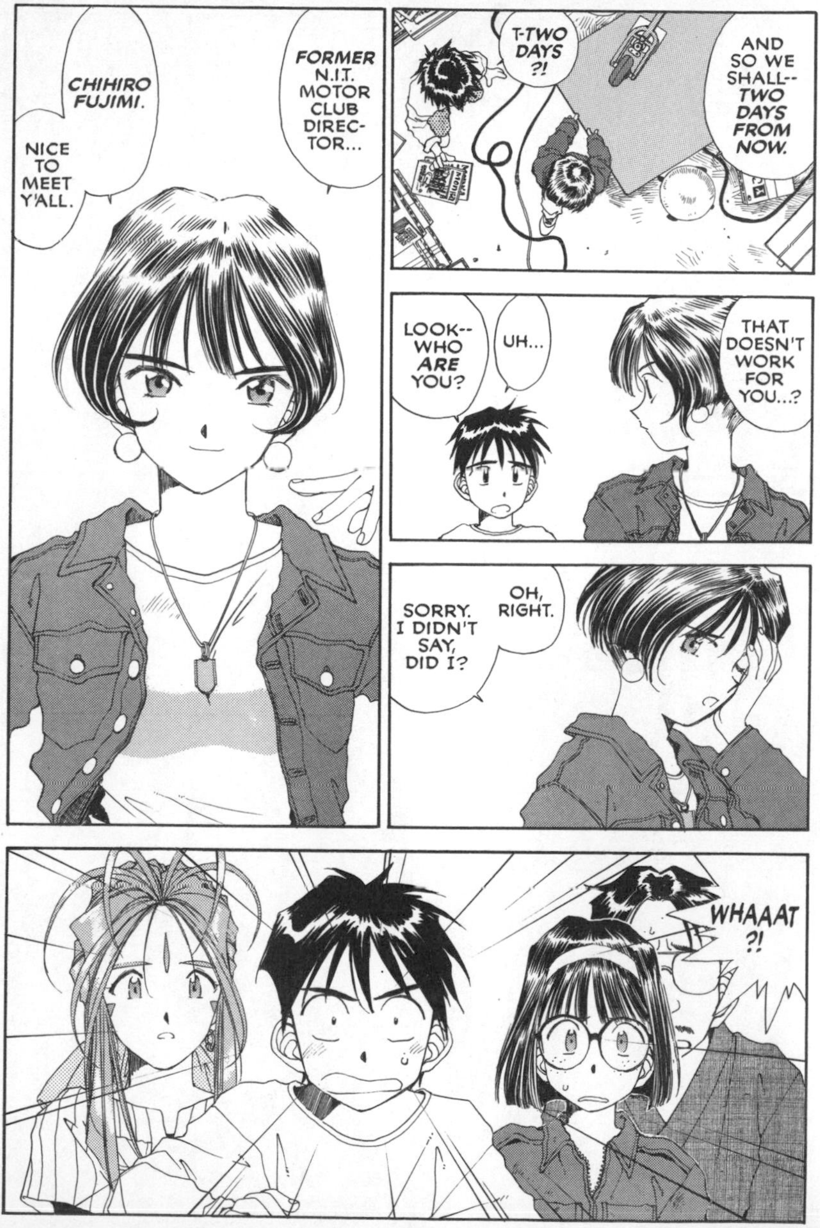
AND SO WE SHALL-- TWO DAYS FROM NOW.
T-TWO DAYS ?!
THAT DOESN'T WORK FOR YOU...?
UH...
LOOK-- WHO ARE YOU?
OH, RIGHT.
SORRY. I DIDN'T SAY, DID I?
FORMER N.I.T. MOTOR CLUB DIRECTOR...
CHIHIRO FUJIMI.
NICE TO MEET Y'ALL.
WHAAAT ?!

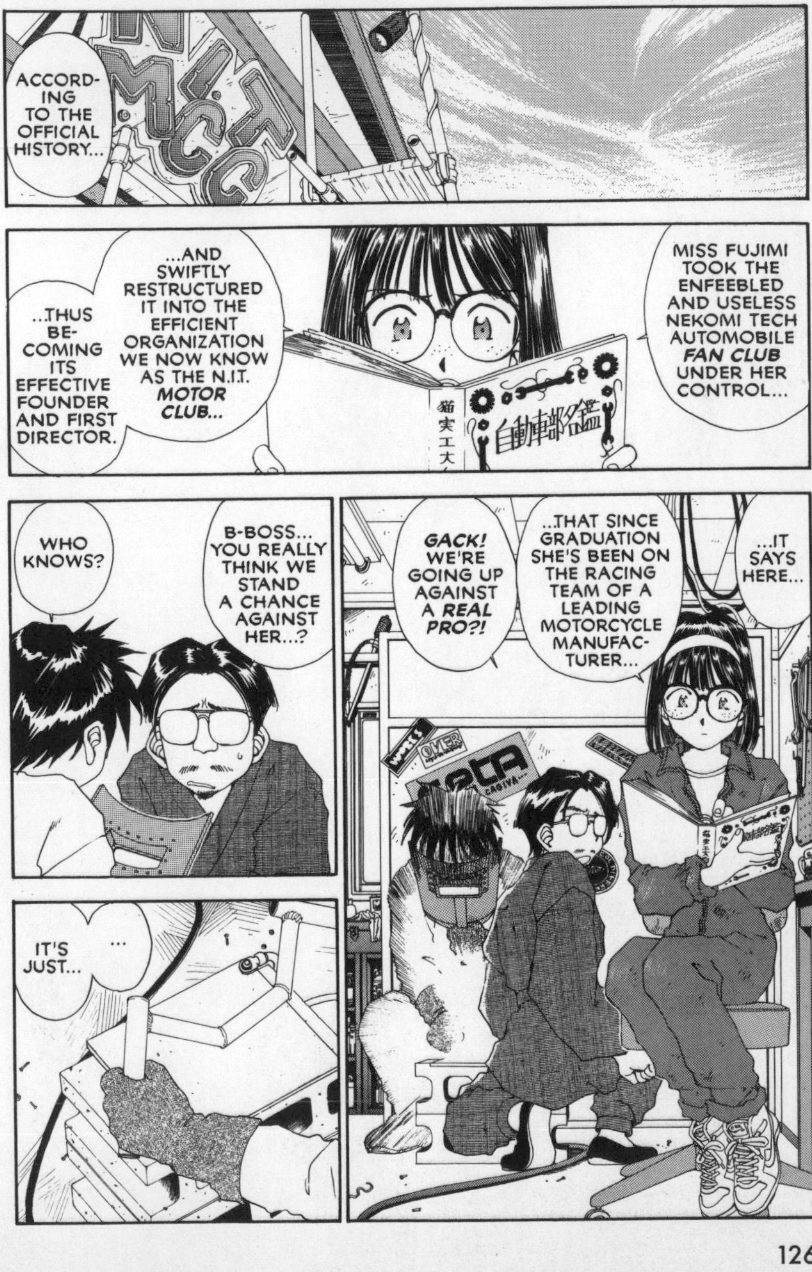
ACCORDING TO THE OFFICIAL HISTORY...
MISS FUJIMI TOOK THE ENFEEBLED AND USELESS NEKOMI TECH AUTOMOBILE ***FAN CLUB*** UNDER HER CONTROL...
...AND SWIFTLY RESTRUCTURED IT INTO THE EFFICIENT ORGANIZATION WE NOW KNOW AS THE N.I.T. ***MOTOR CLUB...***
...THUS BECOMING ITS EFFECTIVE FOUNDER AND FIRST DIRECTOR.
自動車部名鑑
...IT SAYS HERE...
...THAT SINCE GRADUATION SHE'S BEEN ON THE RACING TEAM OF A LEADING MOTORCYCLE MANUFACTURER...
GACK! WE'RE GOING UP AGAINST A ***REAL PRO?!***
B-BOSS... YOU REALLY THINK WE STAND A CHANCE AGAINST HER...?
WHO KNOWS?
...
IT'S JUST...

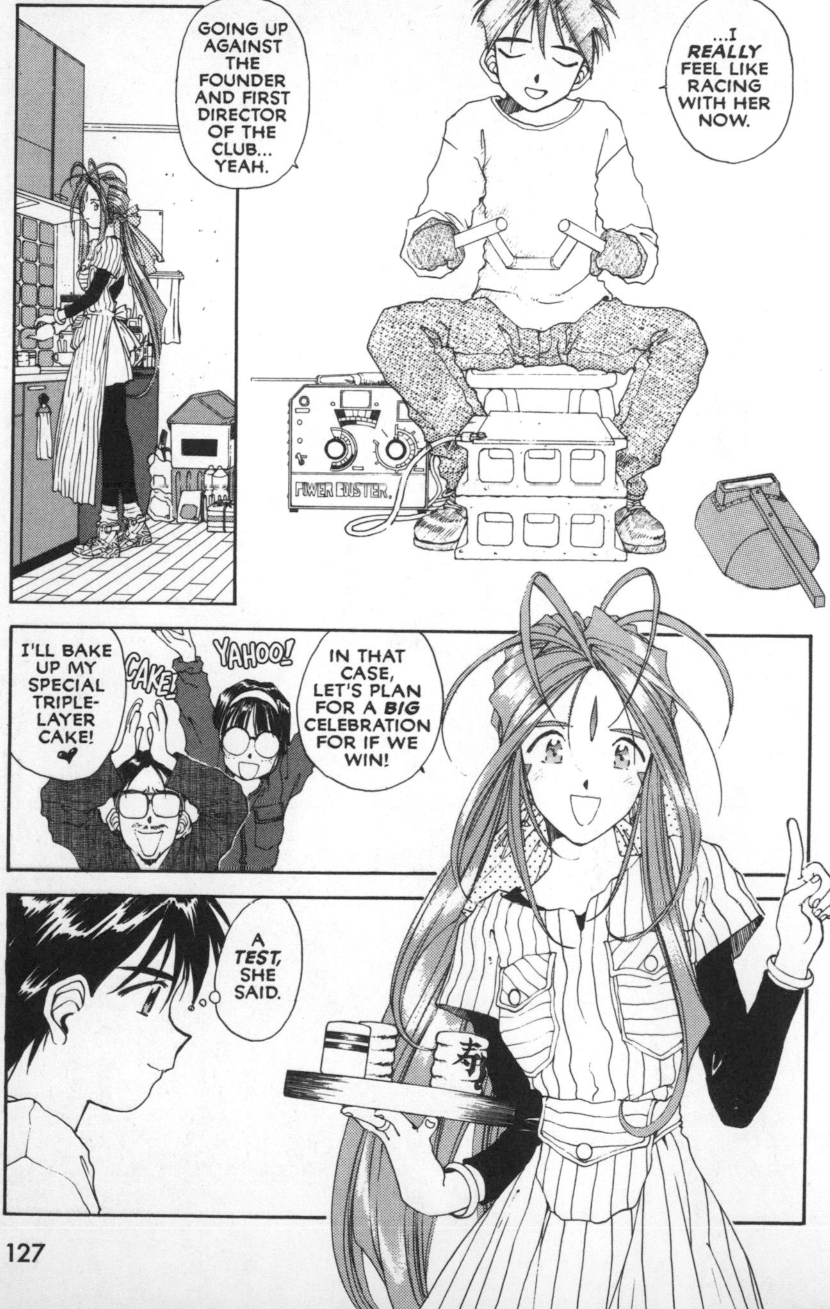
...I *REALLY* FEEL LIKE RACING WITH HER NOW.
GOING UP AGAINST THE FOUNDER AND FIRST DIRECTOR OF THE CLUB... YEAH.
POWER BOOSTER.
IN THAT CASE, LET'S PLAN FOR A *BIG* CELEBRATION FOR IF WE WIN!
YAHOO!
CAKE!
I'LL BAKE UP MY SPECIAL TRIPLE-LAYER CAKE! ❤
A *TEST,* SHE SAID.

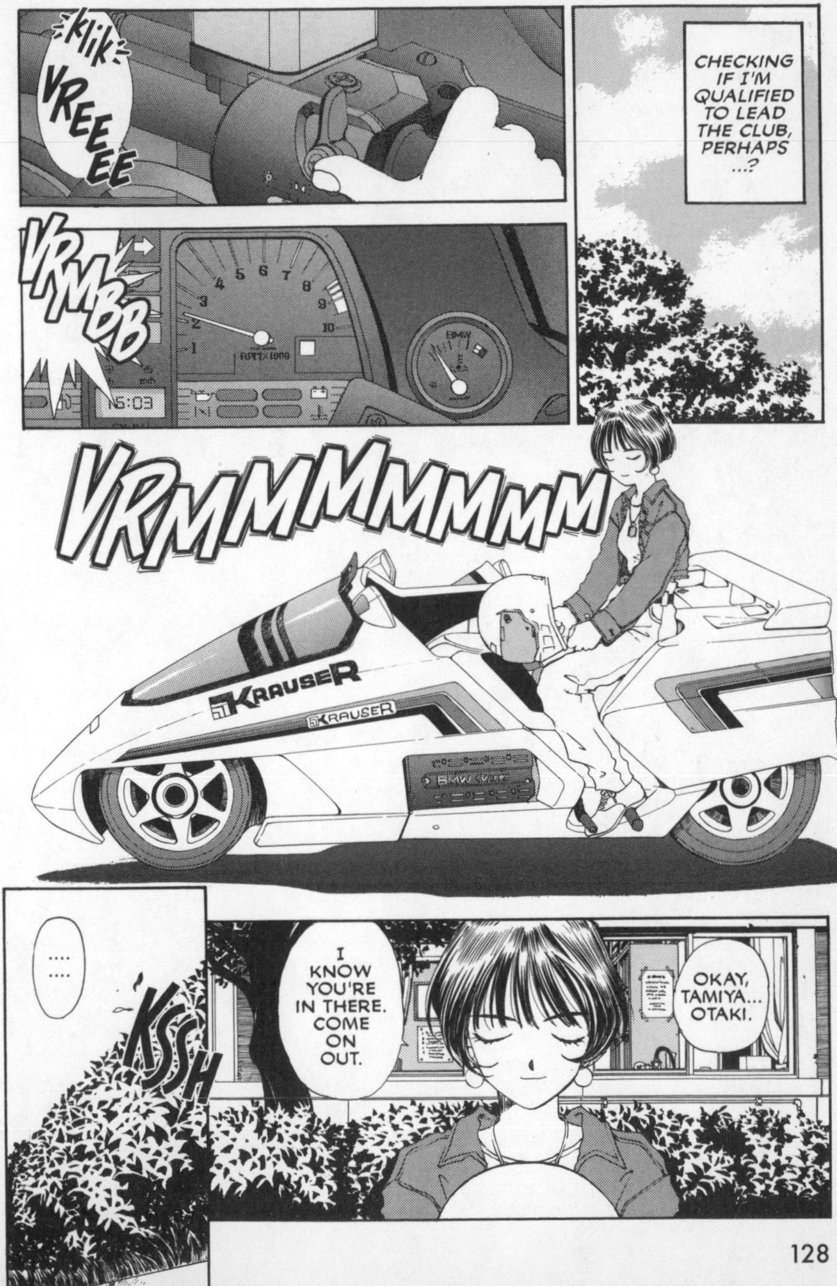
CHECKING IF I'M QUALIFIED TO LEAD THE CLUB, PERHAPS ...?
klik
VREEEEE
VRMBB
VRMMMMMMMMM
KRAUSER
KRAUSER
OKAY, TAMIYA... OTAKI.
I KNOW YOU'RE IN THERE. COME ON OUT.
KSSH
....

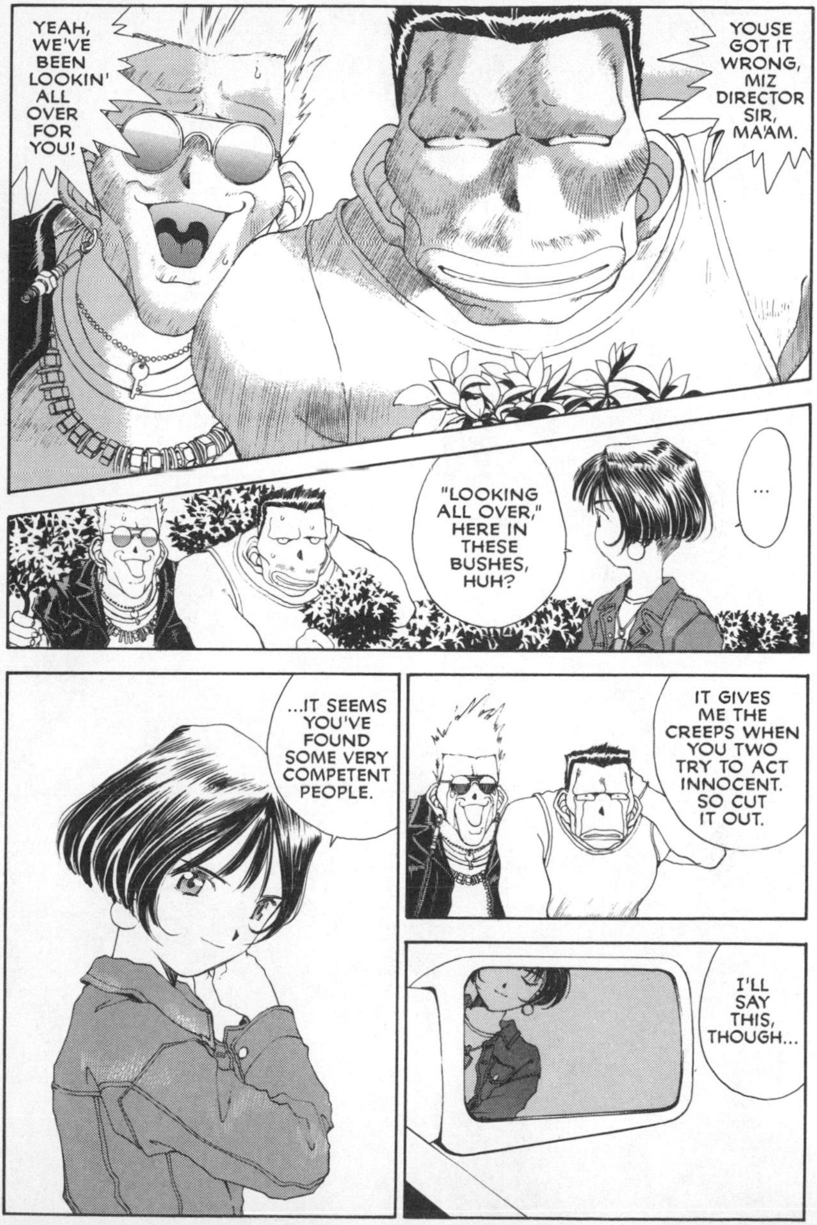

YOUSE GOT IT WRONG, MIZ DIRECTOR SIR, MA'AM.
YEAH, WE'VE BEEN LOOKIN' ALL OVER FOR YOU!
...
"LOOKING ALL OVER," HERE IN THESE BUSHES, HUH?
IT GIVES ME THE CREEPS WHEN YOU TWO TRY TO ACT INNOCENT. SO CUT IT OUT.
I'LL SAY THIS, THOUGH...
...IT SEEMS YOU'VE FOUND SOME VERY COMPETENT PEOPLE.

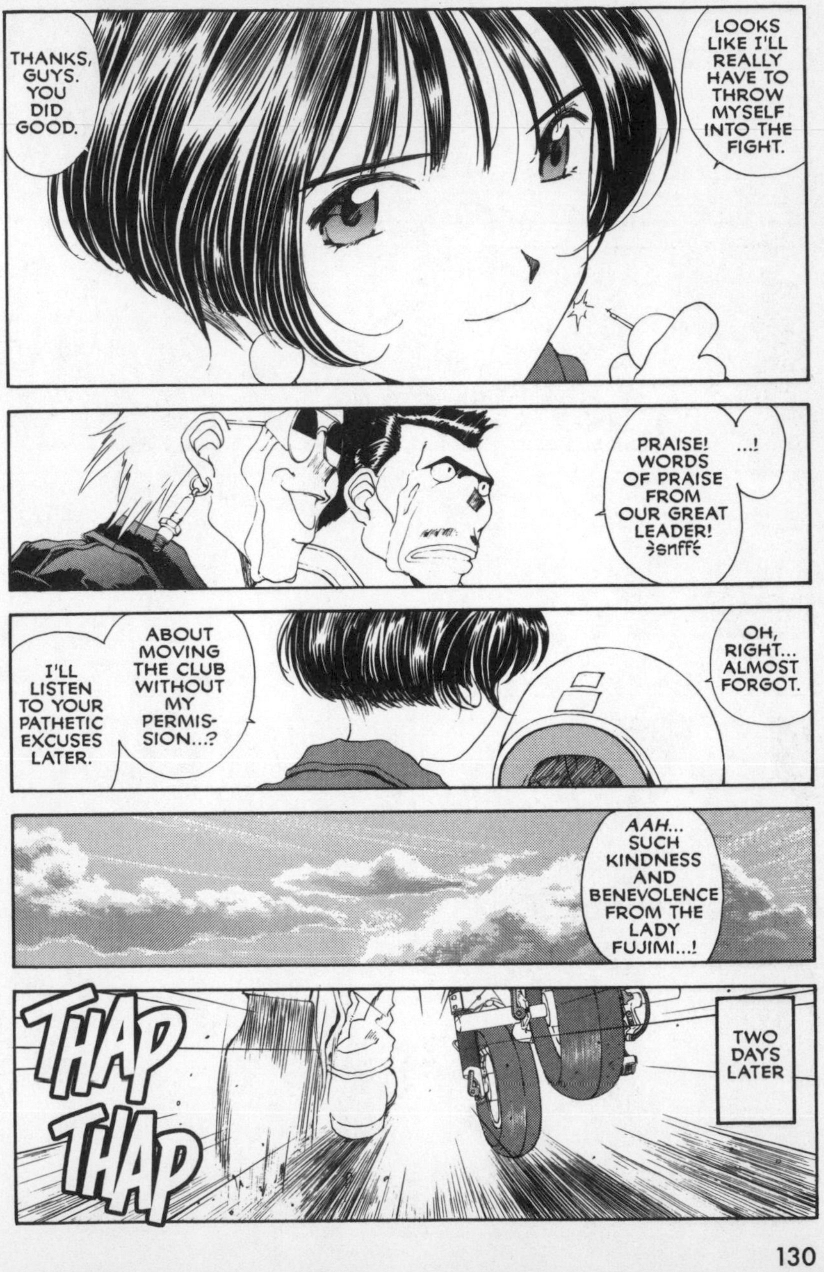
LOOKS LIKE I'LL REALLY HAVE TO THROW MYSELF INTO THE FIGHT.
THANKS, GUYS. YOU DID GOOD.
...!
PRAISE! WORDS OF PRAISE FROM OUR GREAT LEADER! snff
OH, RIGHT... ALMOST FORGOT.
ABOUT MOVING THE CLUB WITHOUT MY PERMIS-SION...?
I'LL LISTEN TO YOUR PATHETIC EXCUSES LATER.
AAH... SUCH KINDNESS AND BENEVOLENCE FROM THE LADY FUJIMI...!
TWO DAYS LATER
THAP THAP

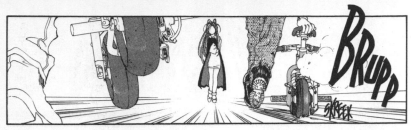

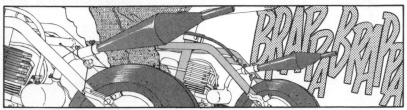

BRUPP
SKREEK
BRAPABRAPA
ALL RIGHT! TWO CIRCUITS AROUND THE CAMPUS!
WIN OR LOSE...
...BOTH RACERS, *WATCH OUT FOR* PEDESTRIANS!
READY
GO

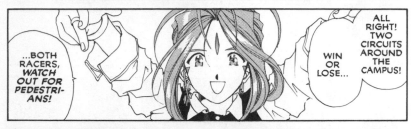

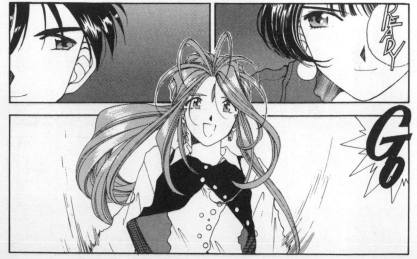

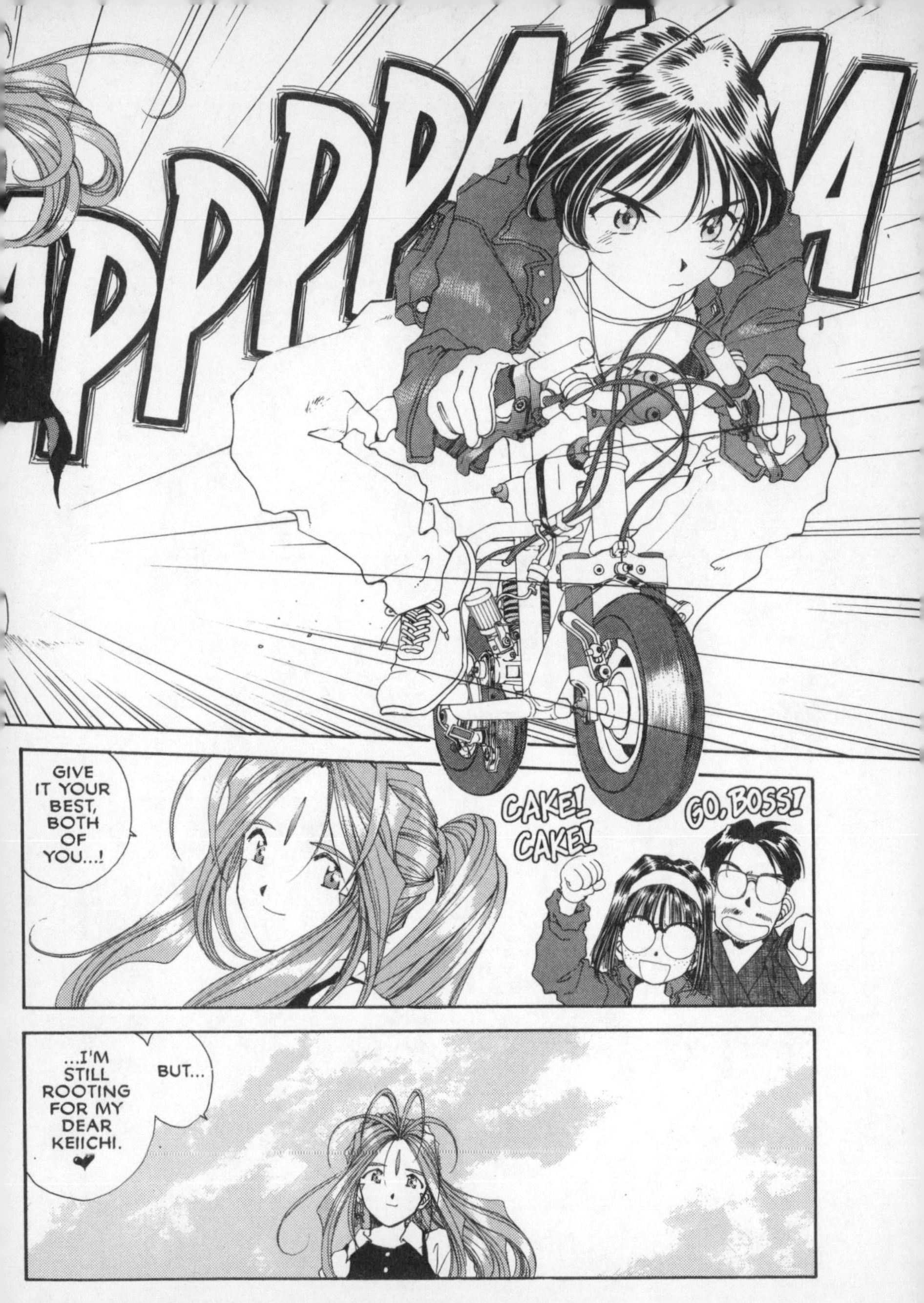

APPPPAAA
GO, BOSS!
CAKE! CAKE!
GIVE IT YOUR BEST, BOTH OF YOU...!
BUT...
...I'M STILL ROOTING FOR MY DEAR KEIICHI. ❤

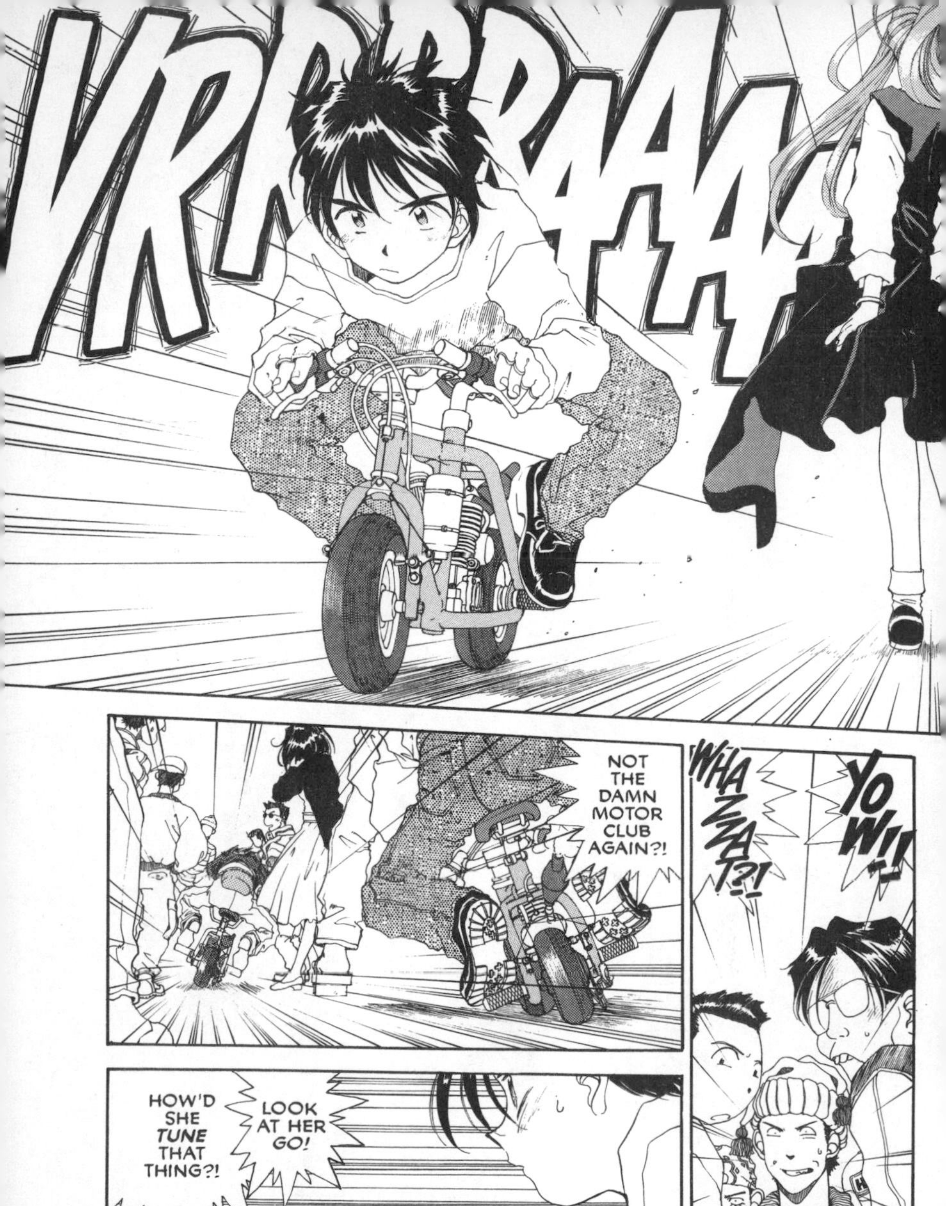
VRRRAAAA
YOWI!!
WHAZZAAT?!
NOT THE DAMN MOTOR CLUB AGAIN?!
LOOK AT HER *GO!*
HOW'D SHE *TUNE* THAT THING?!

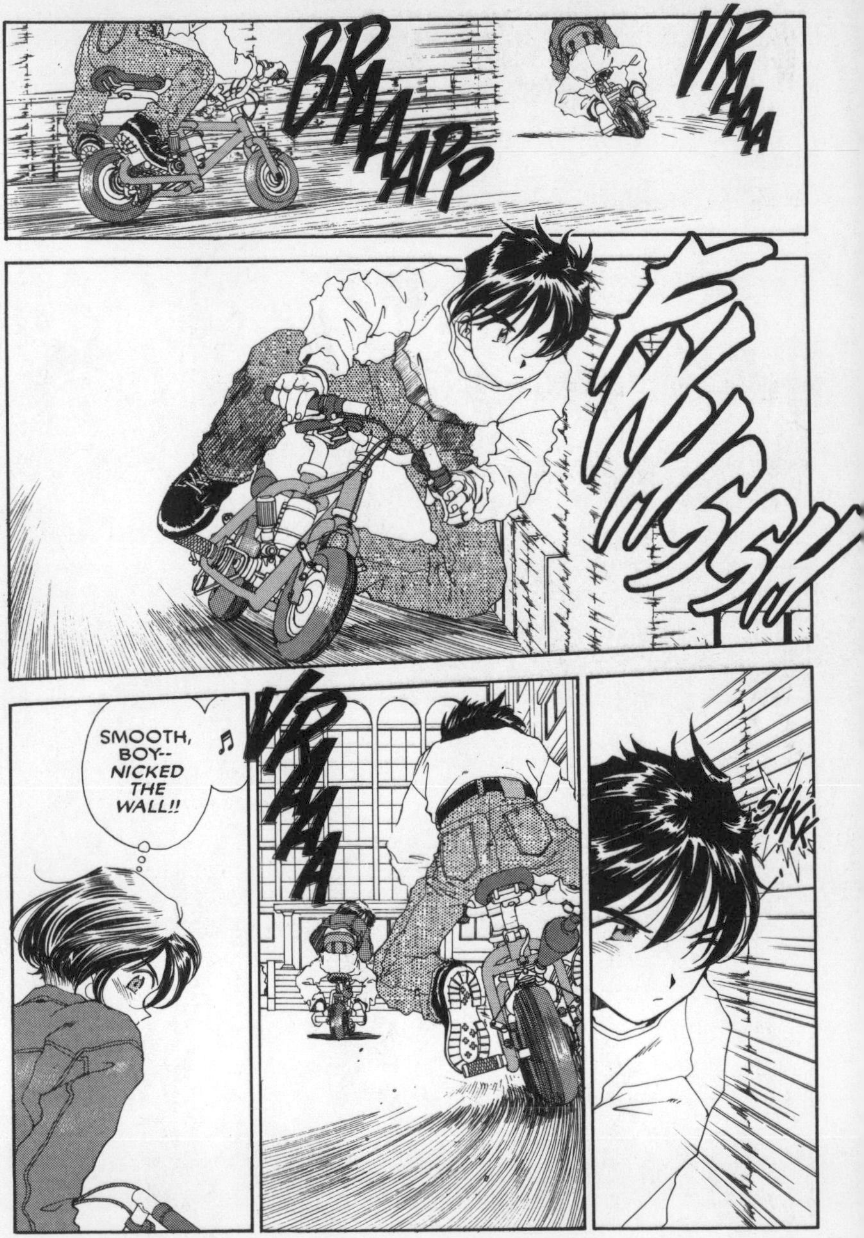
VRAAAA
BRAAAAPP
FWASSH
SHKK
VRAAAA
SMOOTH, BOY-- NICKED THE WALL!! ♪

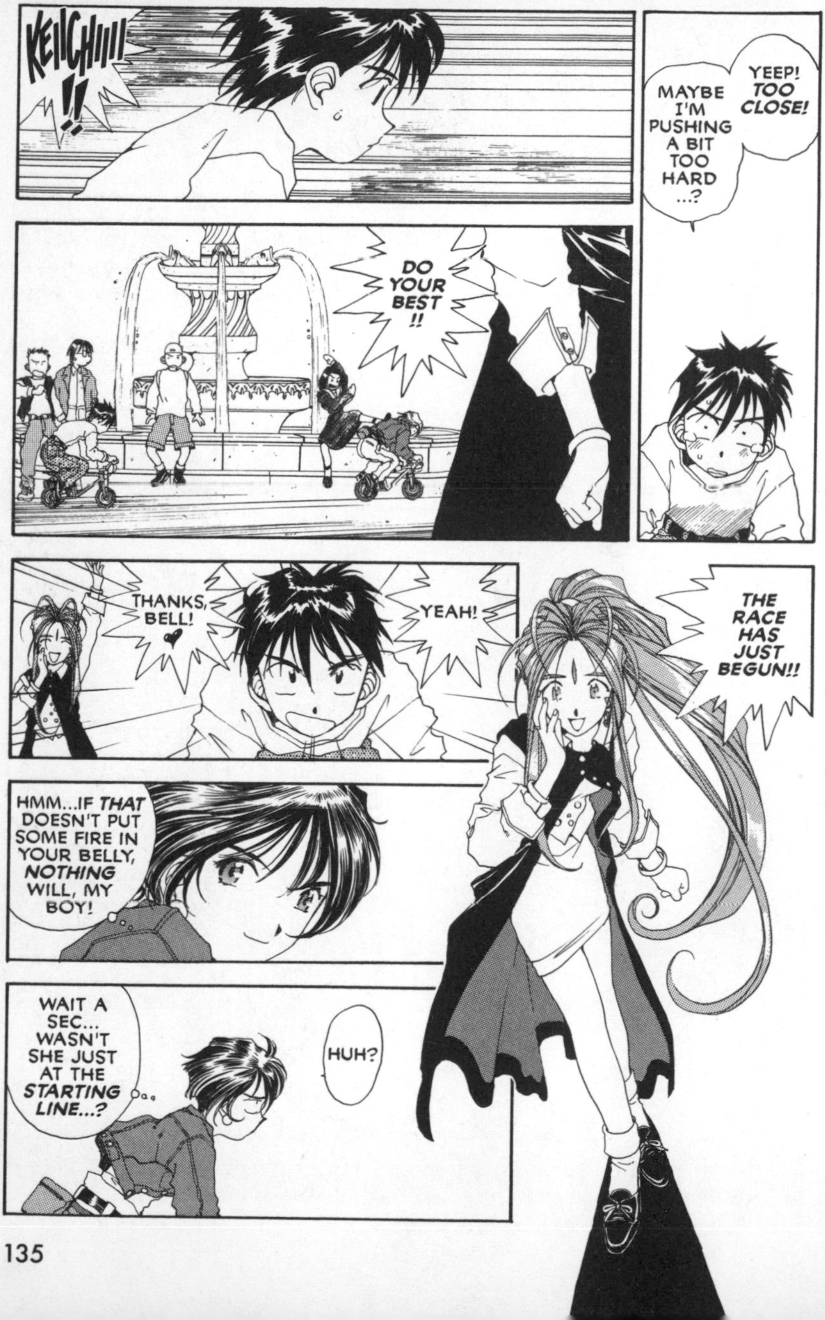
YEEP! TOO CLOSE!
MAYBE I'M PUSHING A BIT TOO HARD ...?
KEIICHIIIII !!
DO YOUR BEST !!
THE RACE HAS JUST BEGUN!!
YEAH!
THANKS, BELL! ♥
HMM...IF THAT DOESN'T PUT SOME FIRE IN YOUR BELLY, NOTHING WILL, MY BOY!
HUH?
WAIT A SEC... WASN'T SHE JUST AT THE STARTING LINE...?

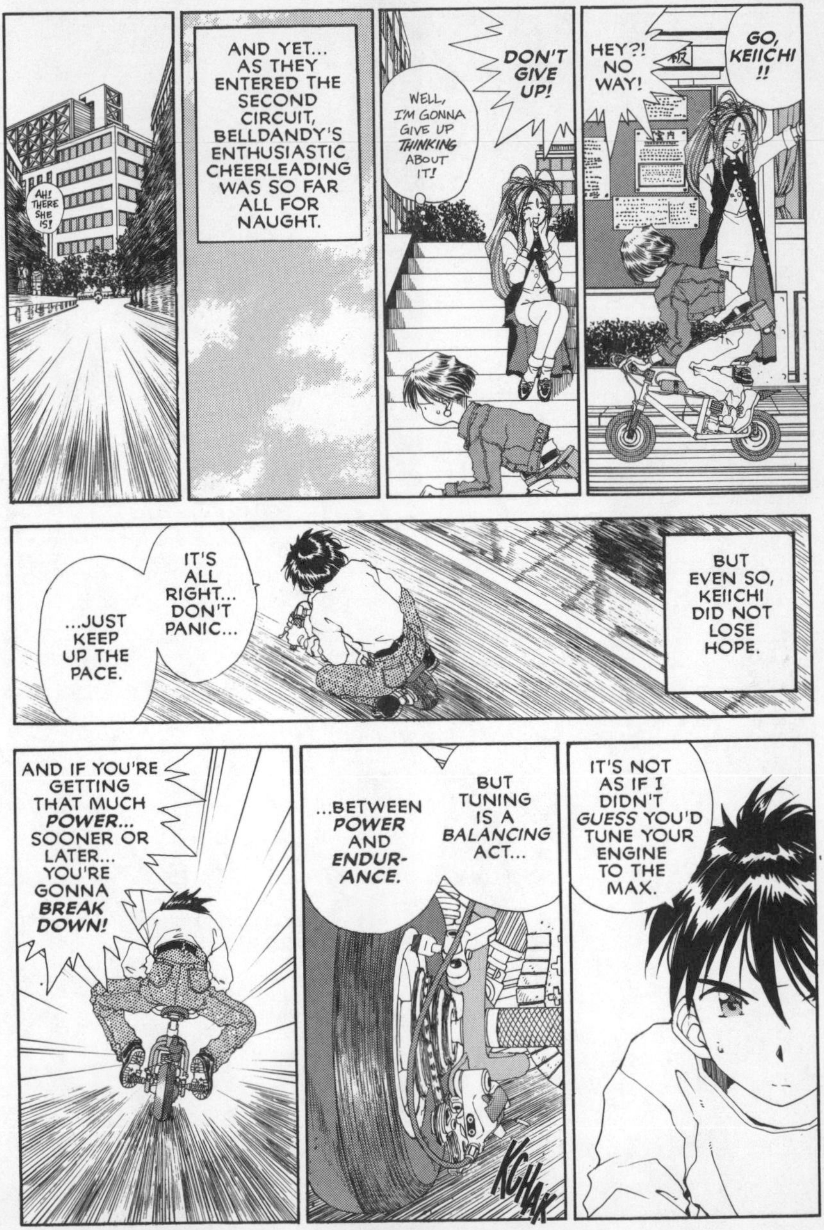
GO, KEIICHI !!
HEY?! NO WAY!
DON'T GIVE UP!
WELL, I'M GONNA GIVE UP THINKING ABOUT IT!
AND YET... AS THEY ENTERED THE SECOND CIRCUIT, BELLDANDY'S ENTHUSIASTIC CHEERLEADING WAS SO FAR ALL FOR NAUGHT.
AH! THERE SHE IS!
BUT EVEN SO, KEIICHI DID NOT LOSE HOPE.
IT'S ALL RIGHT... DON'T PANIC...
...JUST KEEP UP THE PACE.
IT'S NOT AS IF I DIDN'T GUESS YOU'D TUNE YOUR ENGINE TO THE MAX.
BUT TUNING IS A BALANCING ACT...
...BETWEEN POWER AND ENDURANCE.
KCHAK
AND IF YOU'RE GETTING THAT MUCH POWER... SOONER OR LATER... YOU'RE GONNA BREAK DOWN!

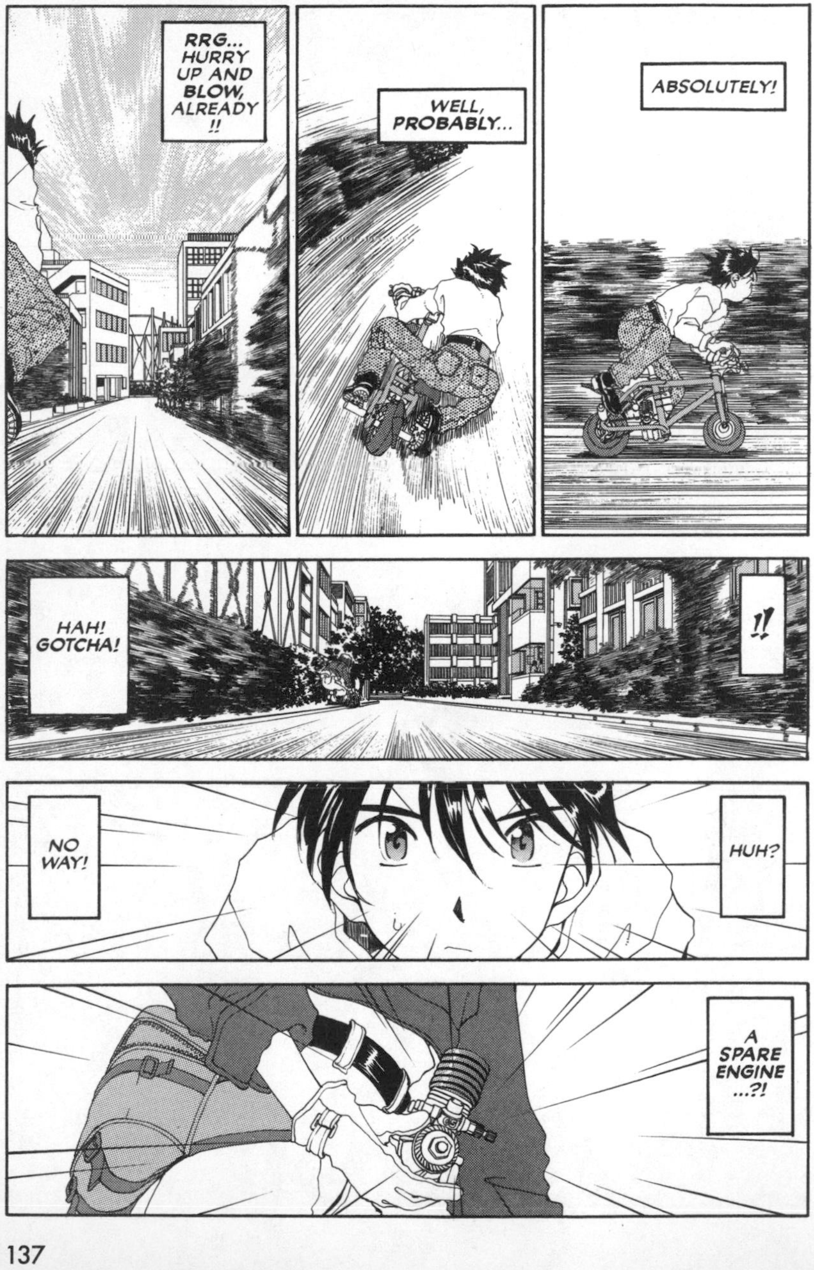
ABSOLUTELY!
WELL, PROBABLY...
RRG... HURRY UP AND BLOW, ALREADY !!
!!
HAH! GOTCHA!
HUH?
NO WAY!
A SPARE ENGINE ...?!

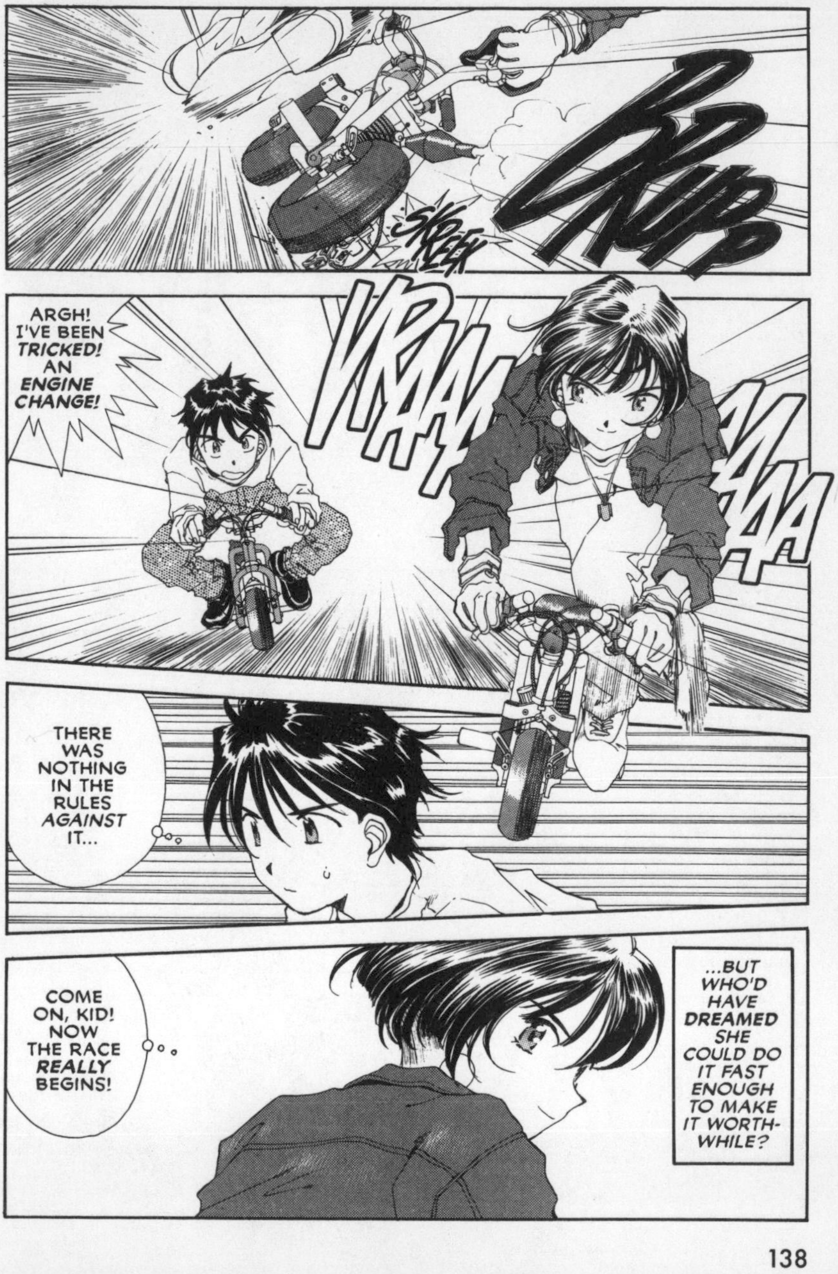
SKREEK
VRAAAAAAA
ARGH! I'VE BEEN TRICKED! AN ENGINE CHANGE!
THERE WAS NOTHING IN THE RULES AGAINST IT...
...BUT WHO'D HAVE DREAMED SHE COULD DO IT FAST ENOUGH TO MAKE IT WORTH-WHILE?
COME ON, KID! NOW THE RACE REALLY BEGINS!

EH?
THE LAST CORNER ALREADY ?!
GOAL!
NOW !!
BRAKE!

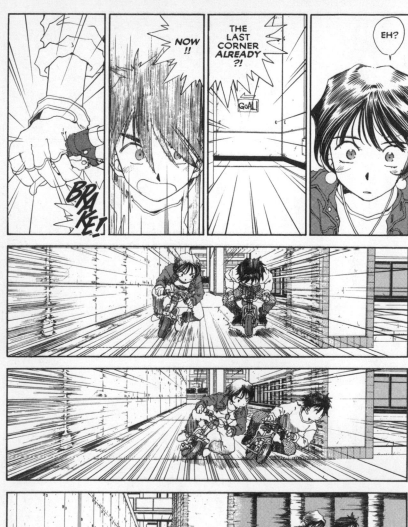

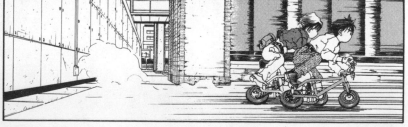

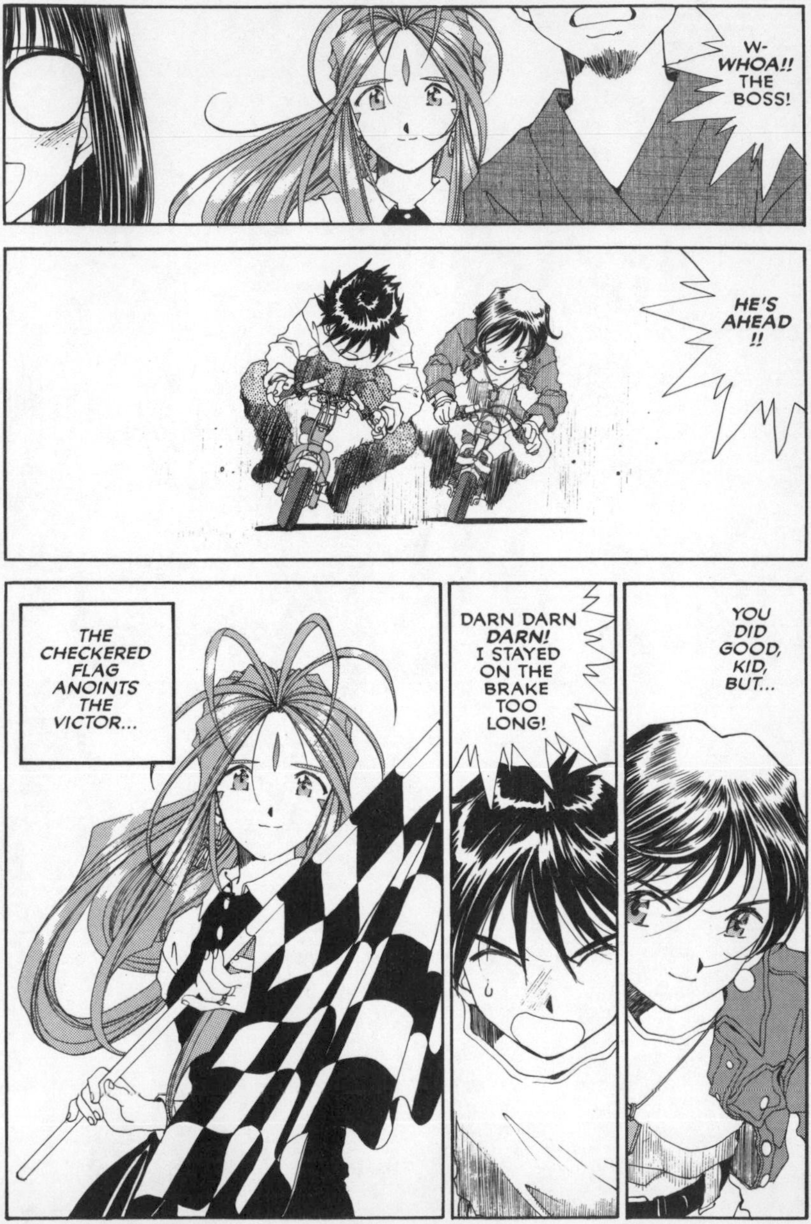
W-WHOA!! THE BOSS!
HE'S AHEAD !!
YOU DID GOOD, KID, BUT...
DARN DARN DARN! I STAYED ON THE BRAKE TOO LONG!
THE CHECKERED FLAG ANOINTS THE VICTOR...

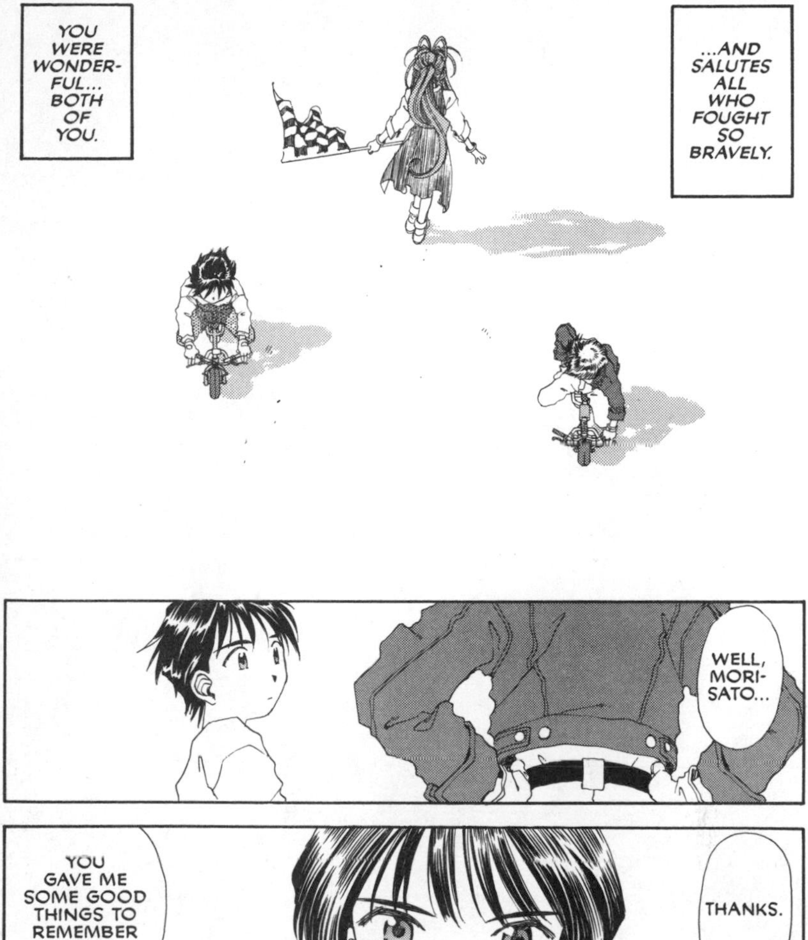
...AND SALUTES ALL WHO FOUGHT SO BRAVELY.
YOU WERE WONDERFUL... BOTH OF YOU.
WELL, MORISATO...
THANKS.
YOU GAVE ME SOME GOOD THINGS TO REMEMBER FOR A CHANGE.

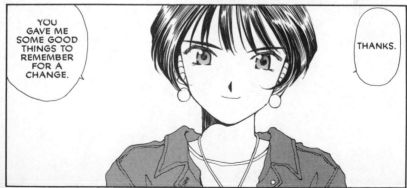

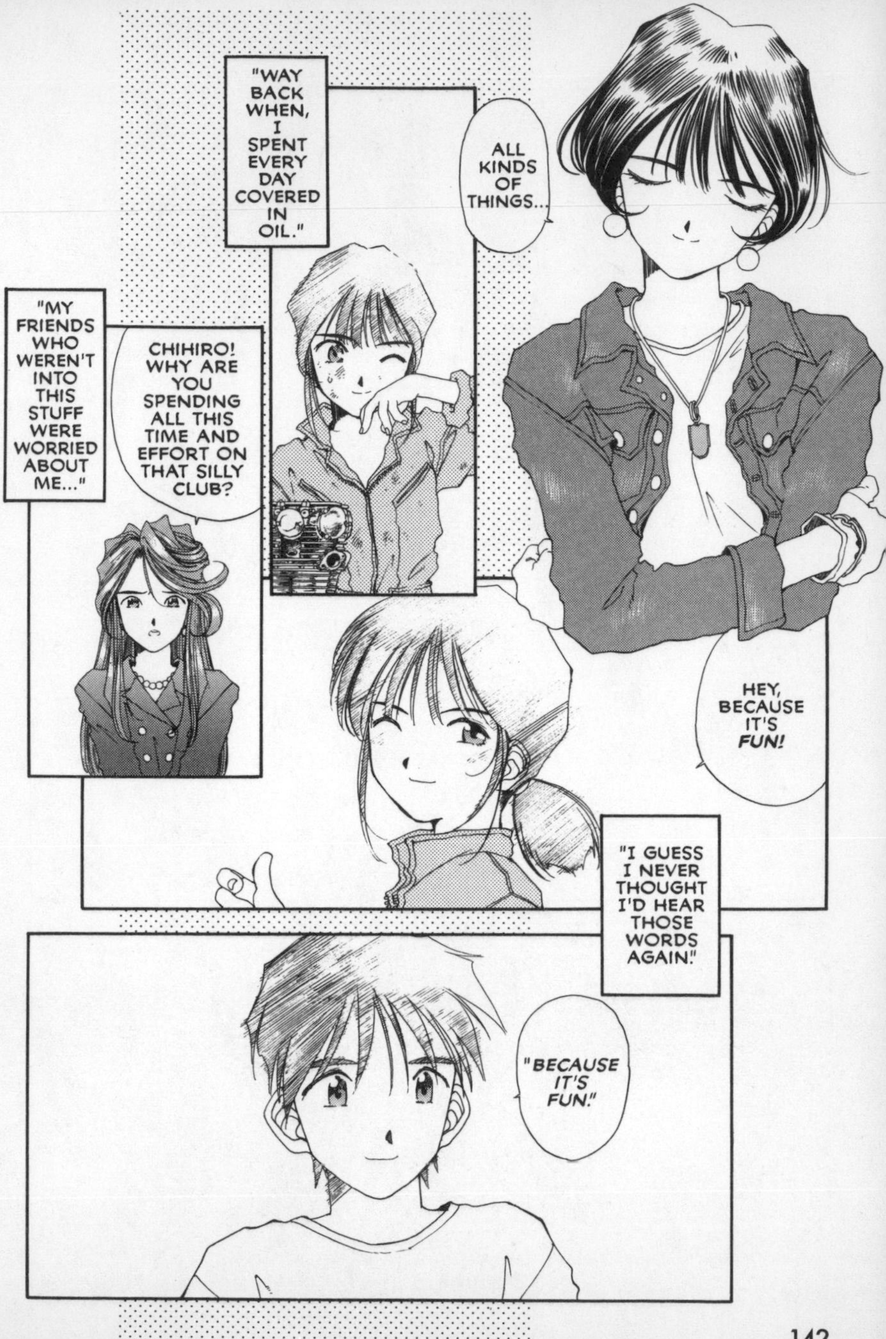
ALL KINDS OF THINGS...
"WAY BACK WHEN, I SPENT EVERY DAY COVERED IN OIL."
"MY FRIENDS WHO WEREN'T INTO THIS STUFF WERE WORRIED ABOUT ME..."
CHIHIRO! WHY ARE YOU SPENDING ALL THIS TIME AND EFFORT ON THAT SILLY CLUB?
HEY, BECAUSE IT'S *FUN!*
"I GUESS I NEVER THOUGHT I'D HEAR THOSE WORDS AGAIN."
"*BECAUSE IT'S FUN.*"

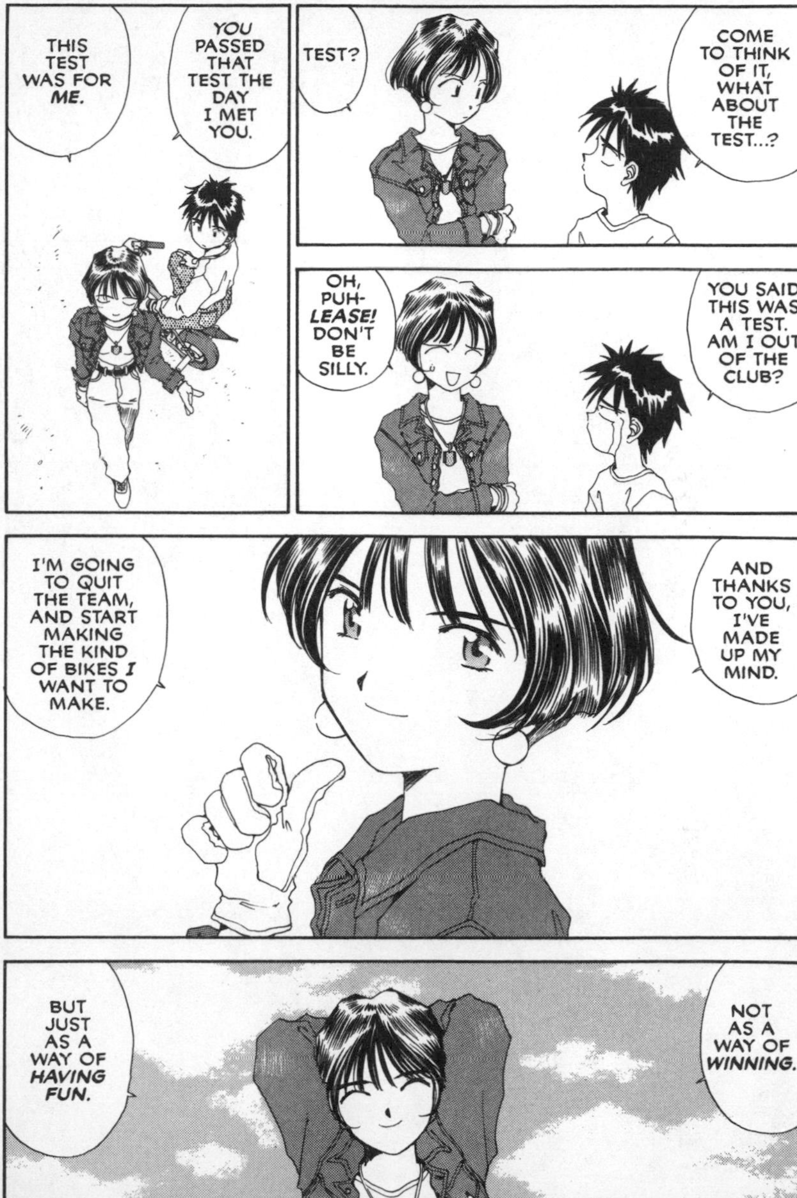
COME TO THINK OF IT, WHAT ABOUT THE TEST...?
TEST?
YOU SAID THIS WAS A TEST. AM I OUT OF THE CLUB?
OH, PUH-*LEASE!* DON'T BE SILLY.
YOU PASSED THAT TEST THE DAY I MET YOU.
THIS TEST WAS FOR *ME.*
AND THANKS TO YOU, I'VE MADE UP MY MIND.
I'M GOING TO QUIT THE TEAM, AND START MAKING THE KIND OF BIKES *I* WANT TO MAKE.
NOT AS A WAY OF *WINNING.*
BUT JUST AS A WAY OF *HAVING FUN.*

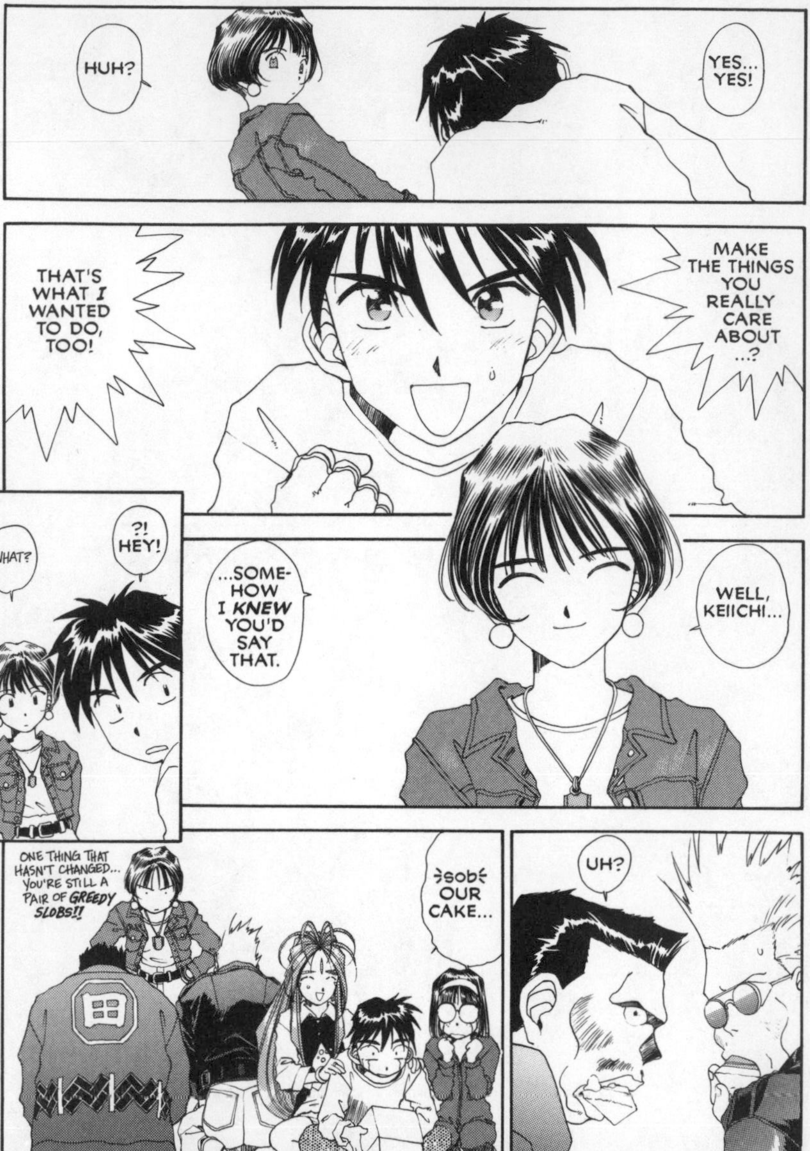
YES... YES!
HUH?
MAKE THE THINGS YOU REALLY CARE ABOUT ...?
THAT'S WHAT I WANTED TO DO, TOO!
WELL, KEIICHI...
...SOMEHOW I KNEW YOU'D SAY THAT.
?! HEY!
WHAT?
UH?
sob OUR CAKE...
ONE THING THAT HASN'T CHANGED... YOU'RE STILL A PAIR OF GREEDY SLOBS!!

CHAPTER 77

Let's Go Feminine!

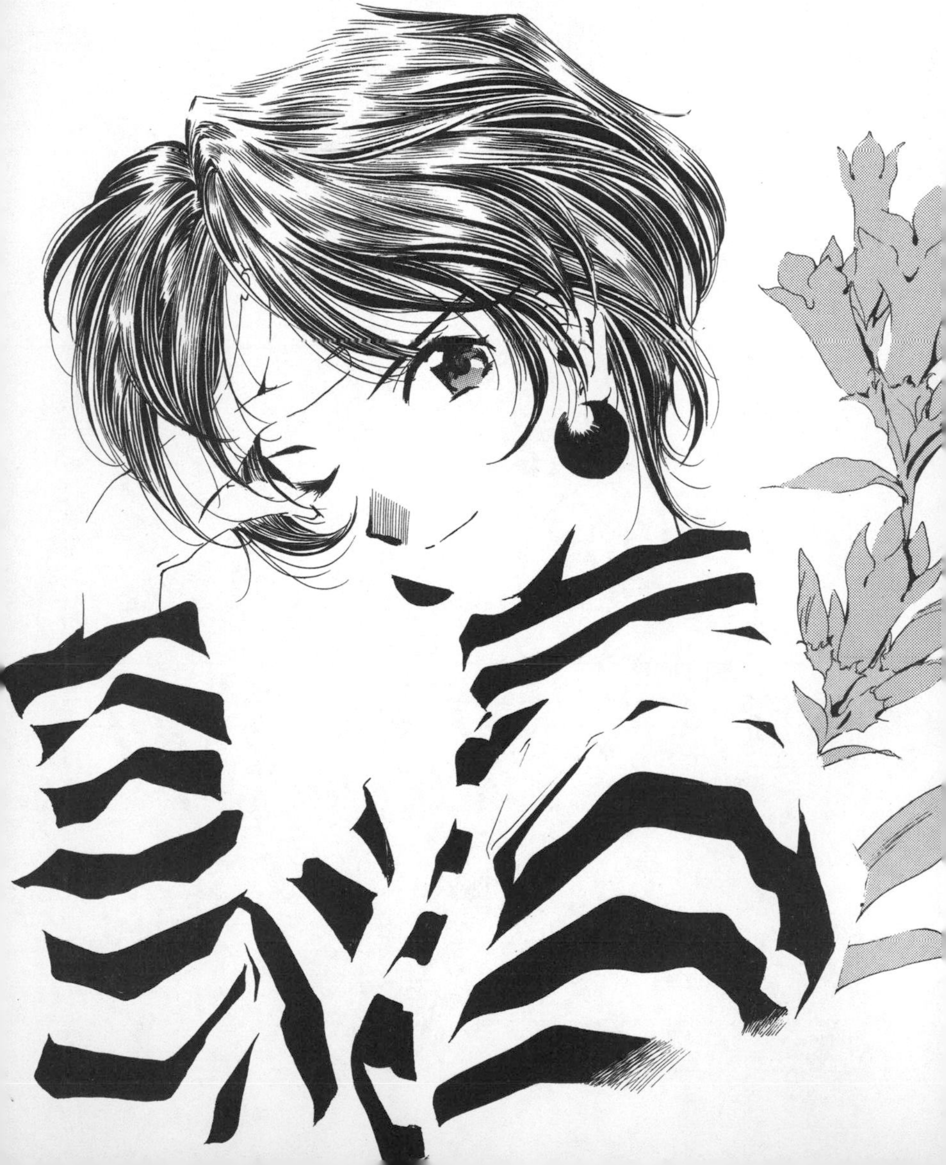

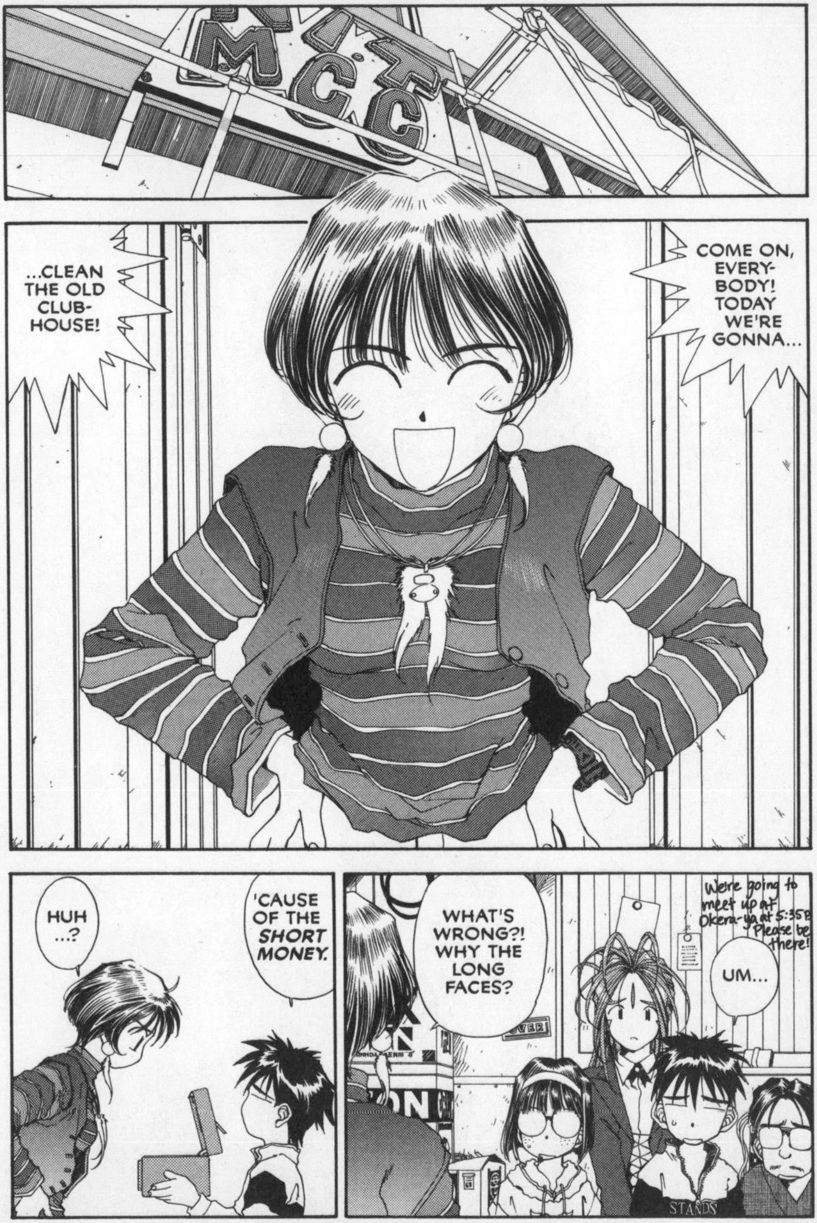
COME ON, EVERYBODY! TODAY WE'RE GONNA...
...CLEAN THE OLD CLUB-HOUSE!
We're going to meet up at Okera-ya at 5:35P Please be there!
UM...
WHAT'S WRONG?! WHY THE LONG FACES?
STANDS
'CAUSE OF THE *SHORT MONEY.*
HUH ...?

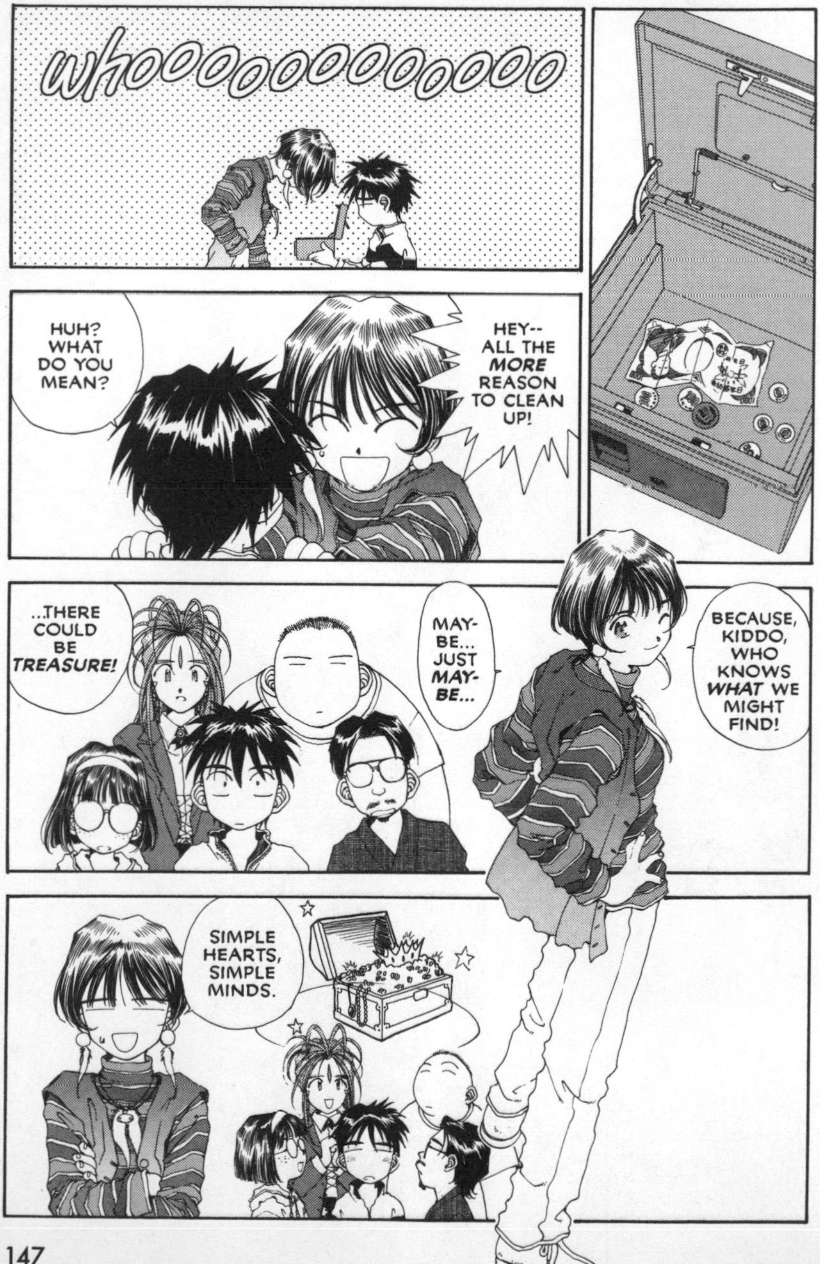
whoooooooooooo
HEY-- ALL THE MORE REASON TO CLEAN UP!
HUH? WHAT DO YOU MEAN?
BECAUSE, KIDDO, WHO KNOWS WHAT WE MIGHT FIND!
MAY-BE... JUST MAY-BE...
...THERE COULD BE TREASURE!
SIMPLE HEARTS, SIMPLE MINDS.

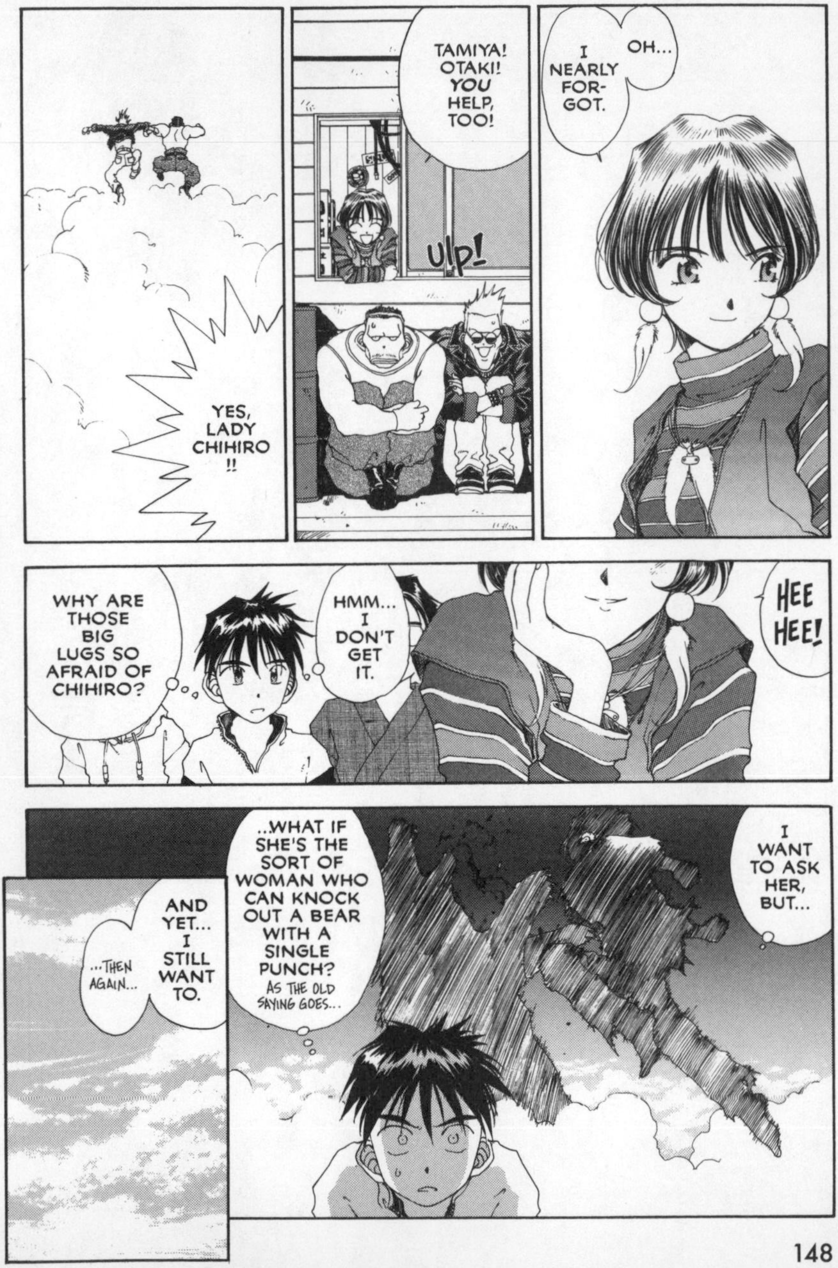
OH... I NEARLY FORGOT.
TAMIYA! OTAKI! *YOU* HELP, TOO!
ULP!
YES, LADY CHIHIRO !!
HEE HEE!
HMM... I DON'T GET IT.
WHY ARE THOSE BIG LUGS SO AFRAID OF CHIHIRO?
I WANT TO ASK HER, BUT...
...WHAT IF SHE'S THE SORT OF WOMAN WHO CAN KNOCK OUT A BEAR WITH A SINGLE PUNCH?
AS THE OLD SAYING GOES...
...THEN AGAIN...
AND YET... I STILL WANT TO.

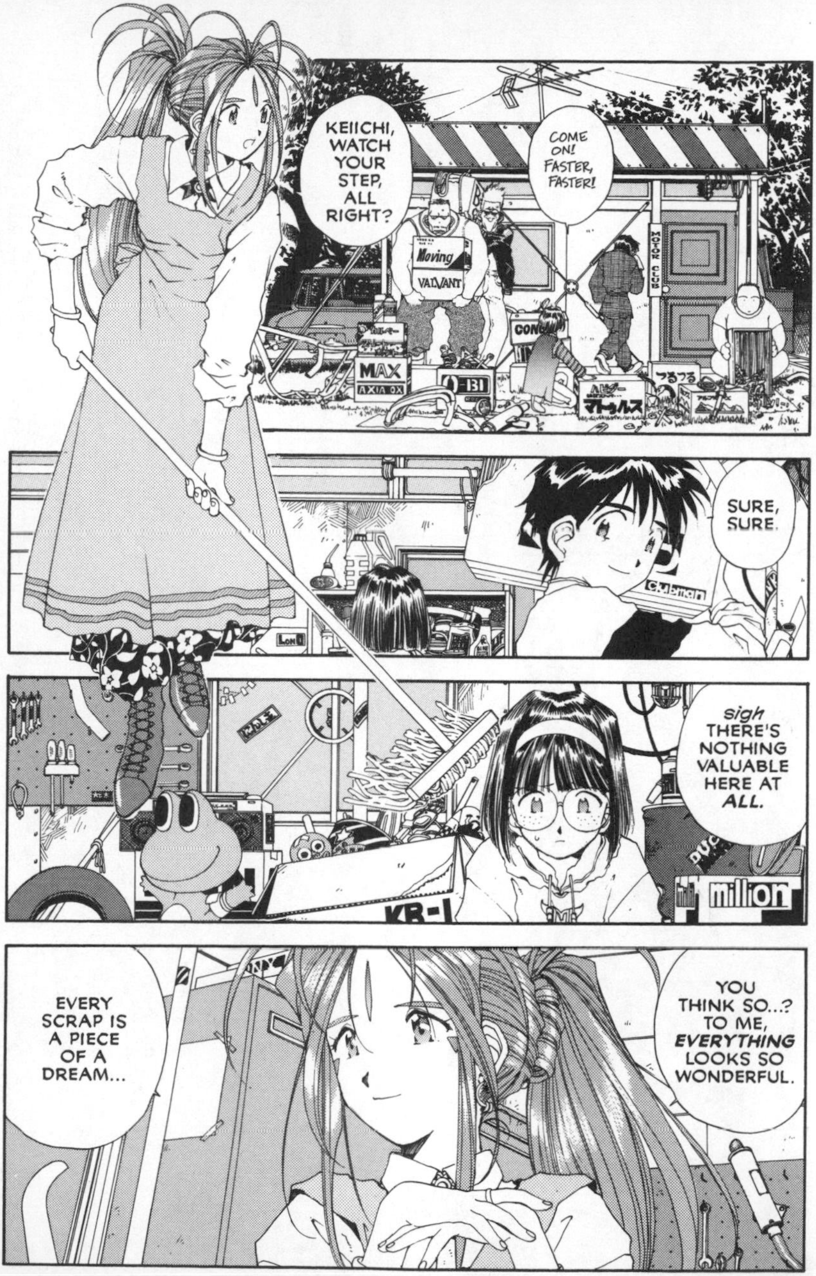
COME ON! FASTER, FASTER!
KEIICHI, WATCH YOUR STEP, ALL RIGHT?
MOTOR CLUB
Moving
VALVANT
MAX
AXIA OX
SURE, SURE.
sigh THERE'S NOTHING VALUABLE HERE AT ***ALL.***
million
KB-1
YOU THINK SO...? TO ME, ***EVERYTHING*** LOOKS SO WONDERFUL.
EVERY SCRAP IS A PIECE OF A DREAM...

YES.

WHAT?! D-DID YOU ACTUALLY *FIND* SOME-THING?!

K'TAK

ISN'T THAT ...?

OH, MY ...?

SUMM

WOW!

A PIGGY BANK!

A BIT ON THE LOW SIDE.

WOW. ¥325.

...

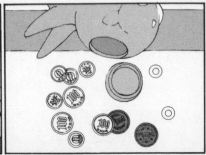

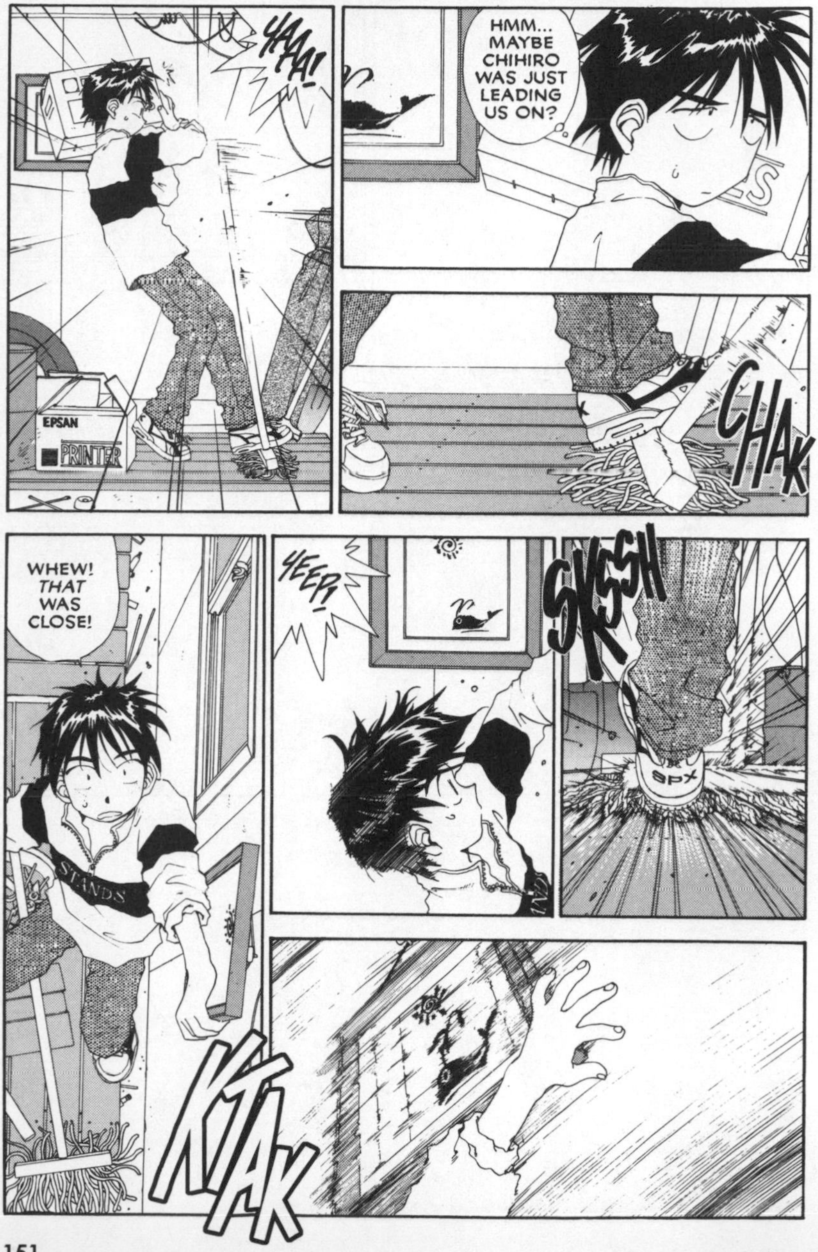
HMM... MAYBE CHIHIRO WAS JUST LEADING US ON?
CHAK
YAAAA!
SKSSH
YEEP!
KTAK
WHEW! *THAT* WAS CLOSE!

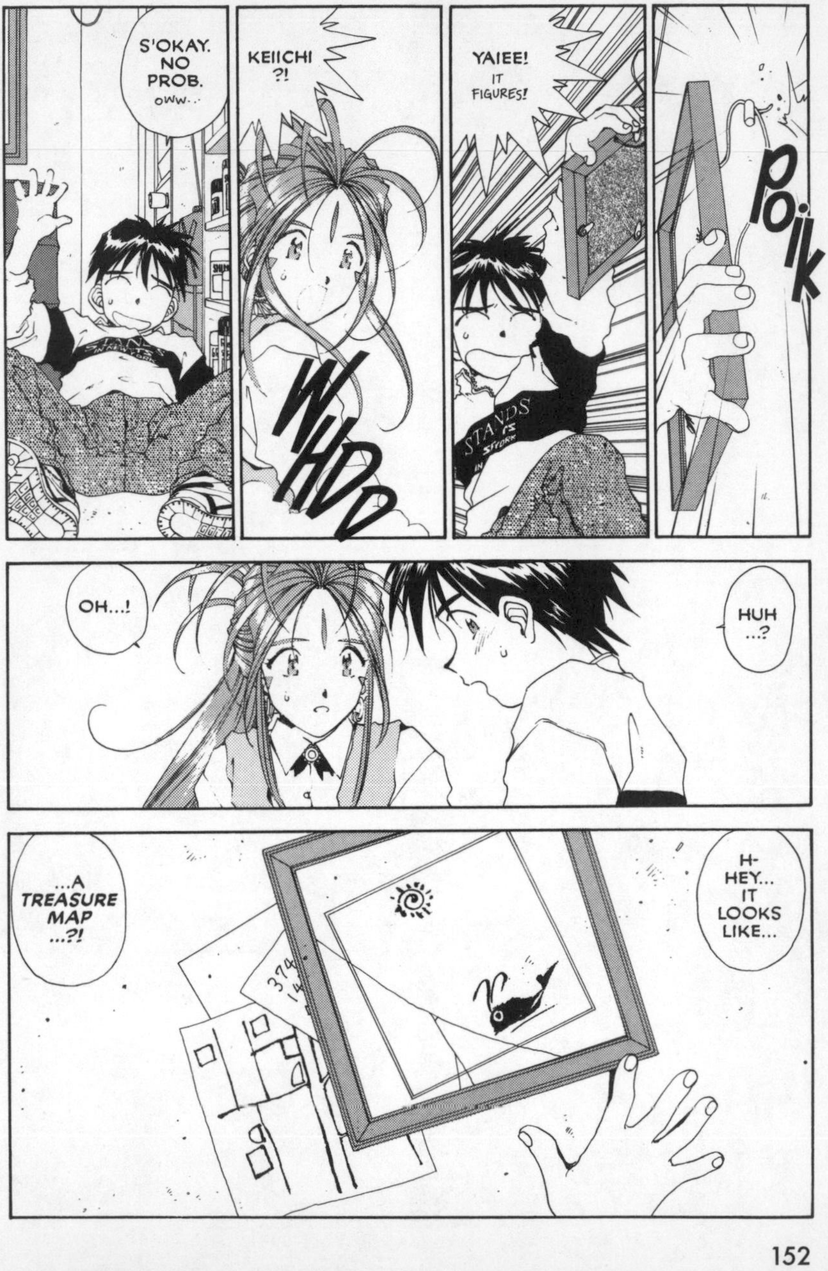
POIK
YAIEE! IT FIGURES!
KEIICHI ?!
WHOO
S'OKAY. NO PROB. OWW...
HUH ...?
OH...!
H-HEY... IT LOOKS LIKE...
...A TREASURE MAP ...?!

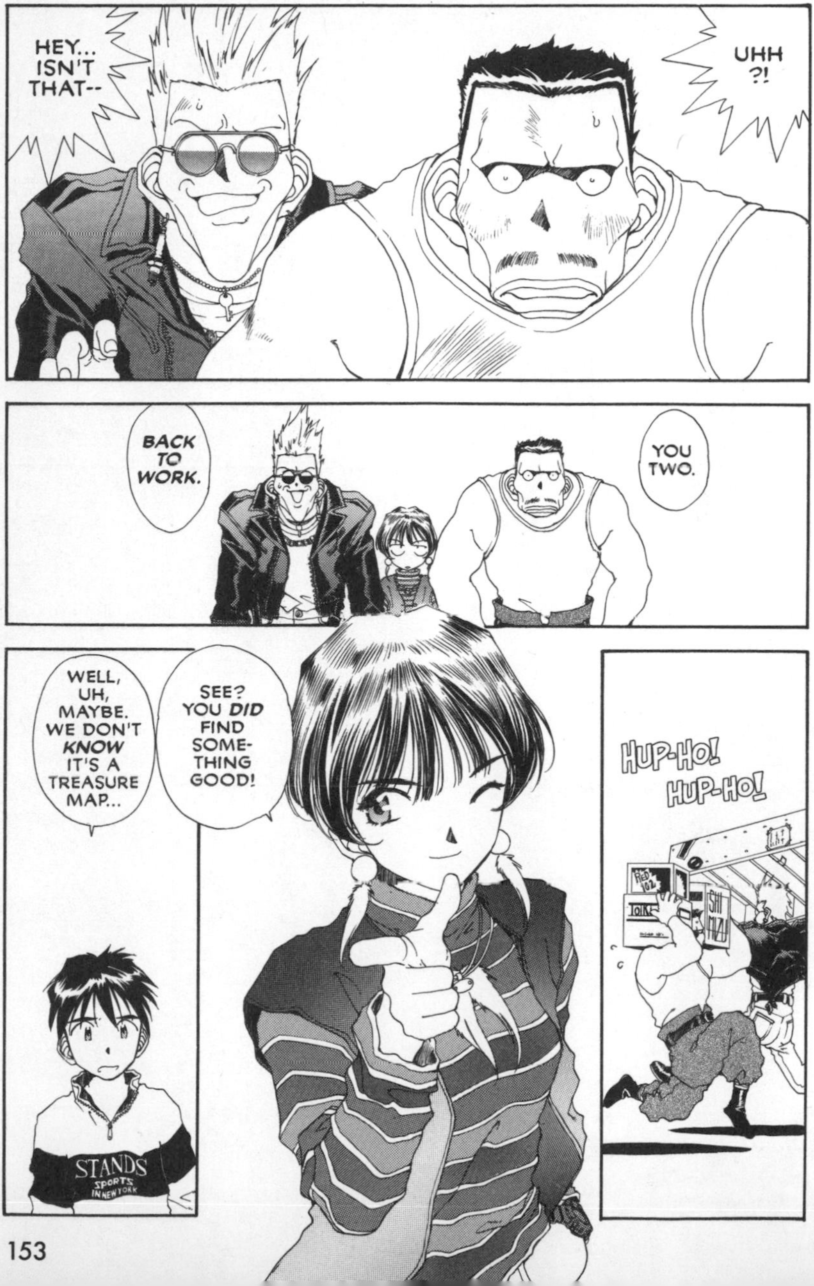
UHH ?!
HEY... ISN'T THAT--
YOU TWO.
BACK TO WORK.
HUP-HO!
HUP-HO!
SEE? YOU *DID* FIND SOME-THING GOOD!
WELL, UH, MAYBE. WE DON'T *KNOW* IT'S A TREASURE MAP...
STANDS SPORTS IN NEW YORK

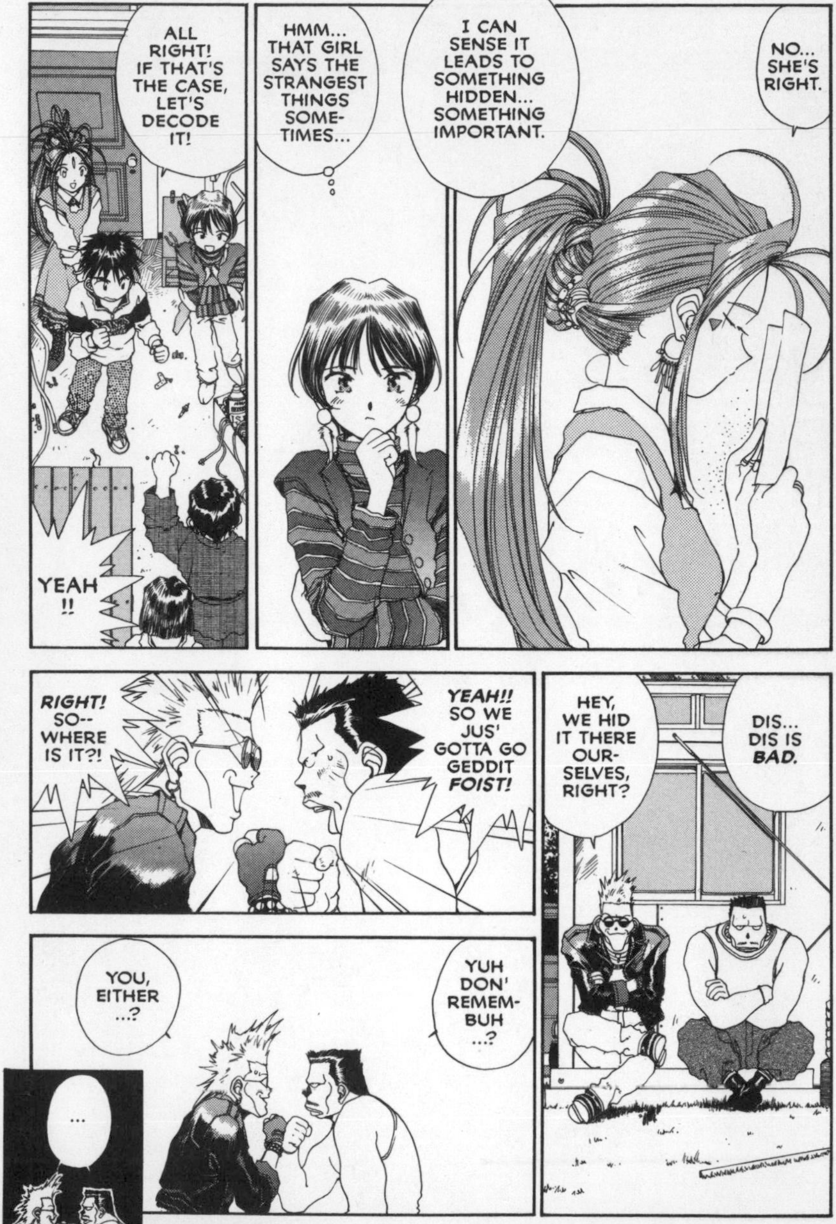
NO... SHE'S RIGHT.
I CAN SENSE IT LEADS TO SOMETHING HIDDEN... SOMETHING IMPORTANT.
HMM... THAT GIRL SAYS THE STRANGEST THINGS SOME-TIMES...
ALL RIGHT! IF THAT'S THE CASE, LET'S DECODE IT!
YEAH !!
DIS... DIS IS *BAD.*
HEY, WE HID IT THERE OUR-SELVES, RIGHT?
YEAH!! SO WE JUS' GOTTA GO GEDDIT *FOIST!*
RIGHT! SO-- WHERE IS IT?!
YUH DON' REMEM-BUH ...?
YOU, EITHER ...?
...

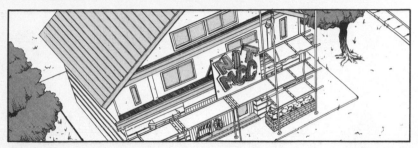

37421
143586
451327869
91243876
751439
143586
751439
7216349
58927
143586

THIS MAP DOESN'T TELL US WHERE TO START, *OR* THE GOAL!

YEESH ...!

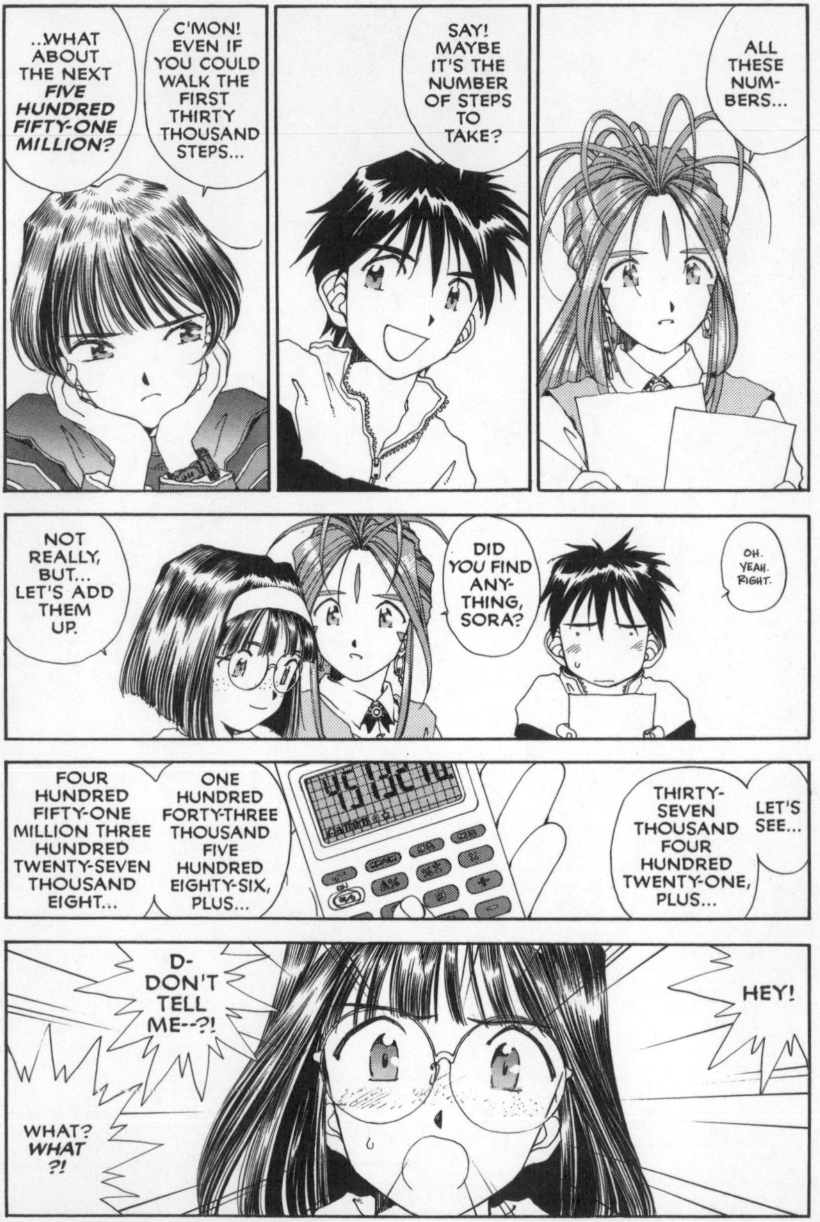
ALL THESE NUM-BERS...
SAY! MAYBE IT'S THE NUMBER OF STEPS TO TAKE?
C'MON! EVEN IF YOU COULD WALK THE FIRST THIRTY THOUSAND STEPS...
...WHAT ABOUT THE NEXT *FIVE HUNDRED FIFTY-ONE MILLION?*
OH. YEAH. RIGHT.
DID *YOU* FIND ANY-THING, SORA?
NOT REALLY, BUT... LET'S ADD THEM UP.
LET'S SEE...
THIRTY-SEVEN THOUSAND FOUR HUNDRED TWENTY-ONE, PLUS...
ONE HUNDRED FORTY-THREE THOUSAND FIVE HUNDRED EIGHTY-SIX, PLUS...
FOUR HUNDRED FIFTY-ONE MILLION THREE HUNDRED TWENTY-SEVEN THOUSAND EIGHT...
HEY!
D-DON'T TELL ME--?!
WHAT? *WHAT ?!*

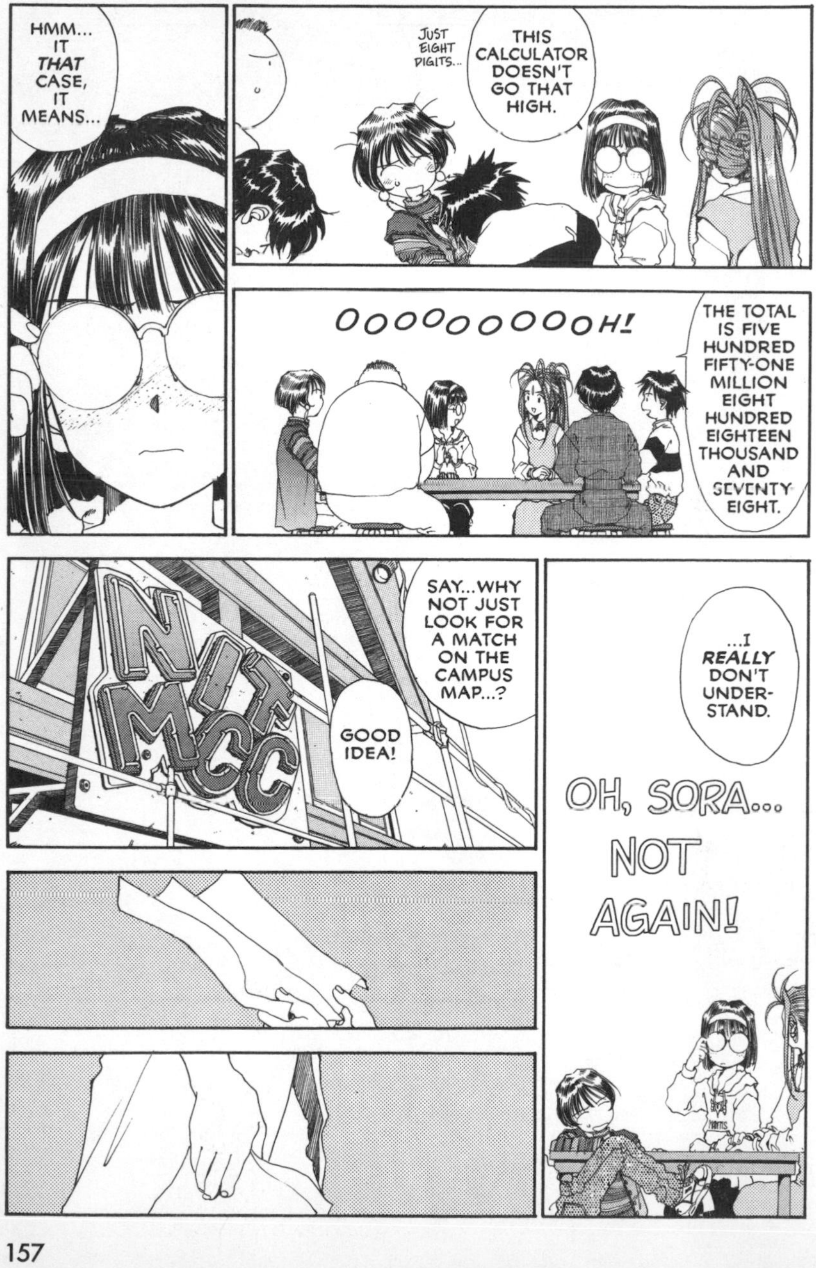
THIS CALCULATOR DOESN'T GO THAT HIGH.
JUST EIGHT DIGITS...
THE TOTAL IS FIVE HUNDRED FIFTY-ONE MILLION EIGHT HUNDRED EIGHTEEN THOUSAND AND SEVENTY-EIGHT.
OOOOOOOOOOH!
HMM... IT *THAT* CASE, IT MEANS...
...I *REALLY* DON'T UNDER-STAND.
OH, SORA... NOT AGAIN!
SAY...WHY NOT JUST LOOK FOR A MATCH ON THE CAMPUS MAP...?
GOOD IDEA!
NIT MCC

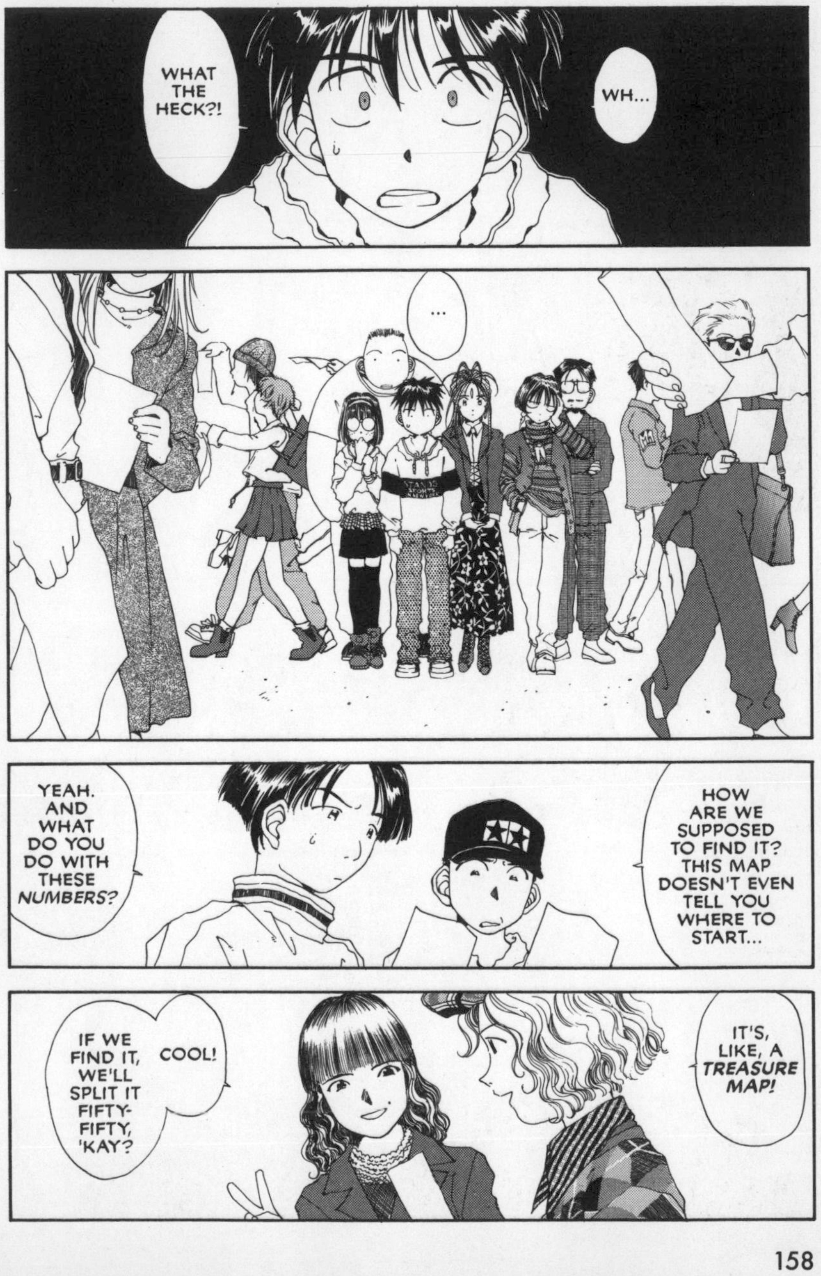
WH...
WHAT THE HECK?!
...
HOW ARE WE SUPPOSED TO FIND IT? THIS MAP DOESN'T EVEN TELL YOU WHERE TO START...
YEAH. AND WHAT DO YOU DO WITH THESE *NUMBERS?*
IT'S, LIKE, A *TREASURE MAP!*
COOL!
IF WE FIND IT, WE'LL SPLIT IT FIFTY-FIFTY, 'KAY?

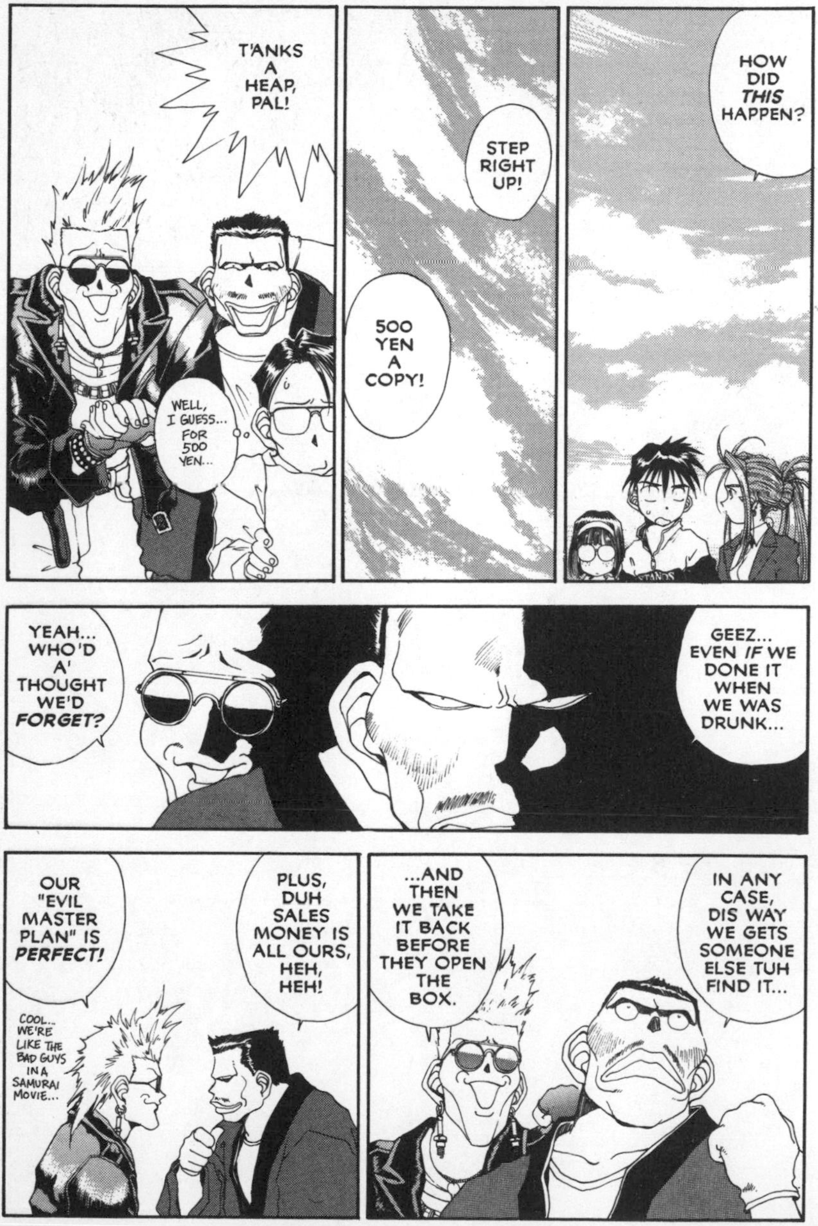
HOW DID *THIS* HAPPEN?
STEP RIGHT UP!
500 YEN A COPY!
T'ANKS A HEAP, PAL!
WELL, I GUESS... FOR 500 YEN...
GEEZ... EVEN *IF* WE DONE IT WHEN WE WAS DRUNK...
YEAH... WHO'D A' THOUGHT WE'D *FORGET?*
IN ANY CASE, DIS WAY WE GETS SOMEONE ELSE TUH FIND IT...
...AND THEN WE TAKE IT BACK BEFORE THEY OPEN THE BOX.
PLUS, DUH SALES MONEY IS ALL OURS, HEH, HEH!
OUR "EVIL MASTER PLAN" IS *PERFECT!*
COOL... WE'RE LIKE THE BAD GUYS IN A SAMURAI MOVIE...

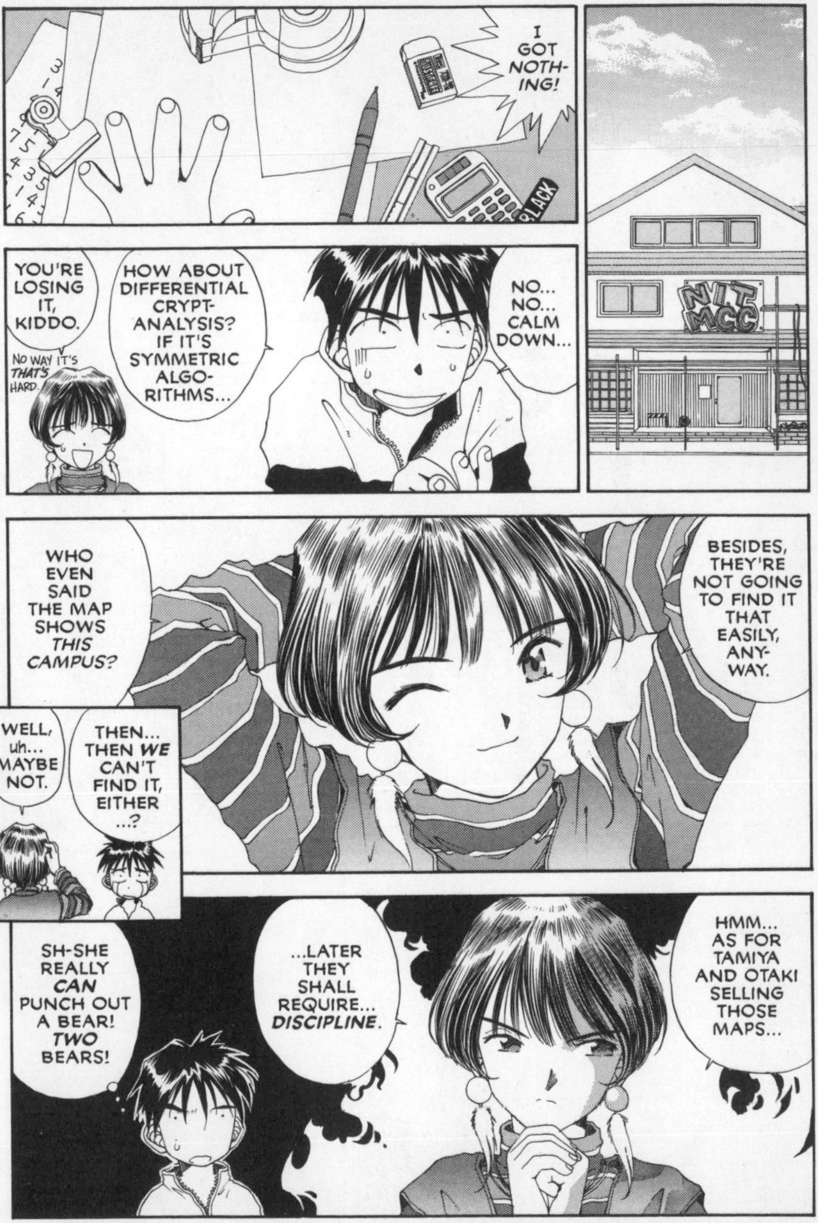
I GOT NOTHING!
NO... NO... CALM DOWN...
HOW ABOUT DIFFERENTIAL CRYPT-ANALYSIS? IF IT'S SYMMETRIC ALGO-RITHMS...
YOU'RE LOSING IT, KIDDO.
NO WAY IT'S THAT'S HARD.
BESIDES, THEY'RE NOT GOING TO FIND IT THAT EASILY, ANY-WAY.
WHO EVEN SAID THE MAP SHOWS THIS CAMPUS?
THEN... THEN WE CAN'T FIND IT, EITHER ...?
WELL, uh... MAYBE NOT.
HMM... AS FOR TAMIYA AND OTAKI SELLING THOSE MAPS...
...LATER THEY SHALL REQUIRE... DISCIPLINE.
SH-SHE REALLY CAN PUNCH OUT A BEAR! TWO BEARS!

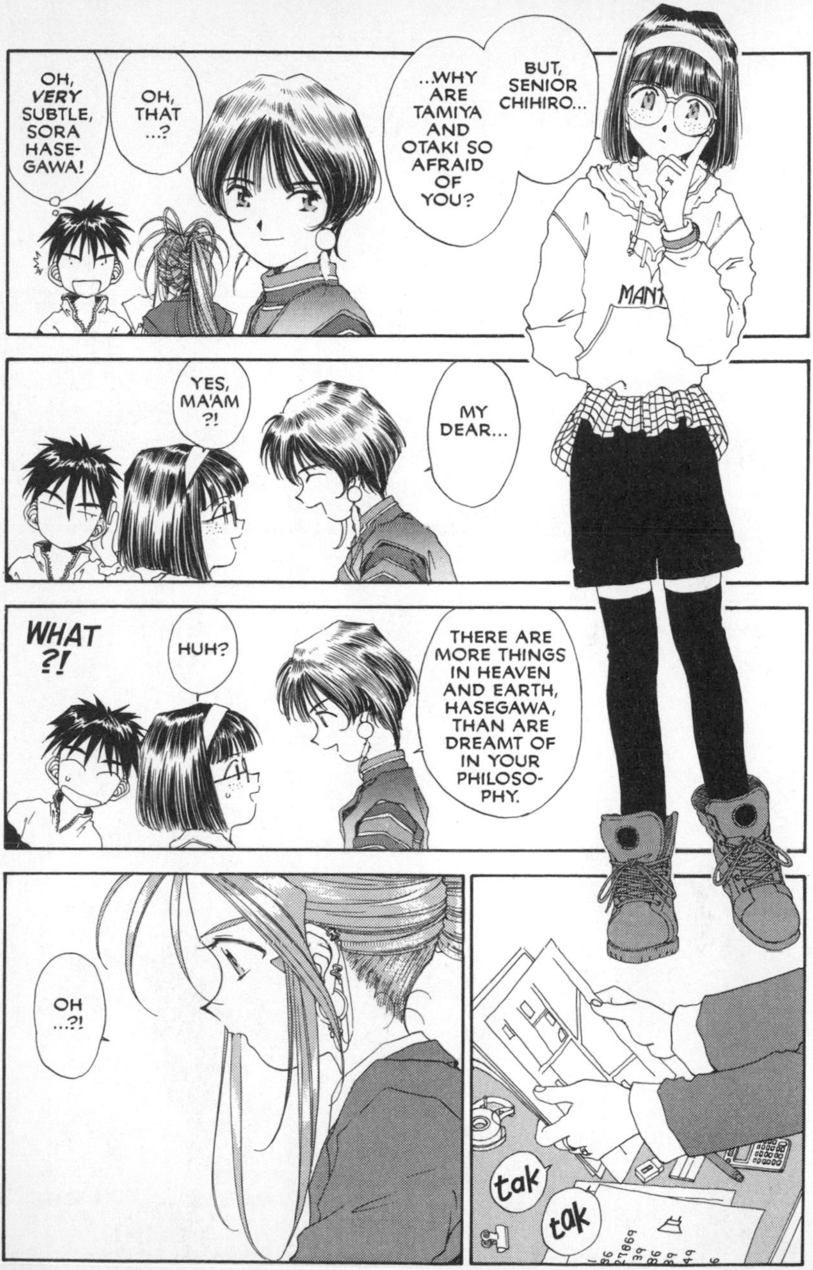
BUT, SENIOR CHIHIRO...
...WHY ARE TAMIYA AND OTAKI SO AFRAID OF YOU?
OH, THAT ...?
OH, *VERY* SUBTLE, SORA HASE-GAWA!
MY DEAR...
YES, MA'AM ?!
THERE ARE MORE THINGS IN HEAVEN AND EARTH, HASEGAWA, THAN ARE DREAMT OF IN YOUR PHILOSO-PHY.
HUH?
WHAT ?!
tak
tak
OH ...?!

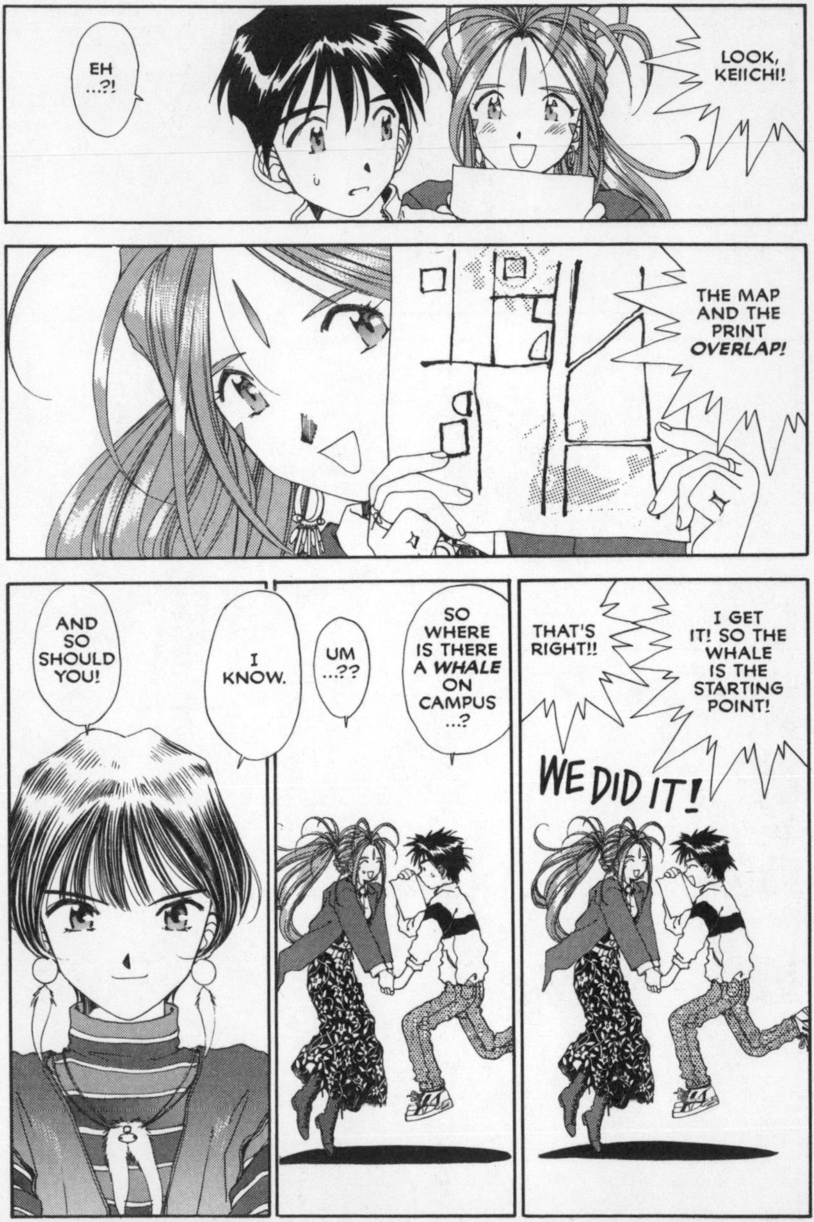
LOOK, KEIICHI!
EH ...?!
THE MAP AND THE PRINT *OVERLAP!*
I GET IT! SO THE WHALE IS THE STARTING POINT!
THAT'S RIGHT!!
WE DID IT!
SO WHERE IS THERE A *WHALE* ON CAMPUS ...?
UM ...??
I KNOW.
AND SO SHOULD YOU!

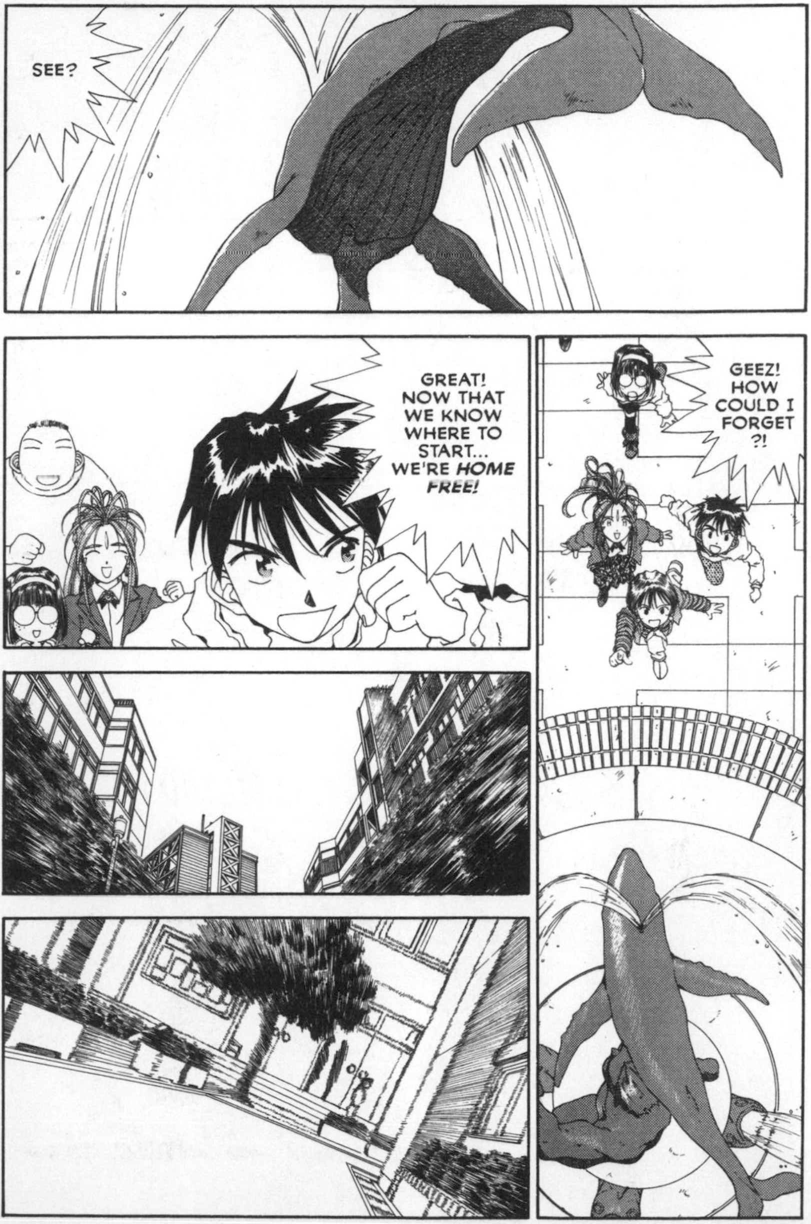
SEE?
GEEZ! HOW COULD I FORGET ?!
GREAT! NOW THAT WE KNOW WHERE TO START... WE'RE *HOME FREE!*

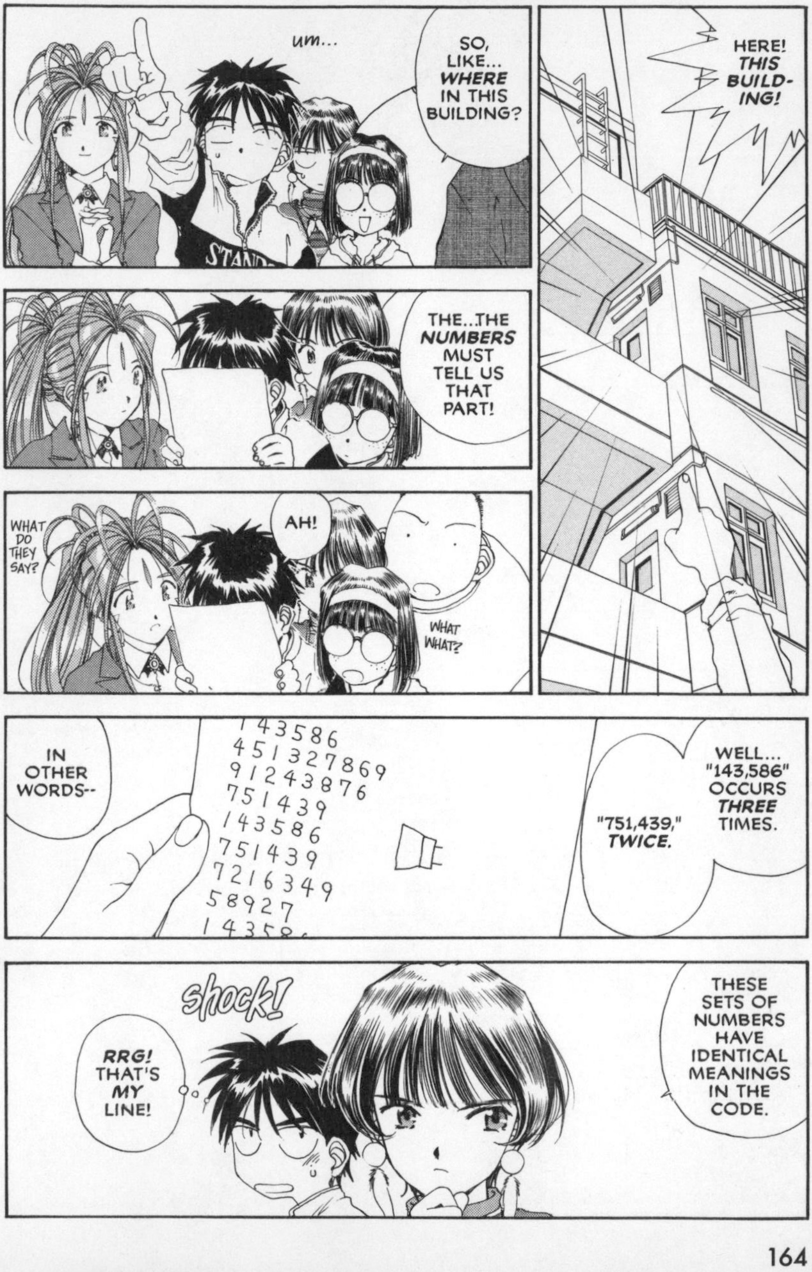

HERE! *THIS* *BUILD-ING!*
SO, LIKE... *WHERE* IN THIS BUILDING?
um...
THE...THE *NUMBERS* MUST TELL US THAT PART!
AH!
WHAT WHAT?
WHAT DO THEY SAY?
WELL... "143,586" OCCURS *THREE* TIMES.
"751,439," *TWICE.*
IN OTHER WORDS--
143586
451327869
912433876
751439
143586
751439
7216349
58927
THESE SETS OF NUMBERS HAVE IDENTICAL MEANINGS IN THE CODE.
shock!
RRG! THAT'S *MY* LINE!

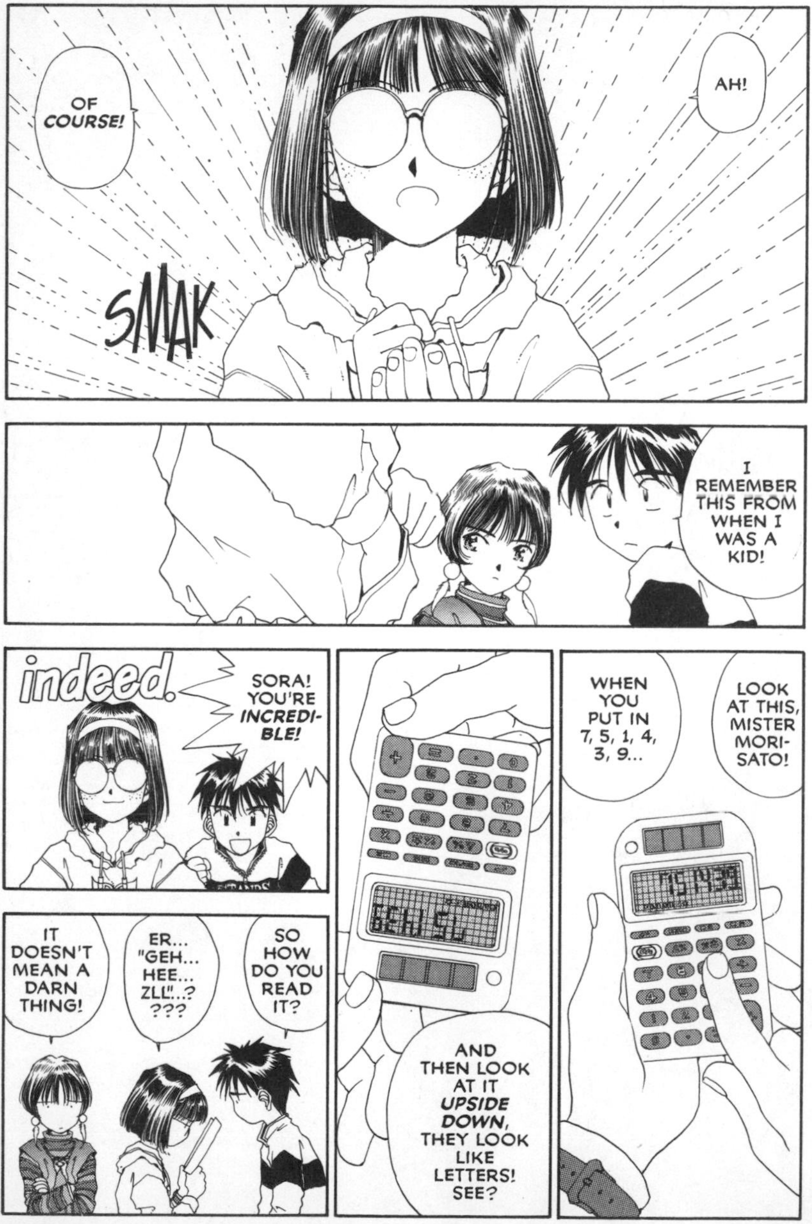
AH!
OF COURSE!
SMAK
I REMEMBER THIS FROM WHEN I WAS A KID!
LOOK AT THIS, MISTER MORI-SATO!
WHEN YOU PUT IN 7, 5, 1, 4, 3, 9...
AND THEN LOOK AT IT *UPSIDE DOWN*, THEY LOOK LIKE LETTERS! SEE?
SORA! YOU'RE *INCREDI-BLE!*
indeed.
SO HOW DO YOU READ IT?
ER... "GEH... HEE... ZLL"..? ???
IT DOESN'T MEAN A DARN THING!

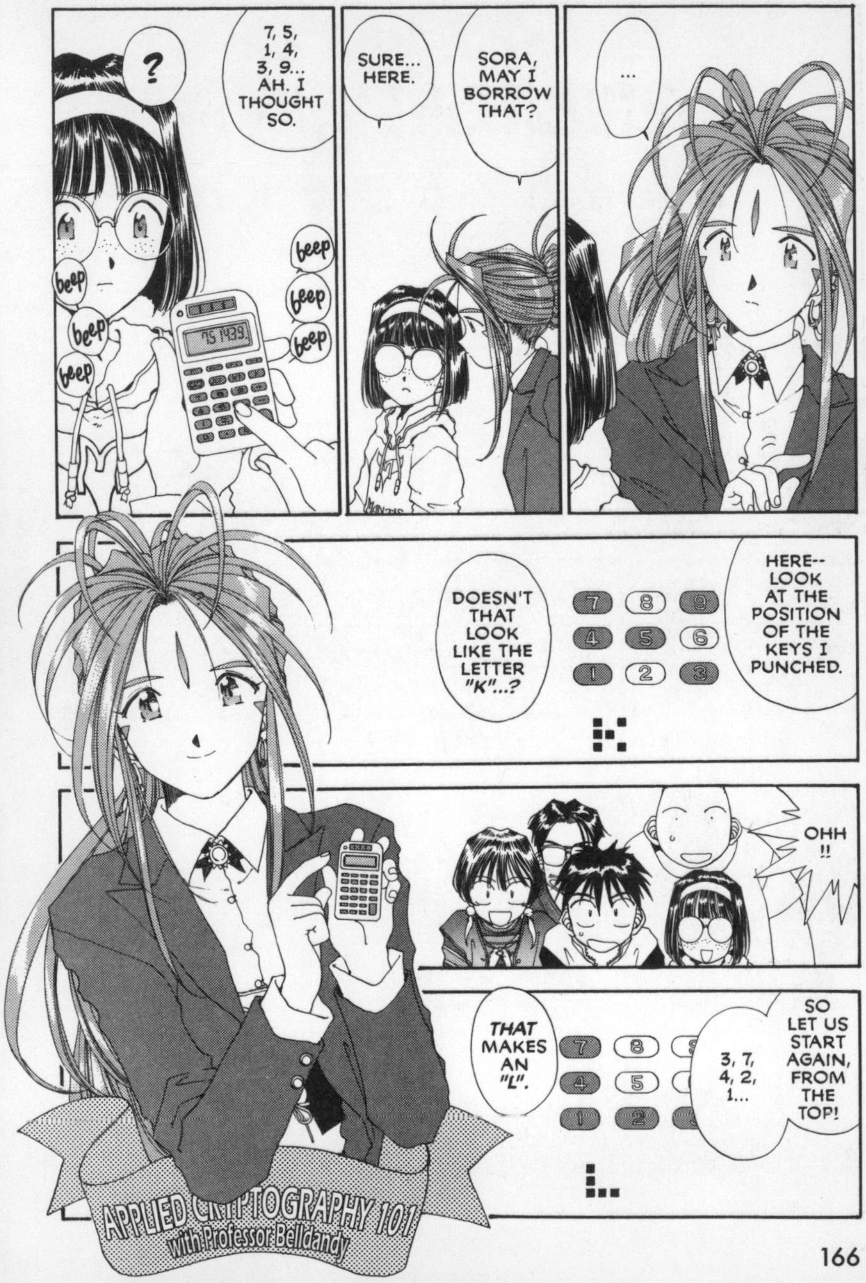
...
SORA, MAY I BORROW THAT?
SURE... HERE.
?
7, 5, 1, 4, 3, 9... AH. I THOUGHT SO.
beep
beep
beep
beep
beep
beep
beep
751439.
HERE-- LOOK AT THE POSITION OF THE KEYS I PUNCHED.
DOESN'T THAT LOOK LIKE THE LETTER *"K"*...?
7 8 9
4 5 6
1 2 3
OHH !!
SO LET US START AGAIN, FROM THE TOP!
3, 7, 4, 2, 1...
THAT MAKES AN *"L"*.
7 8
4 5
1 2
APPLIED CRYPTOGRAPHY 101
with Professor Belldandy

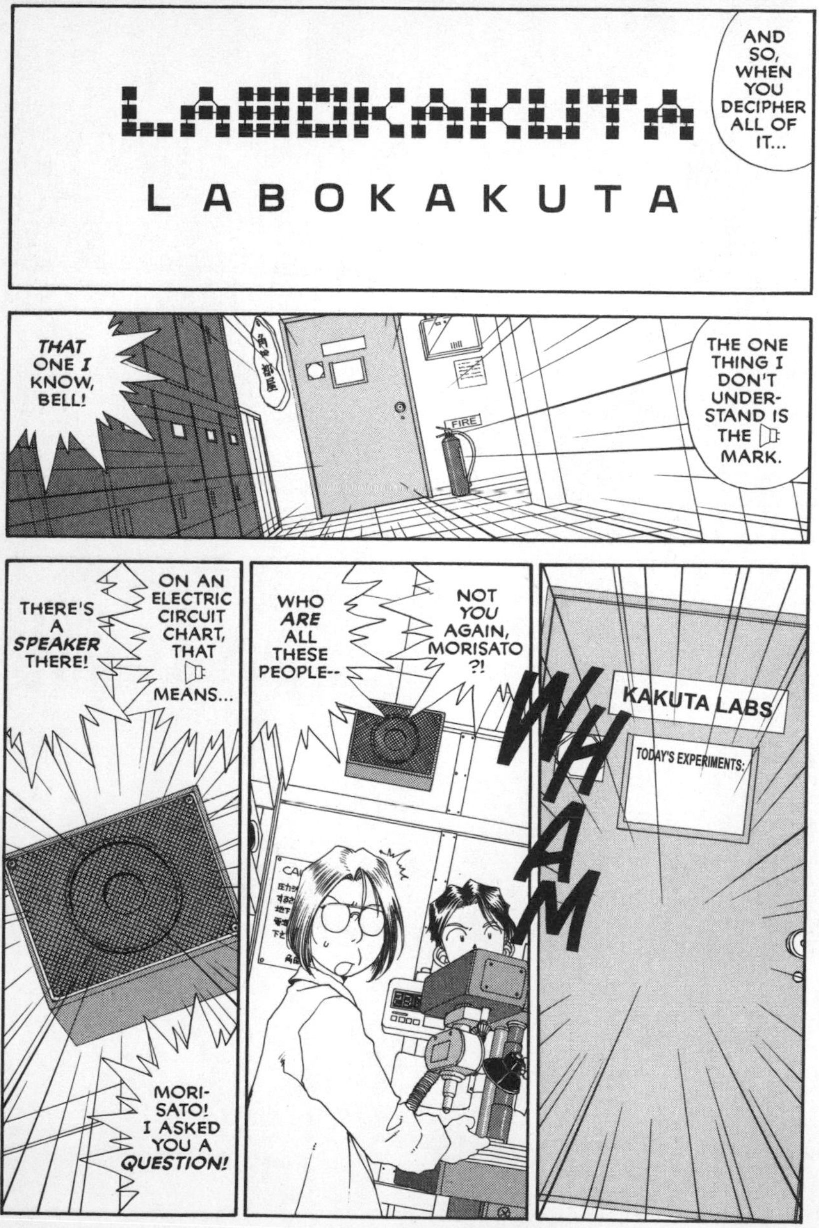
AND SO, WHEN YOU DECIPHER ALL OF IT...
LABOKAKUTA
LABOKAKUTA
THE ONE THING I DON'T UNDERSTAND IS THE MARK.
THAT ONE I KNOW, BELL!
KAKUTA LABS
TODAY'S EXPERIMENTS:
WHAM
NOT YOU AGAIN, MORISATO?!
WHO ARE ALL THESE PEOPLE--
ON AN ELECTRIC CIRCUIT CHART, THAT MEANS...
THERE'S A SPEAKER THERE!
MORI-SATO! I ASKED YOU A QUESTION!

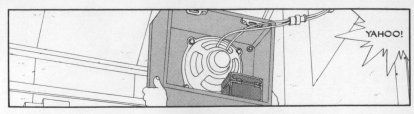

YAHOO!

HERE IT IS!

BUT... IT'S *LOCKED.*

WE DID IT!

OH...? THIS DRAWING...!

UH-OH!

REALLY?!

I THINK I CAN OPEN THIS.

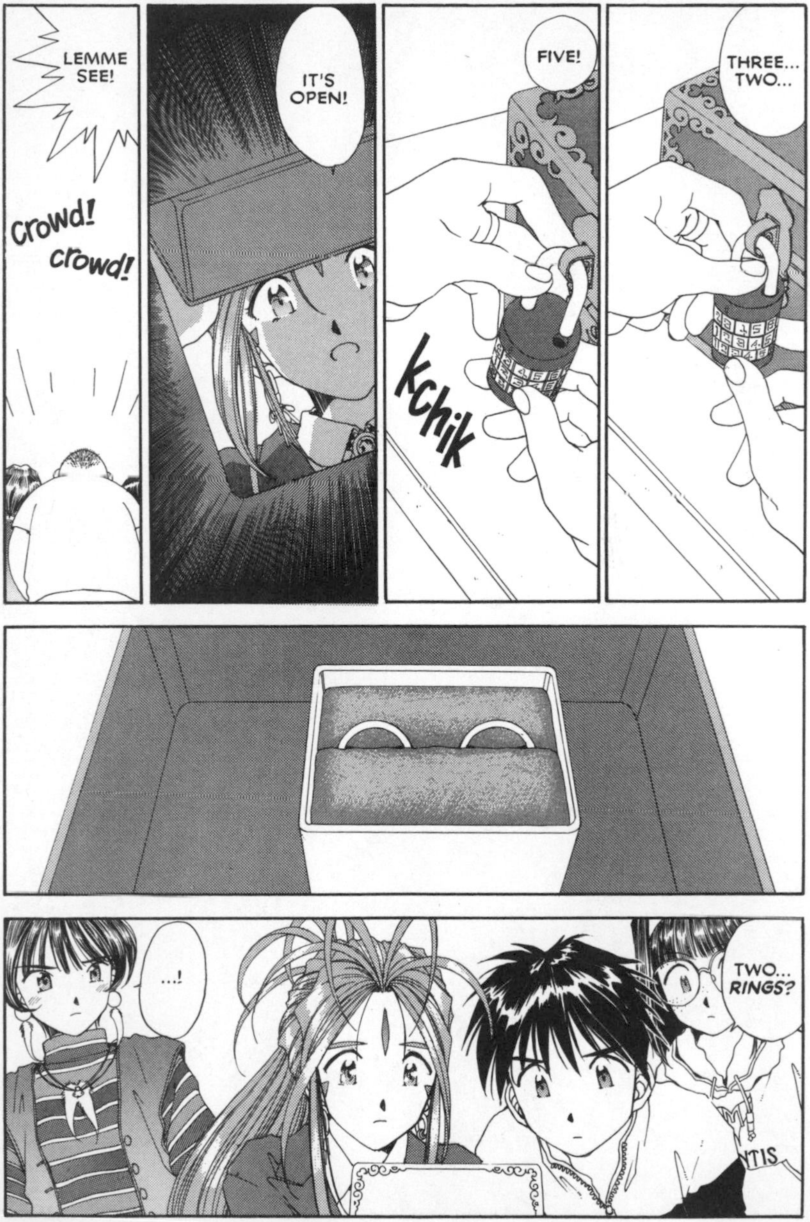
THREE... TWO...
FIVE!
kchik
IT'S OPEN!
LEMME SEE!
crowd!
crowd!
TWO... RINGS?
...!

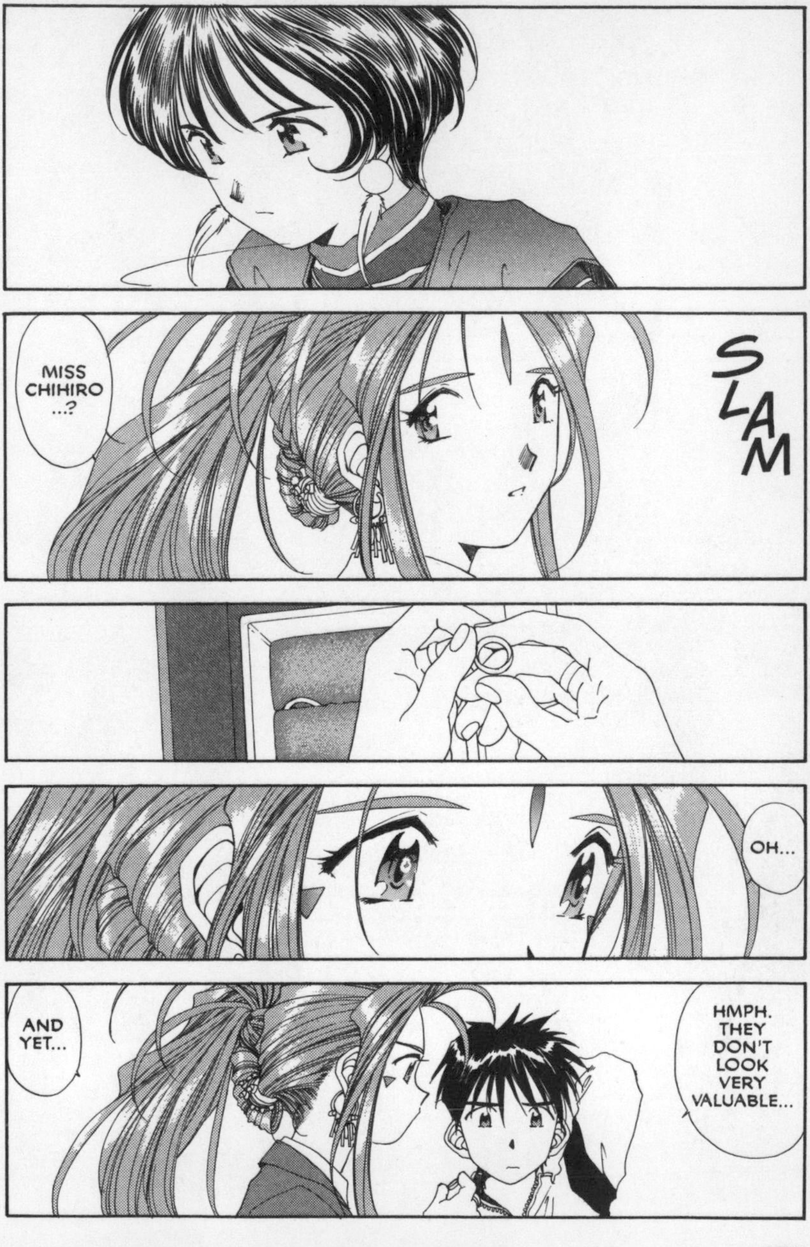
SLAM
MISS CHIHIRO ...?
OH...
HMPH. THEY DON'T LOOK VERY VALUABLE...
AND YET...

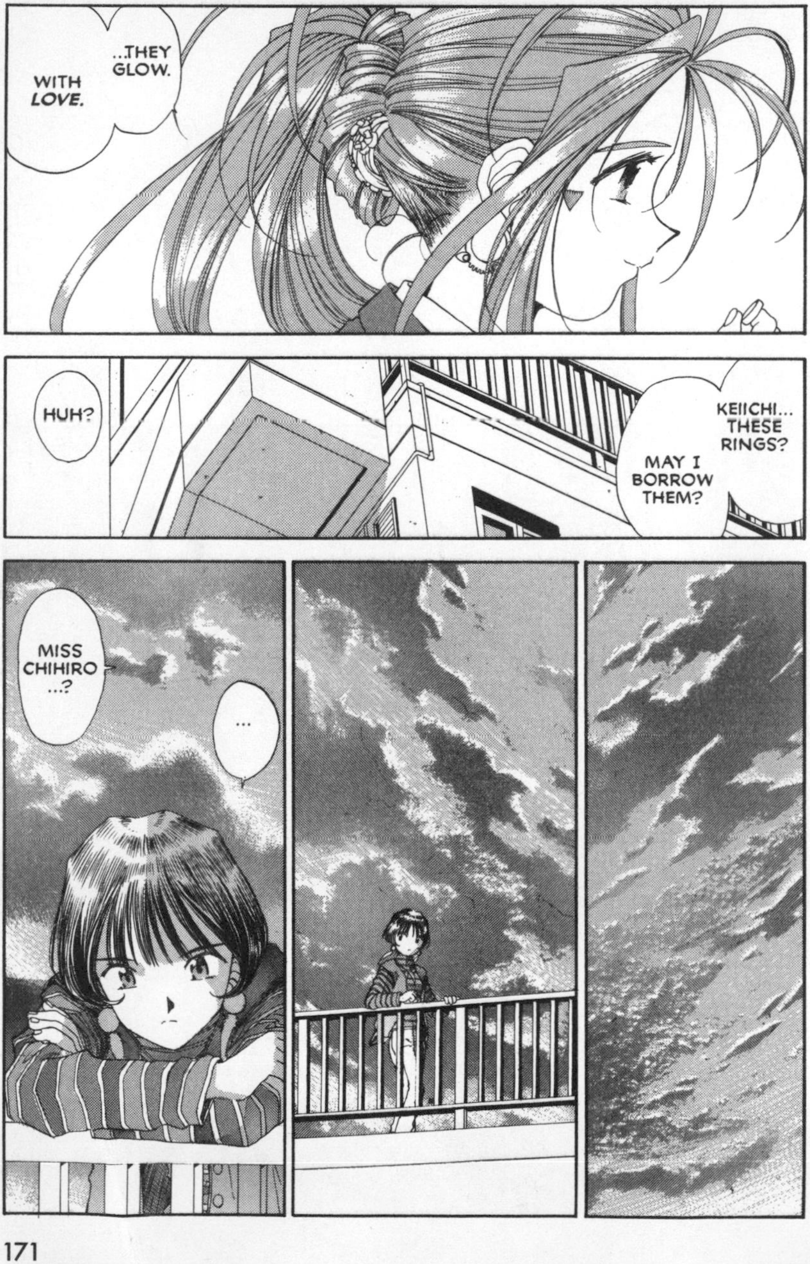

...THEY GLOW.
WITH *LOVE.*
KEIICHI... THESE RINGS?
MAY I BORROW THEM?
HUH?
MISS CHIHIRO ...?
...

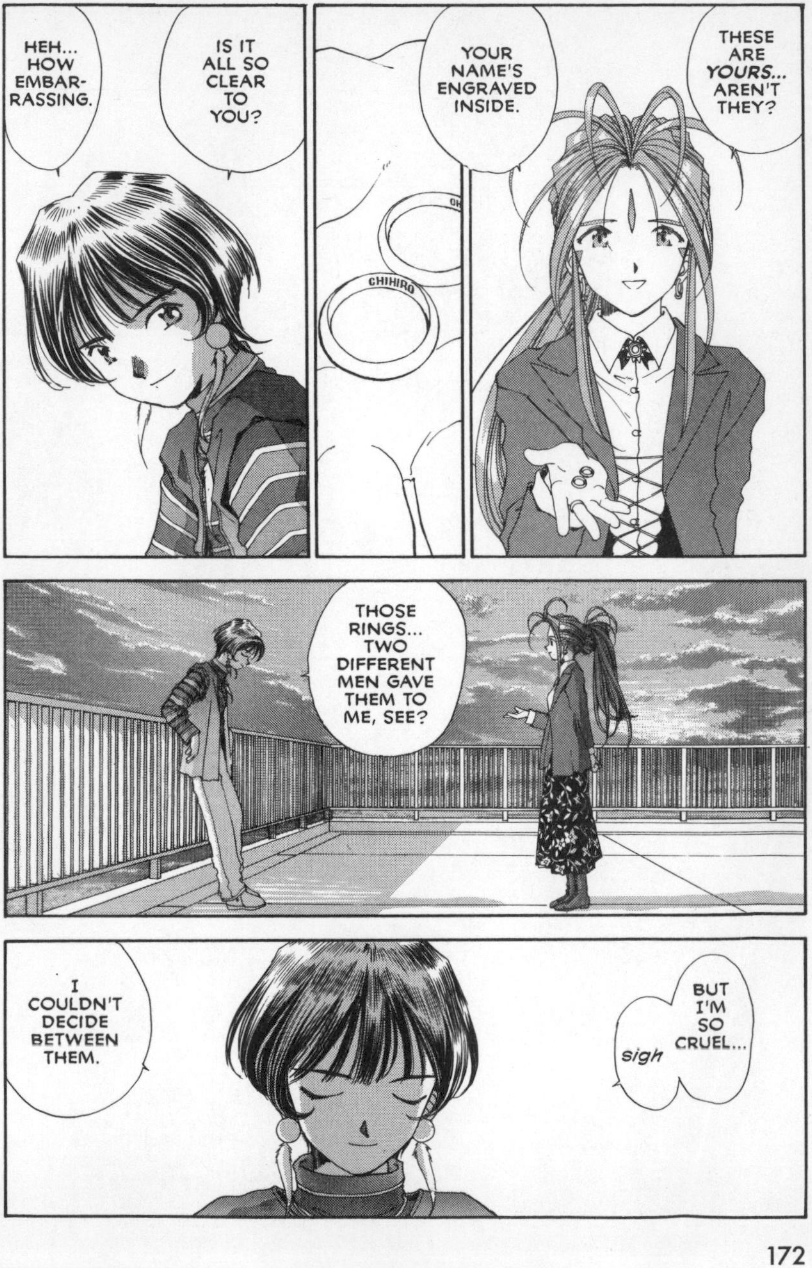
THESE ARE *YOURS*... AREN'T THEY?
YOUR NAME'S ENGRAVED INSIDE.
CHIHIRO
IS IT ALL SO CLEAR TO YOU?
HEH... HOW EMBARRASSING.
THOSE RINGS... TWO DIFFERENT MEN GAVE THEM TO ME, SEE?
BUT I'M SO CRUEL... *sigh*
I COULDN'T DECIDE BETWEEN THEM.

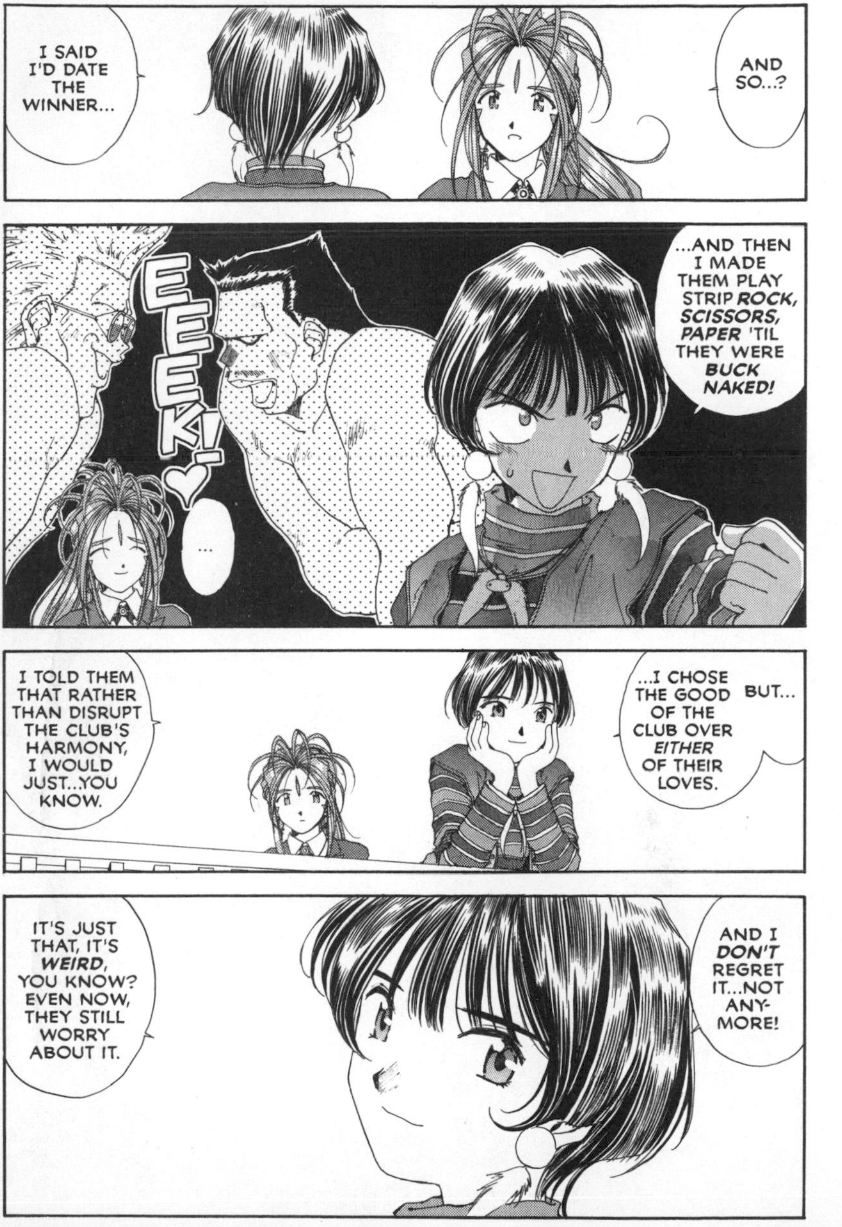
AND SO...?
I SAID I'D DATE THE WINNER...
...AND THEN I MADE THEM PLAY STRIP ROCK, SCISSORS, PAPER 'TIL THEY WERE BUCK NAKED!
EEEK!♥
...
BUT...
...I CHOSE THE GOOD OF THE CLUB OVER EITHER OF THEIR LOVES.
I TOLD THEM THAT RATHER THAN DISRUPT THE CLUB'S HARMONY, I WOULD JUST...YOU KNOW.
AND I DON'T REGRET IT...NOT ANY-MORE!
IT'S JUST THAT, IT'S WEIRD, YOU KNOW? EVEN NOW, THEY STILL WORRY ABOUT IT.

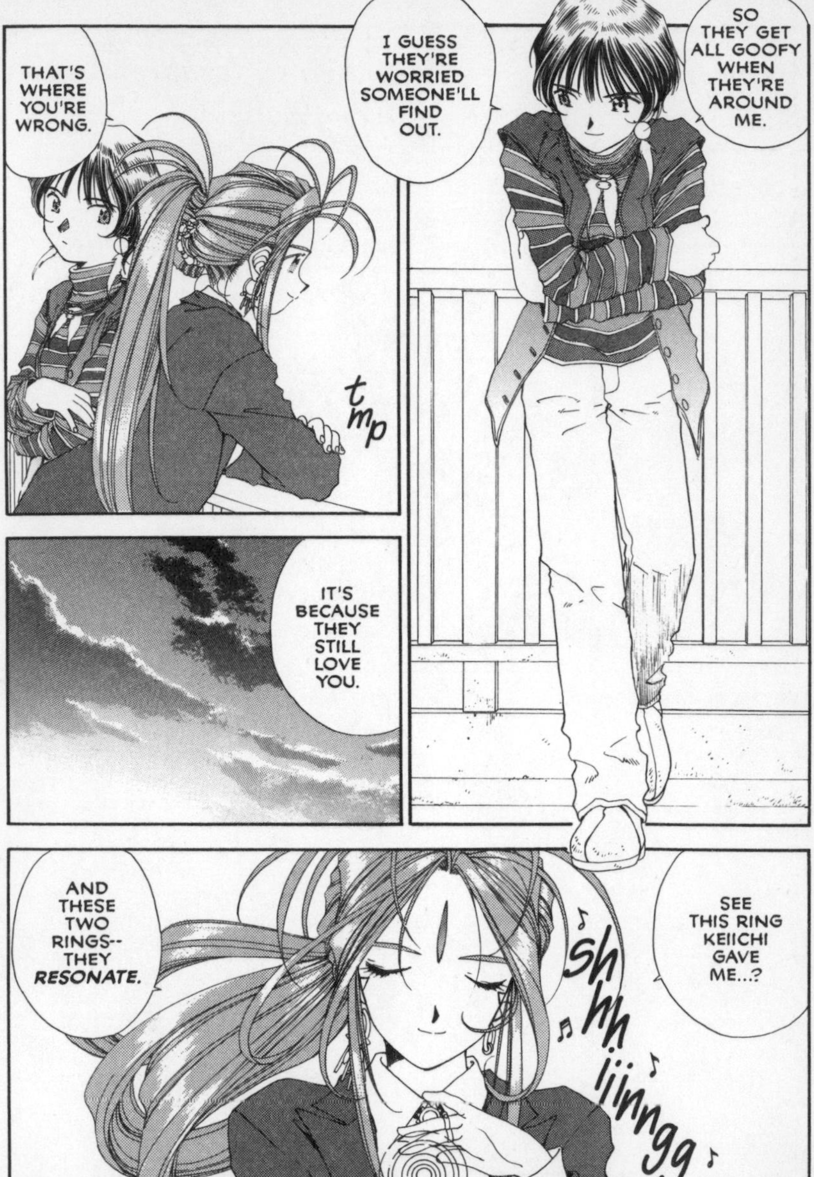
SO THEY GET ALL GOOFY WHEN THEY'RE AROUND ME.
I GUESS THEY'RE WORRIED SOMEONE'LL FIND OUT.
THAT'S WHERE YOU'RE WRONG.
tmp
IT'S BECAUSE THEY STILL LOVE YOU.
SEE THIS RING KEIICHI GAVE ME...?
shhiinnngg
AND THESE TWO RINGS-- THEY *RESONATE.*

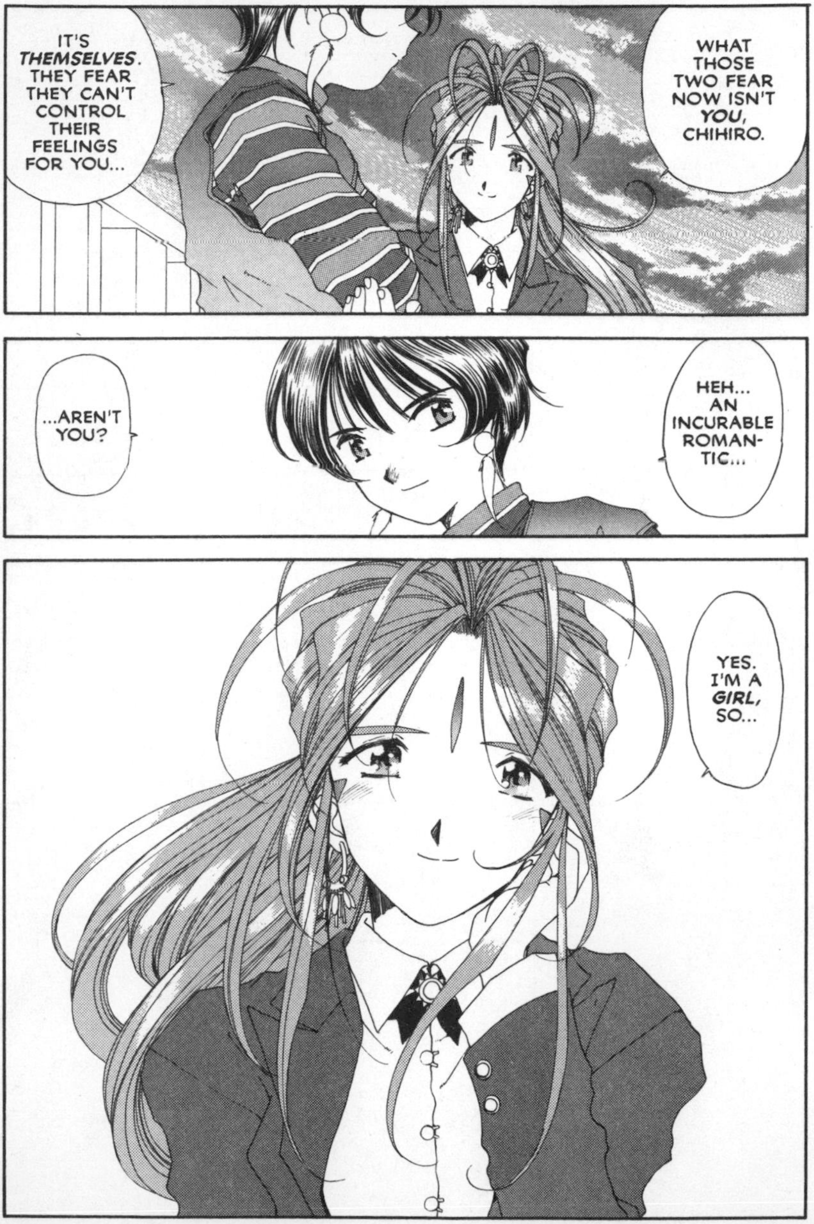
WHAT THOSE TWO FEAR NOW ISN'T *YOU*, CHIHIRO.
IT'S ***THEMSELVES***. THEY FEAR THEY CAN'T CONTROL THEIR FEELINGS FOR YOU...
HEH... AN INCURABLE ROMAN-TIC...
...AREN'T YOU?
YES. I'M A *GIRL*, SO...

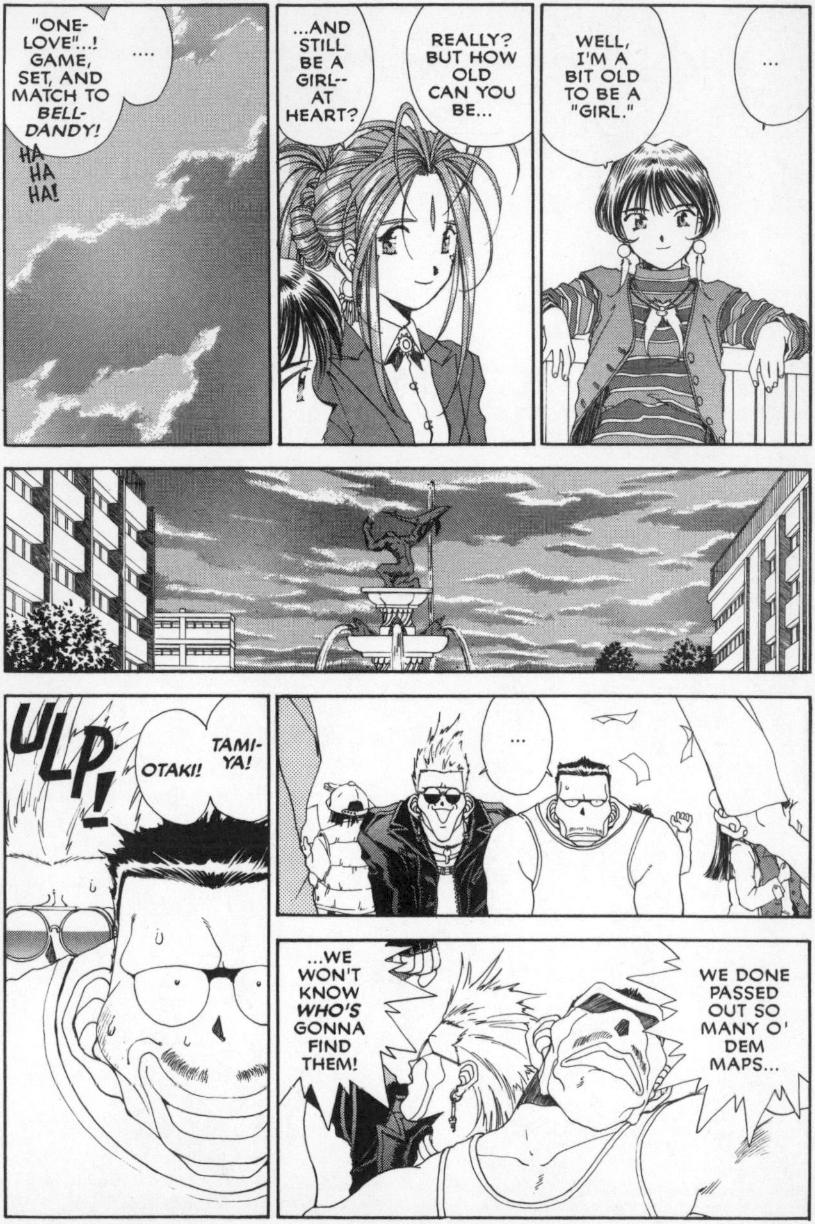
...
WELL, I'M A BIT OLD TO BE A "GIRL."
REALLY? BUT HOW OLD CAN YOU BE...
...AND STILL BE A GIRL--AT HEART?
....
"ONE-LOVE"...! GAME, SET, AND MATCH TO *BELL-DANDY!*
HA HA HA!
...
WE DONE PASSED OUT SO MANY O' DEM MAPS...
...WE WON'T KNOW *WHO'S* GONNA FIND THEM!
TAMI-YA!
OTAKI!
ULP!!

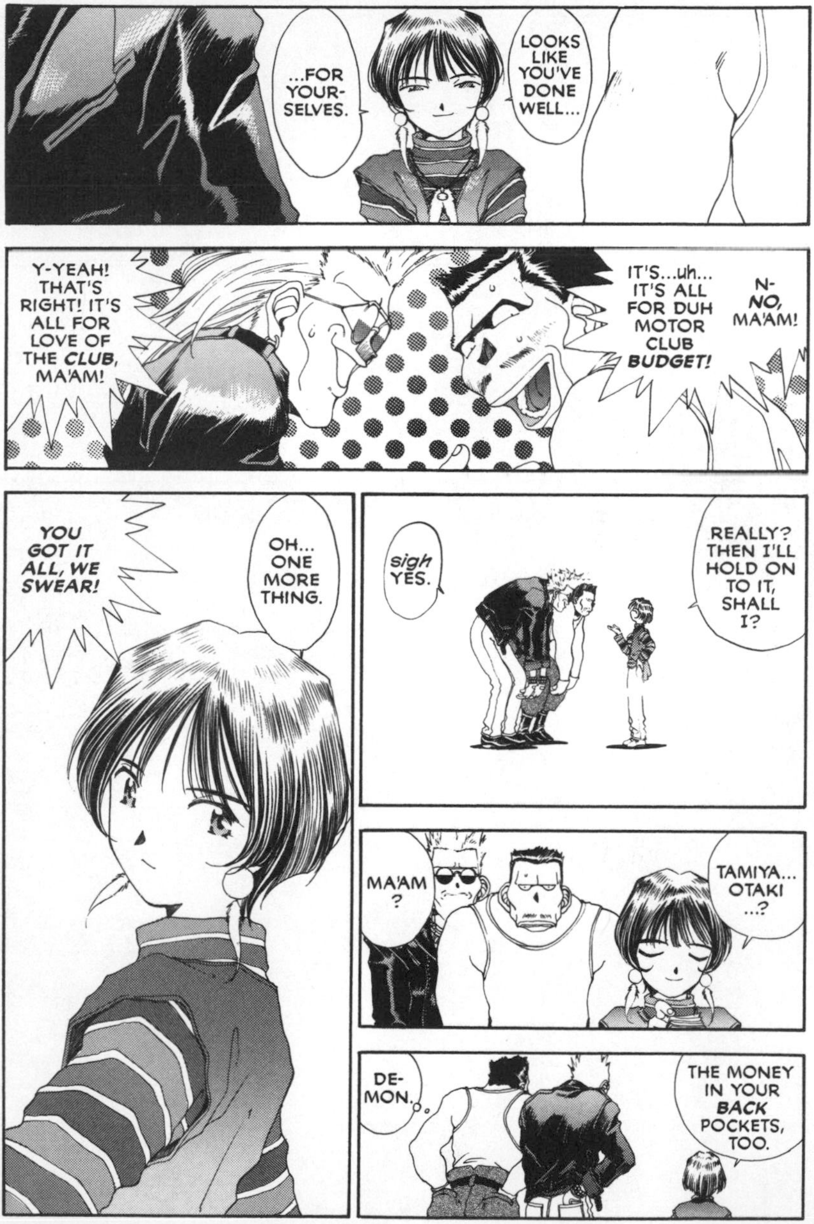
LOOKS LIKE YOU'VE DONE WELL...
...FOR YOUR-SELVES.
N-NO, MA'AM!
IT'S...uh... IT'S ALL FOR DUH MOTOR CLUB BUDGET!
Y-YEAH! THAT'S RIGHT! IT'S ALL FOR LOVE OF THE CLUB, MA'AM!
REALLY? THEN I'LL HOLD ON TO IT, SHALL I?
sigh YES.
TAMIYA... OTAKI ...?
MA'AM ?
THE MONEY IN YOUR BACK POCKETS, TOO.
DE-MON.
OH... ONE MORE THING.
YOU GOT IT ALL, WE SWEAR!

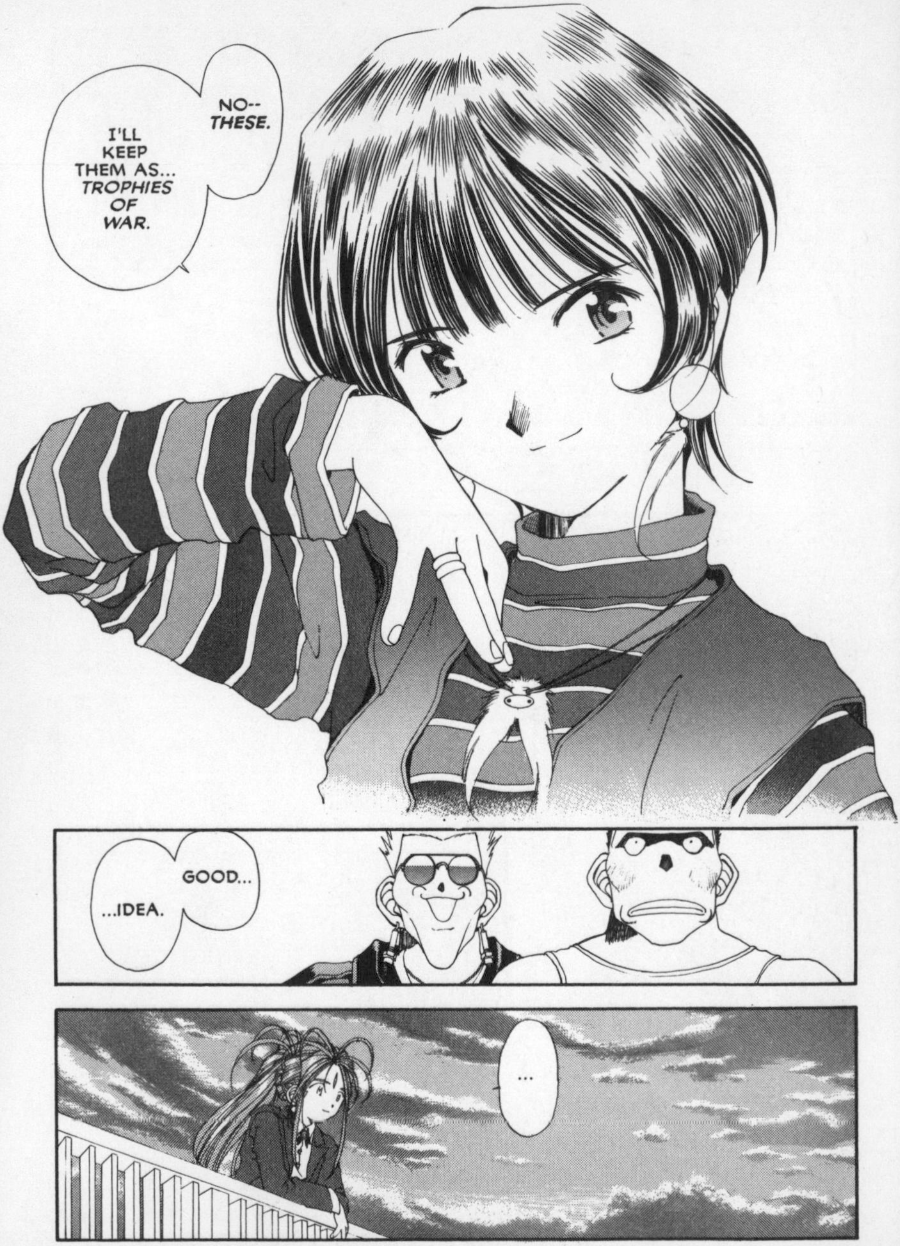
NO--
THESE.
I'LL KEEP THEM AS... *TROPHIES OF WAR.*
GOOD...
...IDEA.
...

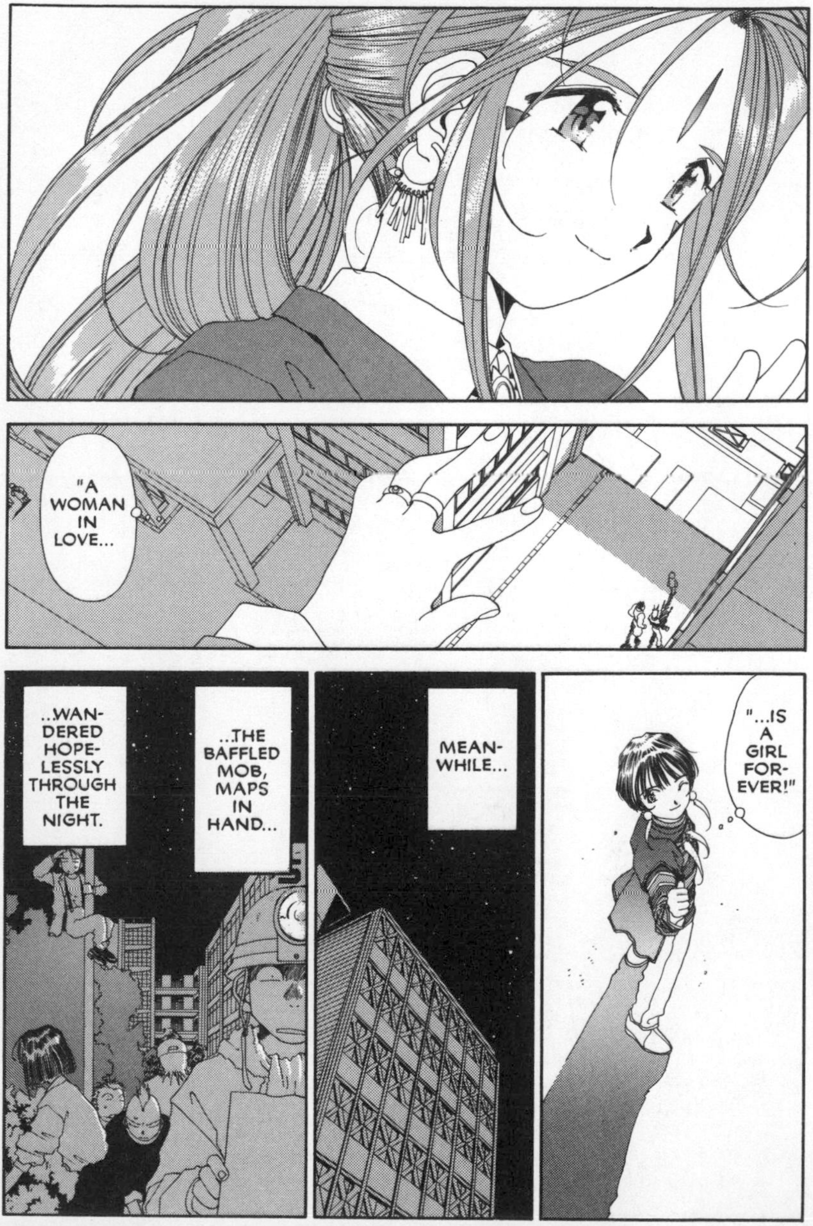
"A WOMAN IN LOVE...
"...IS A GIRL FOREVER!"
MEANWHILE...
...THE BAFFLED MOB, MAPS IN HAND...
...WANDERED HOPELESSLY THROUGH THE NIGHT.

EDITOR
Carl Gustav Horn

EDITORIAL ASSISTANT
Annie Gullion

DESIGNER
Scott Cook

PUBLISHER
Mike Richardson

English-language version
produced by Dark Horse Comics

Published by Dark Horse Manga
A division of Dark Horse Comics, Inc.
10956 SE Main Street
Milwaukie, OR 97222
darkhorse.com

To find a comics shop in your area,
call the Comic Shop Locator Service
toll-free at 1-888-266-4226

First edition: November 2009
ISBN 978-1-59582-386-1

1 3 5 7 9 10 8 6 4 2

Printed in Canada

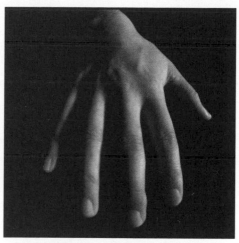

Creator Kosuke Fujishima in 1996!

His message to fans in the original Japanese *Oh My Goddess!* Vol. 13:

Whether revving the throttle on my motorcycle, or pushing the buttons on my game controller, or (with the help of spilled super-glue) bonding all its fingers together, my right hand plays a big role in my daily life. But there's no use I have for it more important than drawing this manga.

P.S. Can you make out the calluses? They're driving me crazy . . .

letters to the
ENCHANTRESS

10956 SE Main Street, Milwaukie, Oregon 97222
omg@darkhorse.com • darkhorse.com

NOTE: Full addresses and e-mail addresses will not be printed, unless you ask! All fan artwork, letters, and e-mails submitted become the property of Dark Horse Comics.

William Levy, who sent a drawing of Urd to vol. 9's "Letters to the Enchantress," returns with another, on the next page! Mr. Levy says:

Hi.

Just got my copy of vol. 32 and the *Oh My Goddess! Colors* book.

What can I say, but *Ah!* Not only a delightful treasure of color, but a wonderful reminder of why I fell in love with the series from the first time I saw it at a convention many, many years ago. It inspired me to drop a rose in my schedule and draw a portrait of Peorth, who's always underestimated in fan circles.

I look forward to further special projects in the future.

William Levy
nightmart@aol.com

Peorth is in some ways the most interesting of the five goddesses we've met thus far. Of course, it may not be fair to make a claim like that, because they haven't all gotten equal time—Lind, in particular, has only been seen to date in one story (although, like James Bond—the-don't-mess with Daniel Craig version—she will return), so it's hard to judge how she might be in other situations (especially in the just-hanging-out situations that are common with the other four). But the central question of *Oh My Goddess!* is

Keiichi and Belldandy's relationship, and Lind has also had the least to do with that issue. Skuld has been jealous of Keiichi, and Urd has been flirtatious, but both of her sisters accepted a long time ago that Belldandy loves Keiichi and intends to be with him as long as he lives (to Skuld, this still doesn't grant K1 any rights of actual physical affection ^_^).

Peorth, however, is the goddess most easily comparable to Belldandy. Both are Goddesses First-Class, like Lind (and unlike Urd and Skuld), but unlike Lind, Belldandy and Peorth also share the same profession—they are both in the "service to mortals" business. Before Peorth was introduced, it might have been natural to assume that Belldandy's more kind, gentle, and temperate manner was part of what set a First-Class Goddess apart from your hijinks-and-tomfoolery types like Urd and Skuld. But Peorth not only had an, uh, very different approach to trying to serve Keiichi, she also didn't see anything wrong with it, and indeed seemed honestly confused at Belldandy's attitude.

If you consider her role in the story, Peorth is interesting in that she revealed Belldandy as a person who is with Keiichi because she loves him, not because she's doing her job as a Goddess. Now, of course, this is something Belldandy had said before in the story (in vol. 6, at the end of the "Lord of Terror" arc). But before Peorth, we never had the chance to compare how Belldandy *is* doing her job as a Goddess to how another Goddess in the same profession might do it.

And this makes Peorth interesting again, because the contrast with Belldandy suggests that Peorth—whom you're supposed to think of as outrageous and disruptive—was only so relative to Belldandy and Keiichi's unusual situation; that is, she was actually being more normal about their profession than Belldandy has been.

Since the entire story of *OMG!* is based on the fact Keiichi chose for his one wish that Belldandy be with him always (technically, he wished for a Goddess "like you" to be with him always—I wonder if that phrasing might one day be used to try to break them apart), we might forget that the sample wishes Bell suggested to K1 when they first met were "if you want to be a billionaire" and "if you want to destroy the world." Now, she said of the latter, "we prefer to avoid doing business with that sort of customer," but the point is she never suggested the wish must, or even should, be used for something selfless and heart-warming; we briefly glimpse the billionaire Keiichi, surrounded by women who presumably love him only for his height.

Remember, Peorth and Belldandy aren't freelancers or self-employed; they work for heavenly agencies. It's been strongly suggested that the normal way they're supposed to do their jobs is to meet one mortal's request, and then move on to help the next mortal, not stay with one mortal "always." It's interesting that Heaven never sanctions Peorth for her supposedly disruptive actions, whereas Belldandy has gotten into trouble with her "superior" on more than one occasion. Of course, a paranoid fellow might theorize it was also because Someone Up There wanted to break K1 and Belldandy apart "legally." As Peorth herself said, what are the odds of a mortal contacting their service twice . . . ?

About page 42: if you, like Mr. Levy, also possess a copy of our recent book *Oh*

My Goddess! Colors, you know there's a section in the back called "The *Goddess! Garage*" that details the history and technical specs of many of the vehicles—cars, bikes, planes, brooms—driven around by *OMG!*'s characters. Now, the Dark Horse version of *Oh My Goddess! Colors* contains everything that was in the Japanese original (and a bit more besides, as the DH version also talks about volumes of *OMG!* that hadn't come out yet when the Japanese version first hit). But I felt bad for Tamiya when I realized that his cute little Honda Motra was never included in either version of *Colors*, and so it appears here on page 42 as a bonus. I wonder why it wasn't featured, though. Don't they like cute things?

—CGH

ROSE BOMB

Peorth

WILLIAM LEVY

STOP! This is the back of the book!

This manga collection is translated into English, but arranged in right-to-left reading format to maintain the artwork's visual orientation as originally drawn and published in Japan. If you've never read comics this way before, take a look at the diagram below to give yourself an idea of how to go about it. Basically, you'll be starting in the upper right-hand corner, and will read each word balloon and panel moving right to left. It may take a little getting used to, but you should get the hang of it very quickly. Have fun! If this is the millionth manga you've read this way, never mind. ^_^

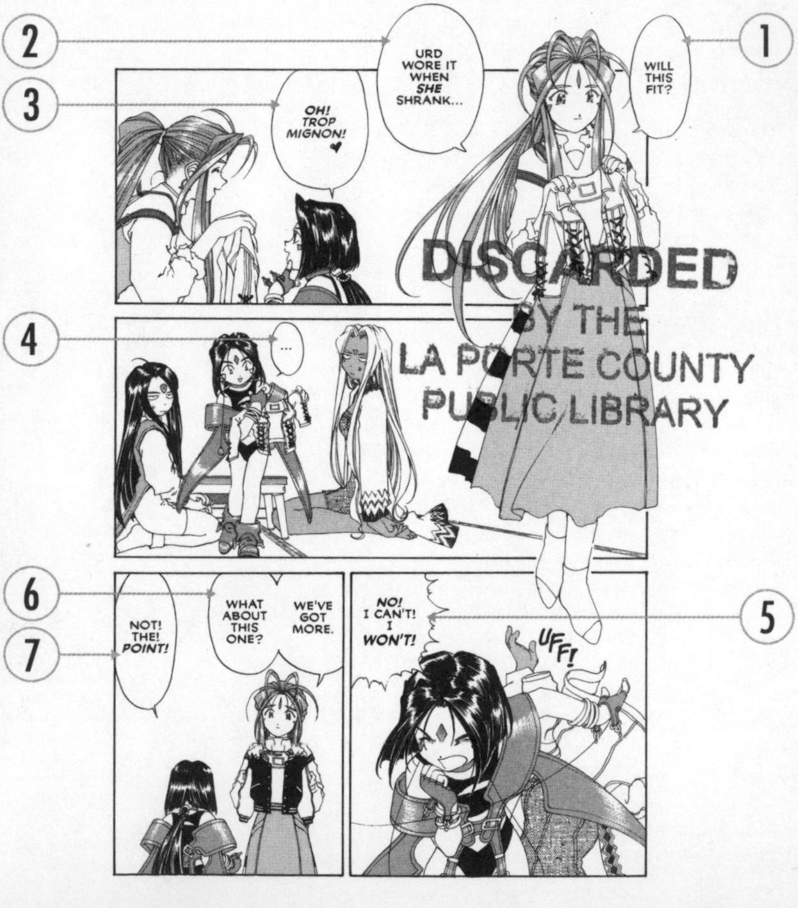
1
WILL THIS FIT?
2
URD WORE IT WHEN SHE SHRANK...
3
OH! TROP MIGNON!
4
...
5
NO! I CAN'T! I WON'T!
UFF!
WE'VE GOT MORE.
6
WHAT ABOUT THIS ONE?
7
NOT! THE! POINT!